THE BOOKLOVERS´
GUIDE TO WINE

*An introductory guide to the history, mysteries, and literary
pleasures of drinking wine*

PATRICK ALEXANDER

BOOKS & BOOKS
PRESS

Published by Books & Books Press, an imprint
of Mango Publishing Group.

Cover Design: Roberto Núñez

Layout & Design: Morgane Leoni

For permission requests, please contact the publisher at:

Books & Books Press
Mango Publishing Group
2850 Douglas Road, 3rd Floor
Coral Gables, FL 33134 USA
info@mango.bz

For special orders, quantity sales, course adoptions and corporate
sales, please email the publisher at sales@mango.bz. For trade
and wholesale sales, please contact Ingram Publisher Services at
customer.service@ingramcontent.com or +1.800.509.4887.

The Booklovers' Guide to Wine

Library of Congress Control Number: 2017906488

ISBN: (paperback) 978-1-63353-606-7, (ebook) 978-1-63353-607-4

BISAC category code PER004010 PERFORMING
ARTS / Film & Video / Direction & Production

Printed in the United States of America

The Booklovers' Guide to Wine is based on the popular six week program the author has been conducting for the past six years at Books & Books in Coral Gables, Florida.

Also by Patrick Alexander

Marcel Proust's Search for Lost Time

Proust on Twitter

The Nigerian Letter

Death on the Eighth

Recollections of a Racketeer

To Jude – for all the days of wine and rosés

And in memory of

Irving Fields – friend, mentor, and mensch (1938 – 2016)

"Great people talk about ideas, average people talk about things and small people talk about wine." — Fran Lebowitz

---

"The discovery of a wine is of greater moment than the discovery of a constellation. The universe is too full of stars." — Benjamin Franklin

---

"Wine is one of the most civilized things in the world and one of the most natural things of the world that has been brought to the greatest perfection, and it offers a greater range for enjoyment and appreciation than, possibly, any other purely sensory thing." — Ernest Hemingway

---

"I can certainly see that you know your wine. Most of the guests who stay here wouldn't know the difference between Bordeaux and Claret." — Basil Fawlty, "Fawlty Towers"

TABLE OF CONTENTS

CHAPTER 1 WINE   **23**

What is Wine?   25

Eyes / Sight (Swirl)   29

Nose / Smell (Snort)   31

Tongue / Taste (Slurp)   34

Mouth / Touch (Slosh)   35

Harmony (All the senses)   36

Describing Wine   36

Scoring and Rating Wine   40

Health Benefits of Wine   45

CHAPTER 2 MAKING WINE   **51**

How Wine Is Made   53

Viticulture: How Vines are Grown (Sun + grape = sugar)   61

Viniculture: Making the Wine (Sugar + yeast = alcohol + CO_2)   70

Oak Barrels   76

Bottling and sealing   79

Aging   80

Wine Bottles   80

Reading Wine Labels   85

CHAPTER 3 HISTORY OF WINE   **91**

Ancient World   94

Roman World   102

Religion and Wine   106

Middle Ages   108

Age of Reason   114

Nineteenth Century   121

Twentieth Century   127

Wine in the Twenty-First Century   136

CHAPTER 4 TERROIR OF EUROPE   **145**

Terroir vs. Varietal   147

France   152

Spain   186

Portugal   193

Italy   198

Germany   211

Eastern Europe   221

CHAPTER 5 THE NEW WORLD   **227**

New World vs Old World Wines   230

Argentina   236

Australia   241

Chile   247

China   252

New Zealand   255

South Africa   258

USA/North America   261

CHAPTER 6 VARIETALS   **279**

Alphabetical list of major varietals—some paired with great writers   282

CHAPTER 7 FORTIFIED WINE

339

CHAPTER 8 WINE PAIRING, SERVING & BUYING

349

What sort of food? 351

Traditional Red/meat: White/fish rule 352

Tannins and Acids 352

National pairings and wine 353

Top Forty Wines to Try Before You Die (24 Varietals) 354

Wine Serving Temperatures 356

Choosing and buying wine 357

ACKNOWLEDGEMENTS

362

APPENDIX

366

APPENDIX A: All 45 Bordeaux AOC Appellations 367

APPENDIX B: All 33 Grand Crus of Burgundy 369

APPENDIX C: 1976 Judgment of Paris final results 372

BIBLIOGRAPHY

374

INDEX

378

EPILOGUE

390

LISTS AND TABLES

Figure 1: The Year of the Vine   63

Figure 2: Transformation of sugar into wine   72

Figure 3: World's top wine import and export nations   137

Figure 4: US Wine Sales by Retail Price   141

Figure 5: Latitude of Northern Vineyards   151

Figure 6: Selection of major wine brands sold in the USA by owner   234

Figure 7: US Wineries by State   264

Figure 8: World's top varietals   282

Preface

We always carry at least one or two copies of Marcel Proust's novel *In Search Of Lost Time* on the shelves of our Coral Gables Books & Books, and over the past forty years we have probably sold on average at least three or four copies each year. So you can imagine my surprise about ten years ago when my store manager asked if we could dramatically increase our Proust inventory. Apparently we had sold more than a dozen copies of this seven-volume novel in the first three months of the year and were still racing to satisfy demand. That's when I discovered that Patrick Alexander was teaching a class on Marcel Proust at the University of Miami. His enthusiasm had created a city of crazed *Proustians*!

Patrick and I have been friends for thirty years now. I first knew him as a voracious reader and eclectic customer; I then knew him as a *Proustian*, and, finally, I discovered him to be a wine expert. While at the University of Miami, among other things, Patrick ran the University's wine appreciation program. After he retired to focus on writing, I suggested he try offering the same wine class at our bookstore; it seemed a pity to waste all that research, and I assumed book lovers might also prove to be wine lovers. Six years, twenty-four classes, and four hundred satisfied students later, it's clear that books and wine do indeed make a fine pairing.

I often enjoy wandering through the bookstore to see the enthralled look on students' faces, surrounded by floor to ceiling books, as they sip at their glasses of wine and listen to Patrick's entertaining stories. If anyone defined the phrase *Renaissance Man*, Patrick is just that person. I don't think I've ever met someone with such a rich intellect, having such diverse interests, and able to pair his love of history, geography, economics, and alcohol with so much humor.

I am proud that my bookstore inspired this book, and I am happy that my friendship made it possible. — Mitchell Kaplan

Foreword

Under the careful supervision of my father, I began drinking wine with meals at the age of five. Although mixed with water, it was unmistakably wine and we would discuss the taste and bouquet while my father would explain where and how it was made. At the same age, with the warm encouragement of my mother, I began a lifelong love affair with books.

My earliest memories involve Christopher Robin, with Pooh and Tigger and then Rat and Mole from the *Wind in the Willows*. Weekends were spent lying on the floor in the local library, lost in the worlds of Kipling and Dickens and, above all, my beloved John Buchan. Another early memory concerns Ernest Hemingway's *For Whom the Bell Tolls*, and asking my mother to explain, *"But did thee feel the earth move?"*

Shakespeare, of course, became an early love of mine, and I still thrill to hear Sir John Falstaff in *Henry IV, Part 2* boldly proclaiming the joys and wonders of a glass, or two, of Sherry. Likewise, in *Richard III*, I still feel a chill when the two murderers arrive at the Tower of London with orders to drown the Duke of Clarence in a barrel of wine. When the unsuspecting Duke asks the men for a glass of wine, the second murderer calms him with a reassuring, "You shall have wine enough my lord, anon."

And it is not just the English who associate wine with books. The twelfth century Persian poet, Omar Kayan, famously wrote:

A Book of Verses underneath the Bough,
A Jug of Wine, a Loaf of Bread—and Thou
Beside me singing in the Wilderness—
Oh, Wilderness were Paradise enow!

Indeed, as the writer Julian Street famously argued in his posthumous book, *Table Topics*: "Blot out every book in which wine is praised and you blot out the world's great literature, from the Bible and Shakespeare to the latest best-seller. Blot out the wine-drinkers of the world and you blot out history, including saints, philosophers, statesmen, soldiers, scientists, and artists."

But of course it is the French, with their unparalleled tradition of winemaking and their glorious history of great writing which, since Rabelais, has always combined that love of books with the mastery of the grape. This combination was enough for me to leave England at an early age and move into the French countryside of southwest France where my wife and I spent the next few years raising children, drinking Bordeaux wines, and immersing ourselves in every writer from Balzac and Flaubert to Rimbaud and Baudelaire.

Ironically, my favorite French writer preferred beer to wine and would even phone the Ritz hotel at any hour of the day or night to order a cold bottle to be delivered to his apartment. Nonetheless, Marcel Proust still wrote a wonderful description of his young hero drinking seven or eight glasses of Port wine to give himself courage to invite a young lady for an amorous assignation. By the time he had drunk enough to make his proposal, the young lady declined. Possibly because he had consumed too much Port wine, or because she had not consumed any.

If Marcel Proust was a wine, I think he would be a Gewurztraminer from Alsace. Despite the wine's underlying acidity, its sharpness and acuity is hidden behind a rich, floral bouquet that charms with a mellifluous harmony that simply overwhelms the senses. In the same way, Proust, the writer, hides his sharp and extremely comic insights into human nature behind a screen of poetically seductive images. The first taste from a glass of Gewurztraminer or a random passage read from *In Search of Lost Time* leaves us standing alone in ecstasy, inhaling through the rain, the lingering scent of invisible lilacs.

Over the years, as I have become more familiar with my favorite authors and have become better acquainted with a wide selection of different grapes, I often find myself pairing wines with writers. In Chapter Six – Varietals, I have therefore described several different grapes in terms of novelists who share similar characteristics with the wine. A literary wine pairing.

Sixty-five years after my first glass, I have become ever more set in my ways, and now I am never happier than with a glass of wine in one hand and a good book in the other.

Introduction

"Wine brings to light the hidden secrets of the soul, gives life to our hopes, bids the coward turn and fight again, drives dull care away, and teaches us new ways to fulfill our deepest desires." —
Horace

———

Wine is an alcoholic drink made from the fermented juice of fruit, specifically the fruit of the grape vine *Vitis vinifera*. Most non-Moslem countries and cultures have evolved social rituals for the consumption of alcohol, using it to celebrate feast days and special occasions such as weddings. In many societies, alcohol is consumed in the form of distilled spirits, drunk in small shots and often accompanied by toasts. In Russia, for example, vodka is widely drunk; in China and Japan it is baijiu or sake. This drinking of distilled spirits, consumed in small shots, is typically limited to groups of males and can often result in public inebriation.

The European tradition of wine consumption is different, in that the wine is sipped slowly, usually accompanied by food, and in social or family groups that include women. Wine drinking is thus regarded as a healthier and more civilized way of consuming alcohol. In modern societies, where women are playing an increasingly independent and important role in business and public life, wine drinking is thus becoming more and more widespread.

Whether for reasons of health, economics, or social change, the consumption of distilled spirits and beer has seen a steady decline in the twenty-first century while the consumption of wine has increased dramatically. Cocktail parties have long been replaced by wine-and-cheese parties, and prime rib dinners are increasingly washed down with Burgundy rather than bourbon. For the world's two largest markets, wine consumption in the US and China is forecast to increase by 25 percent between 2014 and 2018.

CHANGES IN US DRINKING HABITS		
	1982	**2012**
Beer	49%	48%
Spirits	35%	12%
Wine	16%	40%

In 2010, the US became the world's largest consumer of wine, surpassing even France. But while wine drinking in France, as in most of Mediterranean Europe, is part of the traditional culture, in America wine drinking is something new. For a variety of reasons which will be examined later, North America has evolved a long tradition of whisky and cocktail drinking, while wine drinking was regarded with a certain amount of suspicion as being "European" with all the ambivalent connotations that the word implies.

From an early age, most Southern Europeans have been drinking wine with every meal; they drink wine to quench their thirst and to help them digest their food. In France, wine drinking crosses all class divisions; rich and poor, young and old regard wine as the natural accompaniment to every meal. Of the Italians, it has been said that they do not drink wine, they eat it; meaning that, like salt and pepper, wine is regarded as an everyday accompaniment to food. Of course rich Europeans can afford more expensive wine than poor Europeans, but it is believed that no man is so poor he cannot afford a glass of red to aid his digestion.

A two thousand word survey of French wine, *Etude Des Vignobles de France: Regions Du Sud-Est Et Du Sud-Ouest,* published by the eminent Dr. Jules Guyot in 1868, concluded:

"Wine is the most precious and stimulating element of the human diet. Its use in family meals saves a third of bread and meat, but more than that, wine stimulates and strengthens the body, warms the heart, develops the spirit of sociability; encourages activity, decisiveness, courage and satisfaction in one's work."

Many young European children begin drinking wine (mixed with water) at mealtimes. In contrast, Americans prohibit alcohol until the age of twenty-one, often leading to binge drinking at college. Therefore, if only for legal reasons, those Americans who do enjoy wine usually did not start drinking it until they were in their twenties, and then only for special occasions. Consequently, although attitudes are changing, compared to Europeans, Americans are often self-conscious or apprehensive about drinking wine and still regard it as something "mysterious."

This book has been written to dispel those fears and to remove the mystery from wine. Based closely on the very popular six week Wine Appreciation program offered regularly at *Books & Books* in Coral Gables, Florida, the book covers all the basics, from the history of wine to how best to drink and, most importantly, how to discover and appreciate its many pleasures.

"Give me books, French wine, fruit, fine weather and a little music played out of doors by somebody I do not know." — John Keats

---

What is Wine?

Wine is made from the fermented juice of fruit. Any fruit can be used to make wine, and some of it is no doubt delicious. However, for the purpose of this book, our discussion of wine is limited to the fermented juice of grapes made from the *Vitis vinifera* vine which is native to the Eastern Mediterranean but is now planted worldwide.

Fermentation is a naturally occurring process in which the yeast found in the grapes converts the natural sugars into alcohol. The more sugar the grape contains, the higher the level of alcohol.

There are seven basic categories of wine:

Red Wine: Made from dark-skinned grapes when the skins remain with the juice during fermentation.

White Wine: Made from grapes with the (usually pale) skins removed before fermentation.

Rosé Wine: Made from dark-skinned grapes when skins have been allowed brief contact with the juice during fermentation. Obviously, the longer the contact, the deeper the color will be.

Sparkling Wine: Wines which contain small bubbles of carbon dioxide, either as a result of a secondary natural fermentation or through post-fermentation injection. The most famous come from the Champagne region of Northeast France.

Distilled Wine: Brandy is made from fermented wines which have been distilled to 35-60 percent alcohol, and the name comes from the Dutch word *brandewijn*, "burnt wine." The best-known brandies are Cognac and Armagnac, two regions in Southwest France.

Fortified Wine: Made from fermented wine to which some brandy has been added, raising the alcohol level to about 18-20 percent. The most famous fortified wines are from Jerez (Sherry) in Southern Spain and Porto (Port) in Northern Portugal.

Raisinated Wine: Rather than fermenting the juice of the freshly picked fruit, the grapes are allowed to dry in the sun, becoming more like raisins before they are crushed and allowed to ferment. This process, which is called *appassimento* in Italian, concentrates the sugars and thus results in a far higher alcohol level as well as a sweeter wine. Historically, all the best and most expensive wines used to be made this way.

These different categories will be examined in more detail in the chapter on "How Wine is Made."

There are three external factors which affect the taste of wine:

Chemical: Perhaps the most important factor is the chemical composition of the wine. In fact, if the wine is bad, then all the other factors are irrelevant. But assuming the wine is good, that "goodness" is composed of all sorts of qualities, ranging from the type of grape to the minerals from which the roots have derived their taste, and the balance between the sweetness of the residual sugars and the acids and tannins of the skin.

Physical: Even a great wine will be disappointing if it is served at the wrong temperature, while an otherwise mediocre wine, served at the correct temperature and accompanied with food, will taste much better.

Mechanical: As a certain well-known glass manufacturer, Riedel, never fails to remind us in their advertising, each wine improves in the "correct" glass. Certainly, any wine will taste better in a wine glass that tapers toward the opening, rather than one that widens towards the top. The correctly-shaped glass is widest in the middle, where the maximum surface of wine is exposed to the oxygen in the air, releasing the volatile aromatic molecules that rise towards the top of the glass which, tapering to a narrowed opening, concentrates them for the human nose. In order to focus on the color and pleasures of the wine itself, the glass should be clear, un-decorated and certainly not colored.

Alright—four external factors: Dishwashing liquid! Assuming that you follow all the advice and suggestions in this book and put them into practice with a carefully selected wine in an expensive crystal glass, it will all be meaningless if the glass has not been properly rinsed. Wine glasses should be washed by hand if possible, using only the tiniest hint of dishwashing liquid, and then thoroughly rinsed so that no residue remains. The smallest hint of soap in a glass will destroy even the most robust and expensive of wines.

The moment the cork is pulled and the first glass is poured, chemical changes begin which will ultimately affect our appreciation of the wine. As soon as the wine is exposed to the air, it begins to oxidize and evaporate as tiny molecules of aroma are released into the air and give the wine its bouquet.

Tasting Wine

While it is true that the satisfying "pop" of a cork being withdrawn from a bottle, the clink of glasses, the charming gurgle of wine being poured, or the gentle fizz of bubbles in a flute of champagne all involve our sense of hearing, it is the other four senses which are more important for the appreciation of wine: sight, smell, taste, and touch. In my wine class, I make my students follow the same noisy ritual for every glass of wine we taste: swirl, snort, slurp, and slosh. It makes for a somewhat raucous and inelegant class, but establishes good tasting habits which can eventually be discreetly modified to socially acceptable levels.

It is very important to remember that just as we all differ in size, height, weight, hair color, and skin color, so too each one of us has a unique sense of taste. About 20 percent of the population have 150 tastebuds on each square centimeter of tongue. They are known as Supertasters; they react badly to any taste of bitterness and are very sensitive, usually avoiding most red wines and preferring sweet whites. At the other extreme, 20 percent of the population have only fifty tastebuds per square centimeter, and they are very tolerant of tannins and bitter tastes, usually preferring "big" red wines. Most of us are somewhere in the middle, with about one hundred tastebuds per square centimeter. We are known as "tasters" and can enjoy both sweet and bitter tastes, both red and white. Because of these fundamental and natural differences between us, when it comes to wine tasting, there are no "correct" tastes and no "correct" answers. Do not feel bad if your experience is different from your friends or from an "expert." *Vive la difference!*

Eyes / Sight (Swirl)

Our first contact with a glass of wine is with our eyes, which tell us immediately if it is red or white (or rosé). Sight is the most superficial of our senses, but, even before we taste the wine, our eyes give us a hint of the grape the wine is made from and also its age. Pick up your glass and swirl the wine around as you look at it. (Novices may want to practice swirling while the glass sits on the table, moving it in a circular motion so that the wine swirls around, but without spilling over the glass onto a smart white dress or shirtfront.) First look down into the glass, and then tilt it away from you at an angle, preferably against a white background.

By tilting your glass, you will see the variations in color from the center, where the wine is deepest and usually darkest, to the rim or meniscus, where the wine meets the glass and is thinnest. The darker the wine at the meniscus suggests a full-bodied, more intense taste, while a pale color suggests a more insipid wine. A white wine will often have a suggestion of green at the meniscus, a remnant of chlorophyll denoting slightly unripe youth.

A pale red color suggests a lighter grape, such as a Gamay or Pinot Noir, while a dark red suggests a heavier grape, such as a Cabernet Sauvignon or a Zinfandel. A young red wine will show traces of purple, while an old red wine past its prime will be turning brown from oxidization. The best color for a fully mature red wine is a rich ruby.

A pale, almost translucent color tells us the white wine is probably made from a Pinot Grigio or a Sauvignon Blanc grape, while a darker, more golden color suggests a Chardonnay or a Viognier grape. Young white wine shows traces of green, which quickly become yellow as it ages. Except for certain wines like Chardonnay, Viognier, and Gewürztraminer, most wines never darken beyond a pale straw color.

A good Chardonnay, on the other hand, will attain a deep golden amber when it is ready to be drunk. Very few white wines benefit from prolonged aging other than some Chardonnays, Rieslings, and late-harvest dessert wines, which will be discussed later.

Clarity: The wine, whether red or white, should be clear, not cloudy. Some white wines, such as Vinho Verde, Muscadet, and certain Pinot Grigios, have small bubbles visible, but otherwise (with the exception of sparkling wines), the wine should be clear. Obviously, there should be no sediment or impurities floating in the wine. On the other hand, tartrate crystals produced by tartaric acid are perfectly natural and indeed desirable results of fermentation, and can be seen resting at the base of some bottles of wine. Unfortunately, because so many consumers have mistaken them for broken glass or spoiled sediment and returned the bottles, most winemakers now remove them by cold-stabilization or extra-fine filtration which, especially with red wines, detracts from the complexity of the taste.

Legs: Also known as tears of wine, church windows, or curtains, legs refer to the band of clear liquid around the inside of the glass after you swirl it and from which droplets—or legs—reach back down the inside of the glass into the wine. This has nothing to do with the quality or even the sweetness of the wine, but is simply a reflection of the alcohol content. As wine is mainly a mixture of water and alcohol, which evaporate at different rates (and alcohol has less surface tension than water), this phenomenon will be more visible in wine with higher alcohol content. While it is agreeable to swirl a glass of wine and observe that "it has good legs," this has no significance concerning the wine's quality. Just because a wine has good legs does not necessarily mean it will make a great investment, any more than a person with good legs will necessarily make a great spouse.

Color: The color of a wine is a result of the varietal (variety of the grape used), as well as the age of the wine.

Red Wines: A Cabernet Sauvignon, for example, will always be darker than a Gamay, and a young wine will always be darker than an old wine, which, unlike white wine, tends to lighten with age. In general, red wines age from purple when young and ruby or garnet when mature, and become increasingly brown when old.

White Wines: A Chardonnay will always have a deeper color than, for example, a Sauvignon Blanc. White wines tend to age from green when young, to yellow or straw when older, to gold at their prime, and with an increasingly darker, brownish-tint when too old and oxidized.

Sight is the most superficial of all our senses and gives less information than taste or smell, but as we acquire more familiarity with the different grape varieties, the initial judgment based on the color of the wine in the glass will become increasingly informed and useful. Because of the modern taste for powerful, fruit-forward red wines which are usually darker in color, winemakers often use color as a way to imply quality. Adding a touch of such varietals as Alicante Bousquet, Malbec, or Petit Syrah, can make any red wine appear darker and more powerful. The truth is in the tasting. She may have good legs, but can she cook?

Nose / Smell (Snort)

The next and most important contact with wine comes through our nose. By gently swirling the wine around the glass, we are slightly heating it with the warmth of the hand while exposing it to the oxygen in the air, thus evaporating and releasing its aromas. These fragrances consist of the aromatic and volatile chemical molecules, including phenols, which rise to the rim of the glass where our nose captures them with a strong but gentle snort. The second thing to do after examining the color and clarity of the wine is to put your nose as close to the glass as possible and inhale deeply. This first "snort" of the wine is the most important; because of "smell fatigue," the second snort will not be as rewarding and the third even less so.

Smell is the most basic and important of all the human senses. It was our primal ancestors' first sense and is the core sense around which our brain and our consciousness eventually coalesced. Smell is an emotional sense, mixing memory and desire, rather than consciousness and calculation. Smell is the most voluptuous sense; a holdover from our most primitive instincts and the "reptilian" brain that alerts us to food, sex, and danger. Our sense of smell is the most powerful and most evocative of all our senses. The most privately personal and distant memories can suddenly be recalled by the smell of new-cut grass or mushrooms being cooked in some distant apartment. Marcel Proust wrote the world's longest novel, the seven volume *In Search of Lost Time*, based on the smell of a little madeleine cake being dipped into his cup of tea. It is no accident that the global perfume market was estimated to be worth $33 billion in 2015.

Eighty percent of what we call taste is in fact smell. While one in a thousand molecules can be identified by the tongue, the nose is so sensitive that it can identify one in a million molecules. In fact, it's not the nose that is so sensitive; it's the olfactory bulb which is located just behind the nose and between the eyes. The best way to locate the olfactory bulb is to swallow (or imagine swallowing) a large spoonful of very cold ice cream. That "brain freeze" pain you feel just between and behind the eyes is your olfactory bulb protesting the sensory overload of the cold ice cream.

When wine is exposed to the air it begins to evaporate; the phenols and aromatic molecules rise from the surface of the liquid, and are carried through the nose to the olfactory bulb. Wineglasses narrow towards the rim in order to concentrate these molecules as they reach our nose.

Pulling the cork, opening the bottle, and letting it breathe for half an hour before serving is one of the many, meaningless rituals associated with wine. The amount of wine exposed to the air is the half-inch diameter in the neck of the bottle. The rest of the wine is unexposed. Wine only begins to aerate when it has been poured into the glass, ideally half filling the glass to the widest part of the bowl and thus exposing the greatest amount to the air. By cupping the bowl with our hand and gently swirling, we are simultaneously warming and thus evaporating the wine while also aerating it as each swirl brings it into contact with more oxygen. The combined evaporation and aeration raise the aromatic molecules to the rim of the glass where our nose waits to capture them.

This is why, especially for good quality wines, pouring the wine into a decanter is recommended before serving. The very act of pouring it from the bottle will gently aerate it, and the extra exposure to the air the decanter provides will help the wine wake up and begin to reveal its characteristics, to "breathe" and come alive. Any red wine will benefit from aerating before drinking, and there are many inexpensive aerating gadgets on the market which will do this very simply without having to actually pour it into a decanter.

Scientists have isolated seventeen thousand individual smells, and of these, ten thousand can be detected by the human nose. Professionals (actually called "Noses") in the perfume industry, or the wine or tea industries, for example, are able to identify those ten thousand different smells, but even the rest of us can easily identify as many as 1,000.

The only difference between the professional and the rest of us is training. To illustrate this point in my wine classes, I ask my students to close their eyes and imagine moving through their local supermarket. As they picture themselves passing the meat counter, the fish counter, the produce section—passing potatoes, cabbages, tomatoes, pears, apples, peaches, strawberries, and then reaching the cheese section— the students are able to imagine the different smells just by picturing the different sources. Even readers of this book, by closing their eyes and imagining a tour of their local grocery market, will be able to recreate in their minds the smells of the assorted produce. This just confirms how powerful the average person's sense of smell is without him even being aware.

Flavor: Smell and Taste are the senses that determine the flavor of the wine, and of these, the most important is smell in the nose (olfaction), which accounts for about 75 percent, while taste on the tongue (gestation) accounts on average for just 25 percent.

Tongue / Taste (Slurp)

The third step in tasting a glass of wine is to sip a very small amount into the mouth and then breathe in some air, making a slurping noise. As the natural warmth of the mouth heats the wine, the air breathed in will lift the evaporating odor molecules from the wine, carry them to the back of the throat, and then lift them retro-nasally to the olfactory bulb. (Only a small amount of wine is needed for this slurping process, otherwise an elegant wine taster might risk choking and spluttering wine all over the white linen tablecloth.)

Even though the wine is entering our body through the mouth, we still "smell" rather than "taste" it. The small drop of wine in the mouth rapidly evaporates, and the taste is carried to the brain via the nose.

When we smell the wine as it approaches our mouth, and our nose is in the glass, it is called orthonasal olfaction; when we smell it a second time when it's in our mouth, it is called retronasal olfaction, because the odors are rising from the back of the mouth to our brain (thus "retro").

Mouth / Touch (Slosh)

The next step in tasting wine is to sip a second and larger amount of wine into the mouth and to slosh it around. In class, I make my students do this with every glass of wine that they taste just to get them in the habit, but in reality, with most white wines, this sloshing process has little value. However, for red wines, sloshing it around in your mouth tells you a lot about its "mouth-feel." Just as when searching for metaphors to describe smells, we often turn to plants, fruits, and vegetables, so when searching metaphors for mouth-feel, we often use textiles. Pinot Noir is obviously smooth like silk, while Chianti has a warm, flannel feel to it, and a fine Bordeaux feels like soft leather.

The tongue, the roof of the mouth, and the inside of the cheeks all respond differently not only to the relative sweetness, sourness, and acidity of wine, but also to the "feel" of the wine. Does it feel rich and heavy or thin? Do you feel it coating your mouth with a velvety viscosity, or do you feel it stripping away the coating of saliva and leaving you dry and pursed? Does the taste linger so long after you have swallowed the wine; your mouth still retains memories of its presence—or do you need to take another sip just to remind yourself?

Harmony (All the senses)

After we have sniffed, slurped, sloshed and finally swallowed the wine, we can evaluate all these sensory experiences together. First of all, the taste of the wine should linger in the mouth; we may drain the glass but the aroma should remain. Secondly, the various sensations—the smell, the taste, and the flavor of a good wine—should all blend together in a rounded harmony. A good wine might have sharp acids, tannins, and alcohol, but they should be softened and integrated by the fruit and the body of the wine; they should be in balance. When we conduct our initial sniff and taste of the wine, we should be alert for the individual features—the acid, the sweetness, etc.—but when we are actually drinking the wine (if it's a good wine), we should be aware only of the harmony. All these disparate features are finally combined into a balanced whole, with no single aspect dominating the others.

Describing Wine

One of the great challenges of wine appreciation is describing what we taste, not just to other people, but even to ourselves. Translating what we smell or taste into words is far more difficult than translating what we see into words. While dogs, for example, experience the world mainly through their sense of smell, we humans are far more visual and describe the world in terms of what we see with our eyes. From an early age, we are encouraged to"show and tell," but we are never taught to"smell and tell." All languages have a rich and sophisticated vocabulary for describing what we see, and we can be very precise in terms of color, shape, size, and visual distance when communicating with others—but such a vocabulary does not exist for smells and tastes. There is no semantic tradition in any culture or in any language to describe the things we smell, in the way that we are able to identify things we see.

In fact, the whole process of smelling is limited to a single word: smell. There is a smell coming from the mushrooms; I smell the mushrooms; the mushrooms smell. The same single word is used to describe the odor, the detection of the odor, and the action of the odor. Compare that to all the words we have for seeing, looking, watching, gazing, observing, etc. We must therefore look around in our personal memories for similar smells and tastes to compare with the wine, and then, when trying to share our experience, make subjective comparisons: "It tastes like dark chocolate with a hint of mushrooms and damp leaves."

Another problem is that the part of the brain which processes smells also handles emotions and memory; it's not only the most primitive part of the brain, but also the most subjective and personal. Smells are chemicals, and as the wine is exposed to air and evaporates, chemical molecules rise from the glass, through our nose to the receptors in our olfactory cortex.

The olfactory cortex, which evolved over eons into the amygdala, is the very oldest part of our brain, and is where emotions and memories are processed. The very earliest job of the brain was to process smell: does it smell good or bad? Is it something I can eat, something I would like to have sex with, or something I should run away from before it eats me? Memories of smells were therefore critical to survival and, even in the amygdala of the modern brain, the chemical processing of smells, emotions, memory, and desire, are all intimately entwined at a primitive level.

What the olfactory receptors do is transform the chemical information of the wine's aroma molecules into electrical signals. These electrical signals travel into the brain's cerebral cortex: the deepest, most primitive and least "conscious" part of the brain where the electronic impulses are translated back into the memory of our mother's kiss, a feeling of hunger, the desire for a woman, the pleasure of luxury, the terror of darkness, or the lingering scent of invisible lilacs. These involuntary but powerful stirrings of our deepest emotions can all be released by the scent of a loved one's pillow, the fragrance of a rose upon the evening air, or the delicate aromas released by a glass of wine. Nothing is more powerful or evocative and less subject to our verbal skills or logical analysis than our sense of smell.

One of my favorite times of year is fall when I go mushroom hunting in France, combing through the woods of Perigord looking for cèpe mushrooms and truffles, stepping through the fallen leaves and savoring the musky dampness of the decaying vegetation. Most Spanish red wines have an earthy aroma that reminds me of my days in the woods, and so for me the association of earthiness and damp leaves is pleasing and enhances my enjoyment of a good Tempranillo. But to another person, with different memories and experiences, the concept of damp organic decay might be totally disgusting, and my enthusiastic description of the wine might persuade them never to try it. Worse still, because of the unpleasant associations created by my description, a person tasting the wine might possibly dislike it and unfairly discover in it all the bad qualities they imagined I had suggested.

Wine drinkers, therefore, need to consciously train themselves to develop a commonly accepted vocabulary that will allow them to discuss wines with other people. With practice and concentration, they can decide if a wine reminds them of fruit, vegetables, wood, or fresh-cut grass. If it reminds them of fruit, is it a berry fruit, a tropical fruit, or a citrus? Over time, wine drinkers will discover a common language that enables them to share their impressions of a wine with other people using words and allusions that are mutually understood. But to develop such a vocabulary takes practice and conscious effort. The difference between a professional taster and the rest of us is training.

Unfortunately, the best wine class in the world, the best teacher, or the best book, can never impart that knowledge. It has to be accumulated, sip by sip, sniff by sniff, glass by glass, by each individual wine drinker. The UC Davis Wine Aroma Wheel at www.winearomawheel. com is a wonderful tool that will help the true connoisseur differentiate between the aromas of passion fruit and boysenberries, but for the rest of us, just learning to isolate the difference between a fruity taste and an earthy aroma is a good place to begin. Eric Asimov, the excellent wine critic for the *New York Times,* argues that we can divide all wines into sweet or savory. By sweet he does not mean sugary; he is rather referring to the impression of sweet we get from a wine that is intensely fruity, plush, viscous, and mouth-filling. By savory, he means wines which are more austere, with smoky, herbal, earthy, and mineral tastes.

We are not limited to food or taste metaphors; as a visual species we have other tools to describe wine. Karen MacNeil, a well-respected wine critic and author of the *Wine Bible,* quoted a restaurant owner's description of Viognier wine:

"If a good German Riesling is like an ice-skater (fast, racy with a cutting edge), and Chardonnay is like a middle-heavyweight boxer (paunchy, solid, powerful), then Viognier would have to be described as a female gymnast – beautiful and perfectly shaped, with muscle but superb agility and elegance."

Britt Karlson, a Swedish wine critic, once described an unfortunate wine as "ideal for serving at a funeral dinner, because it provokes a fitting mood of sorrow and grief."

Alternatively we can seek our metaphor in music. In one of his Italian detective novels, *A Long Finish,* Michael Dibdin wrote:

"Barolo is the Bach of wine ... strong, supremely structured, a little forbidding, but absolutely fundamental. Barbaresco is the Beethoven, taking those qualities and lifting them to heights of subjective passion and pain ... and Brunello is its Brahms, the softer, fuller, romantic afterglow of so much strenuous excess."

Those people who know their German composers and are familiar with Italian wines will recognize the insightful truth behind Dibdin's metaphors. For those unfamiliar, however, it could sound merely pretentious. And of course, that is the great danger of talking about wine; the metaphors can become too flowery and ostentatious: "This is a cheeky little Pinot; unctuously naughty with a promise of heavenly bliss, like a nun slipping out of her habit."

Roald Dahl, that wonderful British novelist, should really be given the last word on the subject from his short story "Taste":

"Richard Pratt was a famous gourmet.... He organized dinners where sumptuous dishes and rare wines were served. He refused to smoke for fear of harming his palate, and when discussing a wine, he had a curious, rather droll habit of referring to it as though it were a living being. "A prudent wine," he would say, "rather diffident and evasive, but quite prudent." Or, "a good-humored wine, benevolent and cheerful—slightly obscene, perhaps, but nonetheless good humored."

Scoring and Rating Wine

Traditionally, wines are rated on a European twenty point scale:

0-3 points (15%) for sight (color, clarity, etc.)

0-6 points (30%) for smell (bouquet, aroma, etc.)

0-8 points (40%) for taste (tannins, acidity, sweetness, etc.)

0-3 points (15%) for harmony (overall experience and balance)

The value of this system is its "human scale" which is almost intuitive. Without being an expert, anyone knows that a five point score means a weak wine, a ten point score means an average but unremarkable wine, a fifteen point wine will be a memorable experience, and a nineteen or twenty point wine will be absolutely unforgettable.

The influential American wine critic, Robert Parker, introduced his one hundred point system in the 1970s, and unfortunately variants of this system have now taken over and dominate the wine world:

96-100 points: Extraordinary; a classic wine of its variety

90-95 points: Outstanding; exceptional complexity and character

80-89: Barely above average to very good; wine with various degrees of flavor

70-79 points: Average; little distinction beyond being soundly made

60-69 points: Below average; drinkable, but containing noticeable deficiencies

Nowadays the *Wine Spectator, The Wine Advocate, The Wine Enthusiast, Wine and Spirits Magazine,* and every critic and commentator seem to have all adopted a version of this one hundred point scale. The trouble with this one hundred point system is that it has no human scale. What does eighty-nine points mean? Like a German wine label, at first glance it sounds more precise and scientific, but on closer examination it conveys no meaningful or helpful information. It is too vague and abstract.

Numbers satisfy the American taste for quantifying and measuring, and Americans are familiar with the one hundred point scale from their schooldays. Numerical ratings give the impression that wine quality is measurable, and that the experts have scientifically analyzed it and pronounced their judgment. A number makes the critic's opinion sound more objective, and therefore more valid than the consumer's personal opinion. But a ninety-two point score does not tell you if the wine will go with lunchtime pasta, nor does it indicate if it will be better suited for a summer picnic or for a cold winter night around the fire.

The trouble is that because it appears to be a scientific and precise judgment, retailers and consumers treat it as such. Every wine store or supermarket selling wine is now festooned with garish "shelf-talkers"—those little shelf tabs below the bottle—proudly declaiming "Robert Parker 89 points." The implication is that any wine without such a declaration must not be any good. You can see people standing in the aisles debating whether to go for a *Wine Spectator* score of ninety-one or a *Wine Enthusiast* score of ninety-two. It has just become a horrible marketing distraction.

Despite the apparently scientific objectivity of the one hundred point scale, even Robert Parker has admitted it all really depends on his mood and how he got out of bed that morning. "I really think probably the only difference between a 96-, 97-, 98-, 99-, and 100-point wine is really the emotion of the moment," he said to the *Naples Daily News* in 2007.

Robert Parker

I have very mixed feelings about Mr. Parker, which I should explain before proceeding any further. Robert Parker started becoming known for his writing about wine in the mid-70s at just about the time that the Californian wineries began their renaissance; he has written a number of books on wine, and he also edits the very influential *Wine Advocate* newsletter. As mentioned above, Parker's one hundred point scoring system has now become the industry standard. He is a man with a very deep knowledge of and passion about wine, especially the great reds from Bordeaux, the Rhône, and California, and he has reached his position of eminence through hard work, dedication, and simple expertise. Nonetheless, I have two problems with Mr. Parker.

My first objection is personal and selfish. Parker and I share the same tastes; we both like bold, broad-shouldered, swaggering reds. For years, I enjoyed drinking Châteauneuf-du-Pape, Barolo, and Barbaresco, which were all affordable until Parker discovered them. By writing about these wines and bestowing his blessing, he made them insanely popular. As a result, these wines are now extremely expensive and I can no longer afford to drink them.

My second objection owes more to Lord Acton: "Power tends to corrupt, and absolute power corrupts absolutely." I do not in any way mean that Parker himself has become corrupt, far from it; he is rightly proud of his high ethical standards: impartiality and independence from the wine industry. But unfortunately his influence is now so powerful that it has affected—if not corrupted—absolutely everybody else in the industry. For example, one of Parker's early favorite winemakers was Michael Rolland in Pomerol, whose wines Parker always praised. Rolland also worked as a consultant for various other neighboring wineries, creating a similar style wine to his own. These wines also scored well with Parker, and so, inevitably, other winemakers beyond Bordeaux started hiring Rolland as a consultant and very soon Michael Rolland became the first "flying winemaker." Jetting around the world, from Chile and Argentina to Australia and California, Rolland helps fellow winemakers create the style of wine that will score well in Robert Parker's Wine Advocate ratings, and thus be featured on "shelf talkers" in wine stores everywhere. There is even a wine analysis company in Sonoma, CA, called Enologix, which uses complex chemical algorithms to advise winemakers exactly how to manipulate their winemaking techniques in order to get Parker scores in excess of ninety points.

Parker's wine ratings dramatically affect the price of wine on the market. It is claimed that the difference between a Parker score of eighty-five and ninety-five can be $10 million to the value of the wine. A wine rated at less than seventy can bankrupt the winegrower. The prices people pay for wine and the wines retailers and restaurants select to offer for sale are all affected by the judgments of Robert Parker. Even though his judgments may be fair and his opinions correct, I believe that it is wrong and unhealthy for any one individual to have that much power. Of course, there are other wine critics and magazines also rating wines; but not only have most of them adopted Parker's scoring system, most of them have also adopted his tastes and his preferences for the rich and powerful, oaky, fruit-forward reds that he so admires. Consequently, we are seeing an international standardization of taste, a "Parkerization" of wine.

The ripple effect goes even further than the wine market; it reaches as far as the cellar and vineyard. A winegrower who may have a vision of a unique wine he wants to make may hesitate or change his mind when thinking about how Parker might rate it.

Of course, there are many who oppose Parker and the style of wine he promotes; the "hedonistic fruit bombs" as they are called. Parker once referred to such people as an "anti-flavor wine elite," a phrase which went viral on Twitter and which has since been adopted by the very people he criticized. Parker's detractors now sign themselves AFWE.

Hence my ambivalence about Robert Parker; I like his writing, I share his tastes, and I greatly respect his knowledge. Robert Parker should also be admired for making wine popular and accessible to

Americans, and he should be commended for cutting through much of the jargon and Old World mystique of wine and bringing a New World freshness to the business. Unfortunately, the majority of people do not read his thoughtful tasting notes or his informed reviews; they just see the numbers—the Parker Points on the shelf-talkers. That's where power corrupts absolutely.

I just wish there were a couple more Robert Parkers, equally informed and passionate, with similar influence but with different tastes—not to mention a preference for a twenty point scoring system.

For a list of all the French wines that Parker has awarded one hundred points in his system, go to http://tinyurl.com/j5tp4en.

Health Benefits of Wine

Wine has been used as a medicine for more than four thousand years. Ancient Sumerian clay tables and Egyptian papyri, as old as 2200 BC, describe a wide variety of wine-based medicines. The Greek physician Hippocrates considered wine an essential part of a healthy diet, and also as a disinfectant for wounds as well as a cure for everything, from lethargy to diarrhea. The Ancient Greek poet Eubulus also recommended the daily consumption of wine for good health, but only in moderation. For Eubulus, moderation meant three bowls of wine with a meal. The Greek bowl, or *kylix*, contained about 250 ml of wine, so three bowls would be the equivalent of a modern, 750 ml bottle of wine.

The relationship between wine and health was first brought to Americans' attention in a 1991 edition of the TV program *60 Minutes*, when Morley Safer discussed the "French Paradox." The paradox was that the French, who, as a nation, are well-known for enjoying a delicious cuisine high in fats, suffer from a very low incidence of coronary heart disease. The program concluded that although the French diet is indeed high in saturated fats, it also includes a healthy dose of red wine, which obviously counteracts the effects of the fat. Following the TV program, sales of red wine in the USA almost doubled as Americans concluded that the increased consumption of Merlot would make them healthy, slim, and, hopefully, as elegant as the French.

Even if drinking red wine does not make you look like Catherine Deneuve, recent research has shown the health benefits are still not inconsiderable.

Memory Protection: Researchers at the University of Arizona tested women in their 70s and found those who drank wine daily scored much better in memory quizzes than those who did not drink wine. The powerful antioxidant resveratrol protects against cell damage and prevents age-related mental decline such as Alzheimer's. In a study by Loyola University Medical Center, the researchers gathered and analyzed data from academic papers on red wine since 1977. The studies, which spanned nineteen nations, showed a statistically significantly lower risk of dementia among regular red wine drinkers in fourteen countries. The investigators explained that resveratrol reduces the stickiness of blood platelets, which helps keep the blood vessels open and flexible. This helps maintain a good blood supply to the brain.

Longevity: Wine's anti-aging properties have been recognized for more than a thousand years. Monasteries throughout Europe were convinced their monks' longer lifespans, compared to the rest of the population, were partly due to their daily consumption of wine. A twenty-nine-year long Finnish study shows that wine drinkers have a 34 percent lower mortality rate than beer or vodka drinkers. Again, this is attributed to the antioxidant resveratrol, which is found in the skins of red grapes. A study carried out at the University of London found that compounds commonly found in red wine, called procyanidins, keep blood vessels healthy and are one of the factors that contribute towards longer life spans enjoyed by the wine consuming people of the Mediterranean region.

Reduced Infection: British and Spanish studies have shown that people who drink wine daily reduce their risk of infection by *Helicobacter pylori,* the bacteria that causes gastritis, ulcers, and stomach cancer, by as much as 11 percent.

Ovarian problems: When Australian researchers recently compared women with ovarian cancer to cancer-free women, they found that roughly one glass of wine a day seemed to reduce the risk of the disease by as much as 50 percent. Earlier research at the University of Hawaii produced similar findings.

Stronger bones: Women who drink wine daily have higher bone mass than women who don't drink wine. The wine appears to boost estrogen levels, which slow the body's destruction of old bones and cut the risk of osteoporosis, age-related bone thinning related to calcium loss. A report in the *American Journal of Epidemiology* in April 2000 showed that women who drank the daily equivalent of one to three glasses of wine had greater bone mineral density, measured in the hip region of their thighbones, than nondrinkers or heavy drinkers. Bone mineral density is the measure physicians use to determine bone strength and resilience.

Diabetes: A Harvard Medical School study as well as a study by Amsterdam's VU University show that premenopausal women who drink one or two glasses of wine daily are 40 percent less likely to develop type 2 diabetes than women who abstain.

Heart Attack: A Harvard study shows that wine drinkers suffering from high blood pressure are 30 percent less likely to have a heart attack than nondrinkers, while another study conducted by Queen Mary University in London shows that red wine tannins contain procynidins, which protect against heart disease. According to the January 2000 issue of *European Heart Journal*, red wine appears to dilate arteries and increase blood flow, thus lowering the risk of the kind of clots that cut off blood supply and damage heart muscles.

Blood clots and strokes: Polyphenols (antioxidants) in wine help protect the lining of blood vessels in the heart, and the polyphenol resveratrol reduces the risk of inflammation and clotting. A Colombia University study found that wine drinkers have 50 percent less probability of suffering a clot-related stroke than nondrinkers. The polyphenols in red wine appear to boost levels of HDL, the "good" cholesterol, and helps prevent artery-clogging LDLs, or "bad" cholesterol, from causing damage to the lining of arteries.

Cancer: According to the American Cancer Society, an active antioxidant in red wine called quercetin works against certain cancer cells, especially those in colon cancer. A Stony Brook University study shows that the consumption of red wine cuts the risk of colon cancer by 45 percent. It turns out that the same phenolic compounds that lower heart disease risk also may slow the growth of breast cancer cells, according to findings reported by scientists at the University of Crete in Greece. Phenols were also shown to suppress the growth of prostate cancer cells. French scientists found evidence that resveratrol can slow the growth of liver cancer cells. Researchers from the University Of Missouri School Of Dentistry discovered that red wine's antioxidants, resveratrol and quercetin, may inhibit the growth of oral cancer cells.

Cataracts: An Icelandic study published in *Nature* shows that moderate drinkers are 32 percent less likely to get cataracts than nondrinkers are. Wine drinkers are 43 percent less likely to get cataracts than beer drinkers are.

Marriage: A 2016 paper in *The Journals of Gerontology* reports that couples who drink wine together say they are happier over time. Wives reported they were happier when their husbands drank wine and less happy when they didn't. The study was based upon 2,767 married, heterosexual couples with an average length of thirty-three years of marriage.

Erectile Dysfunction: Research, carried out by the University of East Anglia and Harvard University and reported in 2016, found that eating a flavonoid-rich diet and drinking red wine is as beneficial to erectile function as briskly walking for up to five hours a week. The most beneficial flavonoids were found to be anthocyanins (found in blueberries, cherries, blackberries, radishes, blackcurrants, and red wine), flavanones and flavones (both found in citrus fruits).

Social Graces: Preliminary studies conducted by myself and certain associates have suggested that in addition to being good for your health, wine will improve your clarity of enunciation, cognitive functionality, and dancing skills, as well as making you sexually irresistible to other people.

Chapter

2

MAKING WINE

"Athenaeus wrote that Age appears to be best in four things: Old wood best to burn, old wine to drink, old friends to trust, and old authors to read." — Francis Bacon

---

How Wine Is Made

The making of wine involves two complementary arts: viticulture, which means the growing of grapes on vines, and vinification, which means turning those grapes into wine. Very often the grape farmer (the viticulturist) will simply grow the grapes and then sell them to the winemaker (the vintner), and the winemaker will often simply purchase the grapes from the farmer so that the two processes remain separate. But, ideally, the person or team that originally plants the vine and cultivates the grape also produces the final bottle of wine.

The reason the Eurasian vine, *Vitis vinifera,* has evolved as the dominant vine for winemaking, is that it has been affected by human selection for at least ten thousand years, reflecting the human preference for the larger, juicier, and sweeter hermaphrodite grape, which is more suitable for winemaking. In the New World, where human selection did not initially play an important role, the evolution of the grape was more influenced by the taste of birds. Birds preferred small grapes with tough skins, which are easier to carry in their beaks, and blue grapes, which are easier to see from the air; neither quality, however, being conducive to winemaking. Because North American vines, *Vitis labrusca* and *Vitis riparia,* are not really suitable for decent winemaking, the Eurasian *Vitis vinifera* has been imported since the sixteenth century.

Like most living species, the original wild vines, *Vitis silvestris*, are dioecious, meaning they are either male or female. But, because nature is not always perfect, some species are hermaphrodites, meaning they contain both male and female attributes in the same plant and can thus self-reproduce. The pollen from a male dioecious vine might need to travel some distance to find a female plant, and thus its fruit is less predictable. Because the pollen from hermaphrodite plants does not have so far to travel, their fruit is more predictable, more plentiful, and thus more likely to be selected by humans. Over the course of ten thousand years, therefore, it's the hermaphroditic vines which have been selected for the tastiest and most abundant fruit, and the reason *Vitis silvestris* evolved into *Vitis vinifera*.

Tannins: Throughout this book there are many references to tannins. Tannins are chemical compounds known as phenols, which are found throughout nature in most growing plants. In fact, 50 percent of the dry weight of leaves consist entirely of tannins. Tannin is actually tasteless, and is a texture; you feel the coarse particles which stick to the surface of your tongue and teeth. The best way to think of tannins is to imagine sucking on a used teabag. The puckering and astringent sensation in your mouth is the tang of tannin. One theory for the prevalence of tannins is that it is Nature's way to discourage animals from eating the leaves and stalks before the fruit and seeds are ready for dissemination. Some grape varietals, especially white grapes, have little or no tannins, while other grape varietals—most notably Cabernet Sauvignon—have very high levels of tannins in the skin.

The word tannin comes from the German word for oak tree, *tannenbaum*, from which we derive the words tan and tanning. (Oak tannins have always been used for turning animal hides into leather.) As we will see later, the tannins in oak play an important part in the aging of wine in oak barrels. A red wine with very low tannins, such as Beaujolais, can be drunk extremely young. A Bordeaux wine with very high tannins cannot be drunk when young; it would be impossibly astringent. Wines high in tannins need to be aged, preferably in oak, until, with the passing of the years, the harsh taste of tannins has mellowed. Moreover, with age, the Bordeaux wine has not only lost its astringency and become drinkable, it has substantially improved and those initially harsh tannins have added complexity and maturity to the taste. Without tannins, Beaujolais will not age and will deteriorate rather than improve, while, thanks to tannins, Bordeaux wines just get better and better.

Although it's true that thick-skinned grapes such as Cabernet Sauvignon have more tannins than thin-skinned grapes such as Pinot Noir, there are too many other variables to make a definitive list of grape varietals by tannin level. Where and how the actual grapes are harvested, how long the skins are macerated during fermentation, and how the winemaker blends the juices makes it impossible to say that a Sangiovese will always be less tannic than a Syrah or more tannic than a Zinfandel. A selection of grape varietals is listed in Chapter Eight, from light to heavy or full-bodied, but it is a general list and includes more factors than just tannins.

In her splendid *Wine Bible*, Karen McNeil has listed red varietals by tannic level, from least tannic to most tannic: Gamay / Pinot Noir / Sangiovese / Grenache / Zinfandel / Syrah (Shiraz) / Malbec / Merlot / Mourvédre / Cabernet Franc / Cabernet Sauvignon / Petite Sirah / Nebbiolo.

Sulphites: Like tannins, sulphites are often mentioned in connection with wine, and their role and effects are often misunderstood. All wines contain sulphur dioxide, SO_2, in various forms, collectively known as sulphites; even in completely natural wine it is present at concentrations of up to ten milligrams per liter. The most important thing to understand is that sulphites are an entirely natural byproduct of yeast metabolism during fermentation, and would be found in wines even if the winemaker added nothing to the juice. The Romans used to burn sulphur beneath their upturned *amphora*, or wine containers, to sterilize them before use, and winemakers have been adding various amounts of sulphites ever since to prevent bacteria and bad yeasts from developing in the wine. In the late 1840s, European vineyards were nearly all destroyed by a disease called oïdium, and were saved only at the last moment by nationwide applications of sulpher dust. Sulphites play a very important role in preventing oxidization and maintaining a wine's freshness. Even so, compared to processed foods, dried fruit, sodas, packaged meats, or even commercial fruit juice, the amount of sulphites in wine is miniscule. On visits to Europe over the years, I have often been given bottles of wine made by friends for local consumption, not for export. These fresh wines, which were delicious when drunk locally, had been made without the addition of sulphites and were sadly undrinkable by the time I had brought them home to the USA.

US wine labels are required to indicate if the sulphite level exceeds ten parts per million (ppm). Many red wines contain sulphite levels of fifty ppm, but this should be compared with the 2,000 ppm sulphite level of French fries to put it in perspective. Some people blame the sulphites for the headaches they suffer when drinking red wine, but in fact red wine has much lower sulphites than white wine; headaches are more likely to be caused by the tannins, the histamines, or even the extra alcohol in red wines. Despite some of the hysteria about sulphites, the levels of sulpher dioxide in wines is too small to have any adverse health effects, except for those people who are clinically allergic to sulphites; the FDA estimates this to be less than 1 percent of the population. If you have eaten dried fruit or French fries with no ill effects, then continue to drink your wine and not worry about sulphites.

Acids in Wine: While the word "acid" evokes images of car batteries rather than a refreshing beverage, acids play an important role in both the making and tasting of wine. The two major acids, tartaric and malic, are both naturally present in the grapes as they first develop on the vine.

Tartaric acid, unlike malic acid, is not so common in the plant world and, outside the tropics, is almost exclusive to the grape vine. One of the ways that archeologists have been able to identify ancient wine-producing sites is through traces of tartaric acid. Because tartaric acid is unique to the grape vine, residue of tartaric crystals in amphora and other containers provides an indication of a winemaking culture. Depending on the varietal of the grape and the temperature, tartaric acids can sometimes crystallize in the wine. When this happens, the crystals sink to the bottom of the bottles, where they resemble broken glass or "wine diamonds." Although they are perfectly harmless and tasteless, consumers object to these crystals, and so most winemakers try to remove excess tartaric acid before bottling.

Malic acid is found in just about every fruit and berry plant and is most commonly associated with apples, which is where it derives its name, *alum*, the Latin word for apple. It is that sharp astringent taste of green apples which is most recognizable in an acidic wine. The malic acids play an important role in the growth of the vine, providing energy during photosynthesis and, at verison, metabolizing into sugar. It is the malic acid which provides the sharpness to the flavors and which balances the sweetness of any residual sugars, as well as complementing the bitterness of the tannins in red wine. Too much malic acid in a wine will make it tart and unpleasantly astringent and too little will make the wine taste flabby and dead. The correct amount of malic acid is what provides the balance and harmony of a great wine.

57

Lactic acid, unlike the other acids, is not found in the grapes, but is a product of a secondary fermentation. Most white wines and some red wines are not subject to the secondary fermentation, and therefore do not contain any lactic acid. Secondary, or Malolactic Fermentation, is the process by which certain bacteria convert the tart malic acids into the softer lactic acids. Lactic acid was first derived from sour milk in the eighteenth century, and the name comes from the Latin word for milk, *lact*. Most red wines and most Chardonnays undergo malolactic fermentation, partly to soften the tartness of the malic acids but also for the improved "mouth-feel" that results. Unlike, say, a Sauvignon Blanc, which retains the green-apple-sharpness of the malic acids, a Chardonnay following malolactic fermentation will have the softer, more "buttery" feel and flavor of the lactic acid.

Acetic acid is a product of the primary fermentation when the yeasts are converting the sugars into alcohol and carbon dioxide. If the wine is further exposed to oxygen, the alcohol will be converted by bacteria into ascetic acid and eventually into vinegar. Not a good acid.

In addition to balancing the taste of the sugars and tannins in wine to create the complex harmony that wine drinkers so enjoy, acids also play an important role in protecting and stabilizing the wine on its journey from the initial fermentation barrels to its happy arrival in our glass.

Taste & Quality

The eventual taste and quality of a wine depends on a number of factors:

Latitude: Wine-producing vines are grown all over the world in a belt roughly between thirty and fifty degrees latitude north or south of the equator. North of the equator includes the Mediterranean region as far north as Germany, and from southern California as far north as Washington State. South of the equator, the band runs from Central Chile and Argentina, through the tip of South Africa to Southern Australia and New Zealand. The further away from the equator, the less sun there is. Less sun means less sugar and fruit on the vine, and consequently less alcohol and less color in the wine. Wines grown closer to the equator by contrast have more body, a darker color, and higher alcohol content.

Elevation: Where there is less sun, vines need to be grown on a slope so that they catch as much sunlight as possible. This is why German vineyards are all on south-facing slopes of river valleys. Vineyards in the South of France by contrast, already get enough sunlight and so do not need the angled slopes. In California, where fog from the cold Pacific creeps into the valleys most evenings, some types of grapes benefit from the cooling effects of the fog, while other grapes, such as Zinfandel, thrive at a higher elevation above the fog line.

Soil and drainage: Unlike most other crops, good vines do not benefit from rich fertile soil. Most vineyards are found in stony and infertile regions—but with good drainage. Poor topsoil forces the root of the vine to force itself deep into the ground in search of water. This results in stronger and more powerful roots, which can better absorb the complex taste of the minerals through which they dig. Limestone, chalk, volcanic pumice, and gravel are all especially favorable for vines, as they absorb and store rainwater and are rich in complex minerals from ancient marine life.

Climate: The prevailing microclimate of individual regions obviously has a major influence on the cultivation of grapes. The Languedoc region of Southern France has long, hot summers, little rain, and the drying effect of the Mistral winds, thus producing large quantities of dark-red wine with high alcohol. The river valleys of the Mosel in Germany have a much cooler climate with far more rain, and consequently produce pale-white wines which are low in alcohol.

Climate Change: Controversial or not, climate change is having a profound effect on the world's vineyards, especially in Europe, where the boundary for wine growing moves steadily northward. The vineyards of Burgundy, which have always been vulnerable to cold winters resulting in poor harvests, have enjoyed an unprecedented twenty years of perfect growing seasons. The worry is that eventually, as the climate warms, it will become too hot for the Pinot Noir and Chardonnays, which also need cool evenings in order to produce that Burgundian magic. In Germany, too, with the extra sunshine, the Riesling grapes are producing more sugar, and thus the Auslese wines of the Moselle are becoming sweeter and more alcoholic.

The main beneficiaries of climate change are the English, who are finally able to grow their own vines and make their own wine without being beholden to any beastly foreigners. Various French Champagne houses are actually buying land in Southern England and planting vineyards in the same chalky, limestone soil they are used to back home in Northern France. The area of vines planted in England and Wales has doubled from 761 hectares in 2004 to about 1,500 hectares in 2013. The country now has almost 500 vineyards, and English "champagnes" are winning international prizes and being compared favorably—even by the French—to the best French Champagnes. In 1998, an English Classic Cuvée 1993, won first prize at the International Wine & Spirit Competition and was voted best sparkling wine in the world.

Varietal: Varietal refers to the specific type of grape, each of which has different requirements and produce different types of wine. Some varietals need more rain while others need more sun. Some varietals require a longer growing season, some bud early in the year, others reach fruition later. Over the centuries, winegrowers have matched the different varieties of grape with the ideal climate, elevation, and soil type. In Europe, with over 2,000 years of experience, different regions have their own specific grape varietal; in Burgundy, all red wines are made from the Pinot Noir grape, while in Tuscany all red wines are made with the Sangiovese grape. (The major different varietals are described alphabetically starting in Chapter Six.)

Vintner: The vintner, or winemaker, is the person whose decisions affect the final quality of the wine. Until recently, the vintner would rely on tradition, using the wisdom and experience passed down from his father and grandfather who had typically been producing wine in the same place for generations. These days, the vintner is probably university-trained and bases his decisions on the latest scientific research. Another major difference is that these days, the vintner is very often female, as more and more women are running vineyards and directing wineries. Today, there are even "Flying Winemakers" who travel the world, sharing their expertise for the week or two they spend visiting different vineyards and wineries on their travels.

Viticulture: How Vines are Grown (Sun + grape = sugar)

The Vine: The vine is nature's factory that produces the sugar out of earth, air, sun and water which the vintner will ultimately use to make wine. The roots of the vine pull water out of the earth, while the chlorophyll in the green leaves draws carbon dioxide out of the surrounding air. By the magical process of photosynthesis, light from the sun transforms these simple ingredients into sucrose sugars. The rising sap then takes this sucrose into the flesh of the grapes, which is used to provide the seeds with energy. This whole cycle has no other purpose than to provide the seeds with enough food and vigor to start the next generation. The production of juicy grapes or fine wines is purely incidental to Nature, whose only interest lies in propagating the endless cycle of birth and rebirth.

Winter Dormancy: Following the harvest in the fall, the vines are pruned of all signs of life and are left to survive the harshness of the winter on the bare ground. Unlike the luxuriant green plant of high summer, the vine in winter resembles an unattractive piece of dead driftwood. During the winter months, the vine becomes entirely dormant and all the sap descends deep underground to protect the roots. During the growing season, a vine will be destroyed if the temperature falls below 27° F. But during the winter with the sap protecting the roots, the vines can survive temperatures as low as minus 5°F.

Frosts: The vinegrower's year is bookended by the last frost of the spring and the first frost of the fall. If the vines are allowed to bud before winter's final frost, they will not survive. Similarly, if the grapes are not picked before the first frost of the fall, the whole harvest could be ruined. The challenge for the winegrower is to maximize his growing season between those two frosts. The more days of sunshine to which the growing vines are exposed, the more sugar will be produced, and thus the higher alcohol level in the wine.

VITIS VINIFERA				
Month	Weather	Vine	Vineyard Work	Cellar work
January				Malolactic Fermentation
February		Weeping	Pruning	Topping-up / ullage
March	**Spring Frost**	Bud Break	Frost protection	Bottling
April		Shooting	De-suckering	Racking

Month	Season	Vine	Vineyard	Cellar
May		Flowering	Shoot postioning	Assemble & ship orders
June		Fruiting		Binal racking of good wine
July	**Summer Sun**	Veraison	Spraying (disease)	Bottling older wines
August		Ripening	Thining grapes	Clear for Vendage
September			Vendage (harvest)	Vendage
October	**Fall Frost**	Passerillage	Late harvest	Fermenting
November		Botrytis Cinerea	Late harvest	Fining / racking
December			pruning	taste new wines/ malolactic fermentation

Figure 1: The Year of the Vine

Weeping: As winter ends, the ground temperature rises, and once the vine senses the first stirring of spring in the air, it slowly returns to life. As the temperature one foot beneath the surface reaches about 50°F, by a process of osmosis, the sap starts rising from the roots deep in the earth and spontaneously begins to drip from the cuts where the vine was pruned the previous season. It is a beautiful and moving precursor of spring when a whole vineyard begins to glisten with the rising sap, a sign that the cycle of life will begin anew. This natural phenomenon is called "weeping" or "bleeding," and each individual vine is capable of weeping eleven pints of sap.

Bud Break: Within twenty or thirty days of weeping, the first buds begin to form, which means that the vine is at its most vulnerable to late frosts. This is the time of year when the farmer is out in the vineyard, sometimes all night, lighting fires, using smudge-pots, covering the vines, spraying water, blowing fans, or even using the downdraft from helicopters—whatever will best protect the delicate young buds from the damaging frost. An early bud-break is obviously vulnerable to frost, but a late bud-break might mean the grapes will not have a long enough growing season in order to ripen.

Shooting: As the buds produce shoots, these need to be trained onto the trellises which will permit them to spread and support the bunches of grapes. Depending on the grape variety and the wine region, different trellis systems are used; some have just a single strand of wire, while other systems—typically exposed to more sun—allow for several strands, supporting a denser concentration of fruit and a thicker, protective covering of leaves. Buds which do not quickly produce shoots are removed by the farmer in a process called de-suckering, so that only the healthiest buds survive.

In many wine regions, especially in France where the Appellation laws are most strict, there are limits governing how many shoots or buds are permitted on specific vines, and the local "wine police" will inspect vineyards to ensure that the farmer has pruned or de-suckered correctly. The purpose of this is to ensure quality. The less buds and shoots means less grapes and less juice, but also results in a higher concentration of taste—thus ensuring the continuing reputation of the Appellation.

Flowering: Approximately another month or more after the bud-break, the first flowers appear on the end of the shoots as clusters of tiny "buttons." Within a couple of weeks these small buttons grow to become small berries which, being hermaphroditic, immediately begin to self-pollinate. During the pollinating period the vine is very sensitive to outside influences, such as climate and temperature, and, depending on the health of the vine, as little as 30 percent or as much as 60 percent of the flowers may successfully pollinate, producing fruit.

Fruit Set: Following pollination, the berries quickly grow into what are now recognizable grapes, filling with acidic flesh and developing skins with yeasts and tannins. It is at this point, depending on the success rate of the pollination that the farmer can begin to predict the potential harvest crop yield. As spring advances to summer, the chlorophyll in the leaves of the vine start to absorb the light from the sun and, by photosynthesis, to convert the carbon dioxide in the surrounding air into pure energy, which in turn magically converts the flesh of the grape into sugar. The sugar has two purposes: to feed the seed with energy and to make the grape sweet and attractive to birds and animals so they will carry the seeds to a new location to start a new generation.

Veraison: This French term means the beginning of ripening, when the grapes change color as the natural acids in the flesh hydrolyze the sucrose into glucose and fructose to feed the pip with energy to become the seed for a new generation. With veraison, the skin of red grapes becomes darker in color while the skin of white grapes becomes more translucent. At the same time as the skin changes color, the fruit acidity decreases and the sugar level increases by as much as 25 percent. Veraison signifies that the seed of the grape has reached maturity, and as the grape grows fleshier, sweeter, and less acidic, it is obviously more attractive to animals, who, by eating the fruit of the vine, ultimately spread the seeds.

Vendange/ Harvesting: Harvesting traditionally takes place one hundred days after flowering; in the northern hemisphere this occurs between August and October (and between February and April south of the equator). In addition to the latitude of the vineyard and the variety of grape to be picked, the decision of when exactly to begin the harvest depends on the weather and the balance of acid and sugar within the grape. In addition to the sugar/acid balance, the farmer will be judging the taste of the grape to decide if the tannins have begun to ripen and soften. Traditionally, the farmer would make his decision by tasting the grapes on a daily basis, but increasingly these decisions are also being confirmed in the laboratory when random samples of grapes are tested for the correct balance of pH levels and acidity. Typically, a wine-lab will seek a reading of 19-25 degrees Brix, over 0.7 percent acidity and with a pH of less than 3.4. (One degree Brix represents 1 gram of sucrose in 100 grams of liquid juice). The grape is considered ripe when the sugar stops increasing and the acid stops decreasing.

> **Vineyard Yield:** Depending on the size of the grape, about 700 grapes are needed to make one bottle of wine. Different growing regions have different rules concerning the amount of grapes per acre that can be harvested or how much wine can be produced per acre. On average, depending on local rules and conditions, one ton of grapes will produce about 150 gallons of wine, which is about sixty cases, or 720 bottles of wine. Obviously, growing conditions vary enormously around the world, from the rich, condensed vineyards of California's Central Valley to the dry and arid fields of Central Spain where the vines have to be spaced far apart. Consequently, it is much more difficult to discuss average yield per acre when such yields can vary between two tons per acre to ten tons. However, using a conservative four tons per acre, which would result in 600 gallons of wine per acre, or 240 cases, almost 3,000 bottles per acre.

In general, the following can be used for rough calculations:

> *One bottle of wine = 750 ml or one-fifth of a gallon*

> *One Barrel = sixty gallons or twenty-five casesor 300x750ml bottles*

> *One Ton of Grapes = approximately sixty cases or 720 bottles of wine*

*One Acre of Vineyards – Low yield for high quality wines =
two tons*

*One Acre of Vineyards – High yield for less expensive wines =
ten tons*

*One ton of grapes at $1,000 per ton will produce $10 retail bottles
of wine (1 percent rule of thumb)*

In Bordeaux, for example, the permitted yield for red wine is 588
gallons of wine per acre (fifty-five hectoliters per hectare), or slightly
less than four tons of grapes or 240 cases of wine per acre. For
Chianti Classico, the permitted yield is more restricted; 52.5 hectoliters
per hectare, or about 228 cases per acre. For the sweet white wines
of Sauternes and Monbazillac, the maximum yield is even more
restricted, with twenty-five hectolitres per hectare or 1.5 tons (ninety
cases) per acre.

In California's Central Valley, the very efficient and mechanized
vineyards produce ten tons of Cabernet Sauvignon per acre, which
can sell for about $450 per ton (and eventually $4.50 per bottle using
the 1 percent rule of thumb). The same grape grown in the Napa
Valley, often using old vines and manual labor, tightly pruned to
produce less but better grapes, may yield as little as two tons per acre
but which will sell for $4,500 per ton (and eventually $45 per bottle).

Early Frost: Just as a late frost in spring can destroy the budding vines
and ruin a growing season before it even begins, so too an early
frost during the fall can destroy overnight the whole year's work if the
farmer leaves the harvest too late. In choosing when to harvest, the
farmer must be thinking of potential frosts as well as the ripeness of the
grape. However, certain white wines are deliberately left on the vine,
even after the frost, to create a powerful and sweet "late harvest" wine.

Late Harvest Wines:

Passerillage: If picking is delayed and the grapes are left on the vine after the regular harvest has finished, the vine leaves turn yellow and the stems turn woody while the sap stops rising and remains deep below ground to protect the roots through the cold winter months. With no sap rising to nourish the grapes, they shrivel and dehydrate. As the sugar content becomes more concentrated, the flesh of the grape experiences complex chemical changes which adds to the rich taste of the eventual wine. Alternatively, the grapes are placed on straw mats after being picked and allowed to dry in the sun. In Northeast Italy this form of passerillage is called *appassimento.*

Botrytis cinerea (noble rot), similar to passerillage, is actually a fungal infection called *Botrytis cinerea* (or more correctly, if not more improperly, *Botryotinia fuckeliana,* named in honor of a nineteenth century botanist named Karl Wilhelm Gottlieb Leopold Fuckel). This fungal pathogen colonizes grapes in order to glean nutrients from them. The infected pathogens produce the enzymes laccase and pectinase, which help the fungus break down the skin of the grapes to gain access to the inside of the fruit. Botrytis, like most molds, enjoys a humid environment, and in the Sauternes region south of Bordeaux, for example, weather conditions are very specific—with humid, cool mornings and warm, sunny, and dry afternoons—which keep the infection from growing too rapidly and turning into sour rot.

Noble rot uses the pectinase enzymes to break through the skin of healthy grapes, which leads to a natural dehydration of the fruit since the pectins in the skin are what hold in the moisture. This natural dehydration concentrates the sugars, acids, and flavors within the skins, which are then translated into a more concentrated must during the fermentation. Noble rot adds its own influences in the form of additional flavors of marmalade, quince, and mushrooms.

Noble rot also produces gluconic acid, which increases the acid content of the must. It contributes higher glycerol content, leading to a fuller mouth-feel than the fruit would have had without the infection. These traits are particularly desirable for Sauternes, where the tiny, cool Ciron River meets the larger, warmer Garonne, making for cool, foggy mornings and warm, sunny afternoons. The vineyards in this area maximize their exposure to the fungus through multiple picking times (called tries), during which they only choose the most-affected grapes and leave the less-affected ones to increase in concentration. Because the fungus travels through the vines at an unpredictable rate, the grapes have to be harvested carefully, bunch by bunch, when they are ready. For the very best wines, the grapes are harvested grape by individual grape in the early morning before the heat of the sun can affect them. The best and most famous examples of this process are found in the Sauternes and Barsac regions just south of Bordeaux.

Eiswein (Ice-wine): The process is very similar to passerillage, and the grapes are left on the vine to freeze inside the ice while they shrink inside, concentrating their juices and sugars to produce a sweet white wine high in alcohol. This method of making sweet wines is naturally found in colder wine making regions such as Germany, Austria, Hungary, Upstate New York and Canada.

The result of both noble rot and passerillage is a concentrated sweet wine high in sugar content and alcohol; delightfully unctuous and viscous. At their best, these wines are so volatile that no sooner do they enter the mouth than they evaporate. Rising straight to the olfactory bulb, they are immediately absorbed into the deepest recesses of the brain and fill us with a sense of ineffable joy. These late-harvest wines are most traditionally found in Tokaji wines from Hungary, Vendange Tardive wines from Alsace, and Monbazillac,

Sauternes, and Barsac wines from Southwest France. The high cost of labor is reflected in the prices and a single bottle of Château d'Yquem Sauternes was recently auctioned for $115,000.

Dormancy: After all the grapes have been harvested, like a bear in winter the vine shuts down and hibernates until the coming of spring when the cycle begins anew. When the leaves have fallen and the stem shrivels and dries out, it once again resembles a piece of dead driftwood. Looking at a bare and bleak vineyard in winter, it is hard to picture the green and verdant views of the summer. For this reason the vine has always held a sacred, sometimes religious symbolism of rebirth. The Egyptian God Osiris was both the God of wine and the God of rebirth, as was the Greek God Dionysus; features of both were incorporated into Christian symbolism as we discuss in the next chapter, "History of Wine."

Viniculture: Making the Wine (Sugar + yeast = alcohol + CO2)

The Vintner: From the moment the grapes have been harvested, an organic process of decay begins. The natural yeasts in the skin will react with the sugars in the flesh of the grape to produce alcohol and carbon dioxide. When the sugars are all consumed, or the alcohol level reaches about 14 degrees ABV (alcohol by volume), this process of fermentation ends. The next stage in this natural cycle is for the oxygen in the air to transform the alcohol into vinegar, which in turn is transformed by bacteria back into carbon dioxide and water, ready to be extracted from the air and the earth by a new generation of vines. It is the job of the vintner to control this natural cycle and to bottle the wine before the oxygen turns it into vinegar.

Pre-Fermentation: From the moment the grapes are picked four processes can occur:

White Wine: The grapes are quickly crushed, separated from the skins, and the juice is kept at a low temperature and usually protected by an inert gas so that no oxygen can start the fermentation process. Because the skins were immediately removed, the juice is a clear color and will produce white wine. The different shade of white, from pale-straw to rich-golden, depends on the variety of grape used. Before fermentation is allowed to occur, the juice is rigorously filtered until all impurities are removed.

Red Wine: After being separated from the leaves and stems, the grapes are crushed and the juice and skins are allowed to ferment together in the fermenting vat. The skins add color to the juice, resulting in red wine. The skins also contain tannins, which is why red wines are more tannic and need more aging. This mixture of juice and skin is called the must.

Rosé Wine: Prior to fermentation, the juice is exposed to the grape skins long enough to acquire some coloring.

Raisinated Wine: The grapes are left on straw mats to dry out in the sun, becoming like raisins, with a high concentration of sugar later resulting in a powerfully alcoholic wine. This is the process by which the best and most expensive wines used to be made, but these days is usually limited to the shores of the northern Italian Lake Garda where the wines are called Recioto and Amarone.

Fermentation: Fermentation is the process whereby the sugars in the grape juice interact with the yeasts in the skin to produce alcohol and carbon dioxide. As soon as the grape juice is exposed to the oxygen in the air, the naturally occurring yeasts are able to react with the sugars. The carbon dioxide bubbles through the juice and raises the skins and residue of the grape to the top of the vat, where it forms a skin called the cap. The cellar workers stand at the top of the vat and break this cap so the pieces float down in the vat to interact further with the must, which, at the same time, is exposed to more oxygen. Punching down through the cap obviously extracts more tannins and other compounds from the skins as they macerate in the juice, and the cellar master will be constantly tasting the results to know when to stop punching before the wine becomes too dark or too tannic.

COMPOSITION OF GRAPES / WINE		
	Grape	Wine
Water	75.0%	82.9%
Sugars	22.0%	0.1%
Alcohols	0.1%	14.5%
Organic Acid	0.9%	0.6%
Minerals	0.5%	0.5%
Phenols	0.3%	0.3%
Proteins	0.2%	0.1%
	99.0%	99.0%

Figure 2: Transformation of sugar into wine

Although yeasts occur naturally in grapes, modern wineries often also use cultured yeasts for the additional control they bring to the process. The yeasts react with the sugars in the grape juice to produce ethyl alcohol (ethanol) and carbon dioxide, and so the higher the concentration of sugar, the higher the resulting alcohol. This is why juice low in sugar—for example from regions like Germany with less sunshine—produce wines with lower alcohol levels. The yeast continues producing alcohol until there is no sugar left. However, after a maximum alcohol level is reached (usually about 14-15 percent), the alcohol kills off the yeast. A juice with a very high sugar content (such as the late harvest wines discussed above) will thus have residual sugar remaining, even after the maximum alcohol level has been reached. That's why these late harvest wines are celebrated for being sweet as well as powerfully alcoholic.

When the fermentation has finished and all the sugar has been converted to alcohol, the free-run juice (now wine) is run into barrels for the secondary fermentation. The remaining juice and skins in the fermentation tanks are then pressed, and the secondary or pressed-juice will have more body and color than the initial free–run wine and will be used for blending or for distillation into brandy or marc.

Chaptalization: Sugar is sometimes added to the still fermenting wine, not to make it sweeter, but to allow the yeasts to produce more alcohol. Obviously, this occurs only in regions with low sunlight, like Germany or Northern France where the lack of sunshine means the unripe grapes lack sufficient sugar to produce enough alcohol by themselves. The process is named after Napoleon's Minister of the Interior, Jean-Antoine Chaptal, who introduced the concept as a way to improve French wine which had suffered neglect through years of revolution and war.

Secondary (Malolactic) Fermentation: Because most white wines were rigorously filtered prior to fermentation, they can be bottled and shipped as soon as the primary fermentation has been completed. Red wines, however, are subject to a secondary fermentation, called malolactic fermentation. Although it is a naturally occurring process, this secondary fermentation was not really documented until the mid-nineteenth century, when scientists such as Louis Pasteur described the effect of bacteria on wine. It was not until the 1950s that a wine professor at the University of Bordeaux, Émile Peynaud, was able to describe the malolactic process and give winemakers the tools to harness it. Prior to Peynaud's work, the great red wines of Bordeaux needed decades of aging before they were ready for drinking. Thanks

73

to malolactic fermentation, these wines now mature much faster and can be drunk much sooner with no loss of quality.

Malolactic fermentation usually takes place in oak barrels and is the process by which the harsher, naturally occurring malic acids of the grapes are converted by bacteria into the softer lactic acids, and the rough edges of the tannins are rounded out. Lactic acids are actually a bacterium named Oenococcus, which eats and digests the malic acids—but there does come a point when the serious wine drinker says "enough already with the bacteria."

This secondary fermentation is a naturally occurring process which normally takes place after the sugars have been converted to alcohol, and is encouraged by winemakers as it removes the tart, acidic taste of young wine and replaces it with a softer, more buttery taste and increased mouth-feel. Some light reds, such as Beaujolais, which are low in tannins, do not need this secondary fermentation and can be bottled (and drunk) soon after harvesting. Conversely, some white grapes, such as Chardonnay, do benefit from this secondary fermentation and some exposure to oak barrels. Part of the charm of a Sauvignon Blanc is its refreshing acidity, while the pleasures of a Chardonnay come from its rich, mouth-filling softness. Big-bodied reds, such as Cabernet Sauvignon, which are high in tannins and have a harsh, tart taste when young, obviously benefit most from this secondary fermentation.

Post-Fermentation Cellar Work:

Racking and ullage: Just as the grape juice for white wine was carefully filtered to remove any impurities prior to fermentation, so the red wine is filtered after fermentation. The fermentation itself kills the yeast and produces impurities called "lees" which fall to the bottom. Placed in oak barrels, partly to allow the malolactic fermentation—but also to permit the oak itself to impart its own flavor of vanilla, caramel, and cream and to absorb the harshness of the tannins—the wine evaporates slightly in the barrel, thus concentrating its flavors. As the sediments (lees) settle to the bottom of the barrel, the wine is removed and poured into new barrels leaving the impurities behind, a process called "racking." As the wine evaporates through the oak, it leaves an empty space at the top of the barrel which needs to be topped-up regularly with more wine to keep out the air, which would otherwise oxidize and spoil the wine. This process of topping-up is called "ullage." Some white wines, such as Chardonnay, and most red wines, benefit from a certain amount of time in oak, especially those like Cabernet Sauvignon, which are high in tannins. Many of the great Châteaux wines of Bordeaux are aged in oak barrels for as long as two years before bottling. Spanish wines, in order to be classified as Crianza or Reserva, need to be aged in oak for at least six months. As discussed later in the chapter on Spain, the fortified wines of Jerez (Sherry) can be aged in barrels for one hundred years or more under the "solera" process. Oak barrels are discussed in more detail in the next section.

Blending and fining: Blending simply means combining wine from two or more sources and mixing them together. In blending the wines, the winemaker may be trying to enhance the aroma or improve the color, or to lower or raise the alcohol level, the sugar level, the acidity, or the tannins. The blended wines may come from the same vine and the same vintage when the vintner is adding pressed-wine to free-run wine to add more color, for example, but usually the blend will include wines from completely different sources and varietals when the vintner is trying to achieve a balance between the acidity, the tannins, and a lush fruitiness. The classic Bordeaux blend, for example, includes Cabernet Sauvignon for its tannins, Merlot for its softer fruitiness, Cabernet Franc for its earthiness, Malbec for its dark color, and Petit Verdot for its structure and body. In California, this particular blend is called

Meritage; while in England it is called Claret. The racking process, described above, removes most of the sediment from the wine, but fining agents are also added for the final clarification process, as they attract and attach themselves to the microscopic impurities which might otherwise cloud the wine. The most common fining agent is gelatin, but other traditional agents include bull's blood, egg whites, bone char, and even honey.

Oak Barrels

Barrels have been used for transporting, storing, and aging wine since the time of the Romans. Even though modern wineries, with their focus on hygiene and efficiency, use stainless steel for most stages in the winemaking process, top quality wines still spend much of the time in old-fashioned oak barrels. The interaction between the wine and the oak is such an important part of the aging process that when storage in actual barrels is not economically feasible, oak chips are sometimes mixed with the wine in stainless steel vats as a way to imitate the benefit of barrel aging.

There is even an obscure historical relationship between oak and wine caused by the endless rivalry between the English and French. In 1615, England's King James I banned the use of oak to fuel the furnaces used for making glass. The King wanted to preserve England's oak forests for timber with which to build ships to invade France. Unable to use oak, England's glassmakers started using coal in their furnaces, which created much higher temperatures—sufficient to melt sand and thus to produce modern wine bottles, which the French called *verre anglais*—strong enough to store sparkling wines and thus creating Champagne! Two hundred years later, Napoleon Bonaparte ordered the planting of five major forests of oak around France specifically for building a fleet of ships with which to invade

England. These five forests now produce the world's most expensive wine barrels.

Oak barrels offer three unique features: the wood itself absorbs and softens the wine's natural tannins, thus hastening the aging process; the phenols in the oak also impart their own flavors of vanilla, caramel, spice, and smoke; and finally, the oak is porous, allowing the wine to breathe so that it slowly evaporates and thus concentrates its flavors. (This is why oak barrels have to be consistently topped-up.) Serious winemakers—lead by Robert Mondavi—put as much effort and research into selecting the oak for their barrels as they do in planting their vines or blending their wine. Slower growing forests produce tighter grain than forests with more sunshine and longer growing seasons. The tighter the grain of the oak, the more slowly the flavors are imparted; the looser the grain, the more quickly the oak will overwhelm the wine. Cellar masters will select the oak for their barrel depending on the style of wine they wish to make and the length of time they plan to age it.

Traditionally French oak, cut from the five forests planted by Napoleon I for ship-building, have always been favored over American oak, and the price of French versus American oak has reflected this. It has now been accepted that the difference lies not so much in the wood itself but in the way it was treated. The French air-dried their oak for at least two years before working it, while Americans saved time and kiln-dried their oak. To make the staves for the barrels, the Americans cut the wood with a saw, whereas the French always split it along the grain. The French methods imparted a much more subtle effect when aging the wine. Today, however, American wine barrel makers are using French methods and achieving similar results (although French oak is still more expensive).

Each time a barrel is used for aging, the wine will leave a coating of tartaric acid on the inside of the barrel so that after four or five uses the oak will have no further effect on the wine—it becomes a neutral oak barrel which is good for aging a lighter wine when the winemaker wants to retain the taste of fruit. The same is true for very large barrels, since a smaller proportion of the wine is in actual contact with the oak. The reason that German wines during the Middle Ages lasted for so long is that the Cistercian monks stored them in vast, giant barrels called tuns. Many of these tuns could hold over two hundred thousand liters, or over fifty thousand US gallons of wine; indeed some, like the ones in Konigstein and Heidelburg, were so large that they had dance floors built on top of them. It was because the barrels were so vast and the insides so coated with tartaric acid that very little of the wine came into contact with the oak, and so they aged for decades without oxidizing.

However, for top quality, high-tannic wines where the oak is important, smaller barrels are used and used only once or twice before being sold off and replaced with new barrels so the wine can benefit from the intense notes of the fresh, uncoated oak.

The most common barrel size is the Bordeaux barriques style of 220 liters, followed by the slightly larger Burgundy style of 230 liters. Bordeaux's high-tannin Cabernet Sauvignons require more intense oak than Burgundy's Pinot Noirs, hence the smaller sized barrel. In 2011, the cost of a 220 liter French oak barrel was $850. A 220 liter barrel would thus produce almost 300 bottles of Bordeaux at a cost of about $2.90 per bottle. Obviously, this would be an excessive expense for the makers of Two Buck Chuck, but for a Château Latour with an average price of $775 per bottle, it is probably considered an acceptable expense.

Bottling and sealing

Sulphur dioxide is often added just prior to, as well as during, the bottling process, both as a preservative and also to prevent any further fermentation inside the bottle. As soon as the wine has been bottled, the neck is sealed with a cork, and, as a final step, a capsule is added.

Prior to the late seventeenth century, wine was protected from the air by using wooden bungs, cloth, wax, and even olive oil. Cork from the bark of a Portuguese tree was discovered in the seventeenth century and the necks of glass bottles began to acquire a standard size. By the late twentieth century, synthetic corks started replacing natural cork, and in the twenty-first century screw caps are becoming increasingly acceptable. In terms of efficiency at protecting the contents of the bottle from the air, screw caps are far superior to cork—as well as being far cheaper. One of the many meaningless rituals associated with wine occurs in a restaurant when the wine waiter lays the cork down for inspection. Although this once had significance back in the eighteenth century, unless the cork is actually disintegrating and smelly, there is very little you can learn from inspecting it. So just smile politely and say, "Thank you."

Traditional corks are still better for expensive wines, however, which need to be aged for several years because they allow for a certain amount of evaporation, an important factor in the aging process. Since the vast majority of wine produced these days is intended to be drunk within five years of being bottled, the evaporation factor is not important and thus synthetic corks or screw caps make far more sense than more expensive and sometimes tainted natural cork. However, the aesthetic ritual of elegantly removing a cork as opposed to unscrewing a cap is a pleasure not to be easily dismissed. Also, as *The Huffington Post*'s Eleanor Shannon, a sommelier, argues, "Cork is infinitely renewable. Harvesting doesn't harm the trees and it's easy to create more supply by planting more trees. Producing metal screw caps and plastic stoppers requires ten times more non-renewable energy and creates toxic by-products especially from petrochemicals." The debate continues.

Aging

Some red wines, which are high in tannins, actually need to be aged for a long time; they are almost undrinkable when young. Storing the wines in oak barrels and then laying them down in bottles for a few years allows all the youthful harshness to mellow and to become mature— in much the same way that those loud and boisterous medical students eventually become eminent and dignified physicians. Lacking in tannins, very few white wines benefit in the same way, and, with the exception of Chardonnays, most white wines are best drunk young. However, white wines, which are rich in residual sugars, like Sauternes or Tokai, do benefit from aging. Just as the harsh tannins of the reds become softer and more complex with age, so too the sugars of sweet whites become less cloying and more nuanced with age. This is another reason that sweet white wines have always been valued by the aristocracy—because, until quite recently, they were the only wines which aged.

Wine Bottles

Although glass vessels have existed since Roman times, they were generally for household use—serving the wine, rather than buying and selling it. Because glass was so breakable and because hand-blown glass couldn't be made to a standard measure, using bottles as a primary mechanism for storing wine just wasn't practical.

Because the glass was so fragile, wine bottles were wrapped in a protective layer of straw, just as some bottles of Chianti are marketed today. It wasn't until the seventeenth century, when coal-fueled furnaces replaced wood-burning ones, that it became possible to produce thicker and stronger glass. With the addition of the fashion for using cork stoppers, glass bottles suddenly became suitable for the transportation and aging of wines.

Glass bottles were originally shaped like wine skins or sacs and protected with a straw basket, but by the eighteenth century, with stronger glass, bottles became taller and more slender, and could thus be laid on their side for shipping as well as for storage in cellars. Laying bottles on their side also kept the cork moist, ensuring a tighter seal from the air and allowing the wine to age longer.

Because they had to be blown by human glassblowers, all glass bottles, whatever their shape or provenance, have normally held between 600 and 800 milliliters since that is the capacity of the human lung. Following the invention of mass produced bottles in 1903, standard shapes and sizes became increasingly common throughout the twentieth century, and in the late 1970s, the European Union and the USA set a requirement that all wine bottles be a uniform 750 milliliters. A normal serving contains five ounces, or 150 milliliters, of wine, which means a bottle of wine will typically serve five glasses.

The dimple, or concave bump, at the base of many wine bottles is called a "punt." There is no agreement on the original purpose of the punt but there is no shortage of theories. It probably had something to do with the process of blowing glass by hand, and certainly it made the bottle more stable when standing on the table.

Bottle Shapes: There are a number of different bottle shapes, all of which originated in Europe and most of them in France.

Bordeaux: Bordeaux bottles were developed for the English market and needed to be strong and lay flat during the sea voyage. Because the wines were primarily blends of Cabernet Sauvignon with high tannins designed to age, and because the fastidious English like to decant their wine, the high, sharp shoulders help to catch the residue when the wine was being poured. The red wines made with a selection of such grapes as Cabernet Sauvignon, Merlot, and Malbec are bottled with dark green glass while the white wines are bottled in light green glass. Sweet dessert wines from Sauternes and Barsac are bottled in clear glass. Some châteaux, such as Haut-Brion, has its own unique bottle shape, slightly squatter than the norm.

Burgundy: Bottles from Burgundy have gently sloping shoulders and are slightly plumper than the Bordeaux bottles; both reds and whites use dark green glass. Since Burgundy wines are almost all Pinot Noir and Chardonnay, producers of these grapes elsewhere in the world have adopted the Burgundy style of bottle.

Rhône: Wine bottles from the Rhône valley, south of Lyon, are similar in shape to the Burgundy style but slightly less plump and with a slightly longer neck. The bottles are often embossed with a coat of arms, especially those from Châteauneuf-du-Pape—which again often have uniquely-shaped bottles. The green glass is reserved for the red wines such as Grenache, Mourvèdre, or Syrah, while white wines such as Viognier are bottled in clear glass.

Alsace: These tall, slim bottles made of light green glass, known as flûtes d'Alsace, are used for all the noble, white wines of Alsace, such as Riesling, Gewürztraminer, and Sylvaner. The same bottles are also used over the border in the Moselle River Valley of Germany.

Rhine: Very similar in shape to the bottles of Alsace, the bottles of the Rhine are colored amber or brown, are slightly thinner, and are often called hocks. Some of the cheaper wines, especially those made with Muller-Thurgau grapes like Liebfraumilch, are often colored a garish blue. These flute-shaped bottles from the Rhine, the Moselle, and Alsace, all derived their tall, slim design because, unlike the wines of Bordeaux and Burgundy, they were transported on gentle river barges and therefore did not need to be so sturdy, and were thus designed for more economical packaging in crates.

Côtes de Provence: As rosé wines are finally becoming known and popular in America, it is worth including the traditional "flûte à corset Provençal" (also known as a Mae West) from Provence in this list of international bottle shapes. Its distinctive and curvaceous shape is decidedly feminine, and its clear glass shows off the color of the rosé to great advantage.

Chianti: Prior to the seventeenth century when glass was extremely fragile, all bottles were protected with straw baskets. The glass flask or Fiasco itself has a rounded base since it was supported by the straw. Some of the producers of Sangiovese in the Chianti region of Tuscany have continued the tradition, even if only for marketing reasons. It should not be forgotten that the addition of a simple candle to the empty Chianti flask in a student's humble apartment has helped generations of young men persuade generations of young women that deep down, they are sensitive, hopeless romantics.

Port & Sherry: Like Bordeaux wines, the fortified wines of Oporto and Jerez were developed primarily by and for the English market. All three bottles have the high shoulders and straight sides, but the Sherry, and especially the Port bottles, are made of a much darker glass to protect the contents from the light. Port bottles, for whatever reason, are made with thicker glass. They have a bulge in the neck to collect sediment when pouring, and often are stamped with white paint rather than paper labels.

Champagne: Champagne (which used to be part of the Duchy of Burgundy and which is made of the Burgundian grapes of Pinot Noir and Chardonnay) also uses a Burgundy-style bottle. However, because the pressure inside the bottle can be 90 psi (three times the pressure of a normal car tire), the glass needs to be extra thick; the punt is more pronounced, enabling the riddler to turn the bottle in the rack. Most Champagne is bottled in green glass, but pink Champagne is bottled in clear glass to show off the color.

In addition to the standard 750 ml bottle, Champagne also comes in larger bottles—though I suspect the benefits are more visual than gustatory:

Magnum – 1.5 liters (two regular bottles)

Jeroboam (a.k.a. Double Magnum) – 3 liters (four bottles)

Rehoboam - 4.5 liters (six bottles)

Methuselah – 6 liters (eight bottles)

Salmanazar – 9 liters (twelve bottles)

Balthazar – 12 liters (sixteen bottles)

Nebuchadnezzar – 15 liters (twenty bottles)

Solomon – 18 liters (twenty-four bottles)

Goliath – 27 liters (thirty-six bottles)

Melchizedek or Midas – 30 liters (forty regular bottles)

Winegrowers in Burgundy and Bordeaux also produce large format bottles with similarly Biblical names—but not to the extent found in Champagne.

Winegrowers in the New World tend to use the bottle shape most appropriate for the varietal or style of wine they are selling. A

winery in New Zealand or California will use a Burgundy bottle
for its Chardonnay, Viognier, Shiraz, or Pinot Noir, but will use a
Bordeaux-style bottle for its Merlot, Malbec, or Cabernet Sauvignon.

Reading Wine Labels

Although every country has unique rules governing the information
on its wine labels, most labels conform to the laws of the two largest
markets, the European Union and the United States of America. In
general, the label should inform consumers where the wine came from,
how old it is, who made it, and what grapes were used.

Appellation d'Origin Controlée: In 1935, the French government
divided the country into about 300 different wine regions and
subregions. At its simplest level, an AOC (*Appellation d'Origin
Controlée*) designation on a label defines the source or terroir for the
wine in the bottle. For example, Appellation Bordeaux Contrôleee
means that the grapes were harvested and the wine was bottled within
the Bordeaux subregion. At its more complex level, an AOC can
be far more specific. "Batard Montrachet, Grand Cru, Appellation
Contrôleee" specifies not only that the grapes were harvested in the
Batard Montrachet, Grand Cru vineyard in the commune of Chassagne
Montrachet, near Beaune in Burgundy, but also that the grapes are
100 percent Chardonnay with a specific minimum alcohol level of 12
percent and a maximum level of residual sugar of 2 grams per liter
and that only forty hectoliters of grapes per hectare were harvested—
meaning a maximum of about 174 cases of wine per acre. Different
Appellations have different rules; obviously the more expensive
and prestigious the Appellation, the more specific and restrictive
the regulations.

As the European nations joined the European Union, standardized regulations were increasingly adopted and enforced. Most countries adopted the French Appellation system for their wine labels and so, for example, we see DOC - *Denominación de Origen Calificada* in Spain, DOCG - *Denominazione di Origine Controllata e Garantita* in Italy, and DOC - *Denominação de Origem Controlada* in Portugal, all of which specify the origin of the grapes and the local regulations concerning alcohol levels or number of bottles per acre of vineyard. The main exception to this general rule is Germany, which is discussed elsewhere.

Even outside the European Union, the wine-producing nations of the New World have adopted similar classifications, and so Australian wine comes from specific AGIs, *Australian Geographic Indicators,* and even US wine is divided into various AVAs, *American Viticultural Areas,* such as Alexander Valley in Sonoma and Stags Leap in Napa Valley. New World appellations, however, are less well-defined than those in Europe, and typically just refer to the origin of the majority of the grapes—much like the *Indicazione Geografica Tipica* (IGT) certification in Italy.

Date (Vintage): The date on the label refers to the year the grapes were harvested. Some wines, especially white wines and wines from Beaujolais are bottled soon after harvesting, and so the date of harvest and bottling are the same. Other wines may spend several years aging in oak barrels before being bottled. In both cases, the date on the label refers always to the year of harvest. Sherry from Jerez in Spain is made from a mixture of various vintages, some going back one hundred years, which is why bottles of Sherry do not show a vintage date. Likewise, most Champagne is non-vintage and made with a blend of grapes from different years. This is done in order to create a standard house-taste which is consistent over the years, and which is why the label does not show a date. Vintage Champagne is made only when there is an especially good harvest, and then the Vintage Champagne must be made with 100 percent grapes harvested in the year shown on the label.

Grape Varietal: Traditionally, European wines did not show the varietal of the grape used for making the wine. Based on centuries of experience and tradition, it was commonly understood that wines from Chianti in Tuscany were made with the Sangiovese grape, red wines from Burgundy were made exclusively from Pinot Noir grapes, and Bordeaux wines were made from a blend of grapes dominated by Cabernet Sauvignon and Merlot. The only main exception was the wine-growing region of Alsace, which produced a number of different white wines made from an officially approved selection of about six different varietals. Wines from Alsace, therefore, always show the name of the grape varietal.

But as vineyards were planted in the New World, no such traditions existed; Californian and Australian winegrowers had no prior experience to guide them, and so the type of grape varietal planted was more important than where it was planted. Initially, New World wines were described in terms of the European wines they most resembled—so many Californian red wines were called Burgundies and whites were called Chablis. But in the 1970s, Californian winemakers started to identify their wines by the grape variety used. New World wine labels focused on the name of the grape used to make the wine, while European labels focused on the name of the place where the wine was made.

Recently, in order to succeed in the US market, many European growers began adding the name of the grape varietal to the label on the bottle.

Alcohol Level: To comply with US laws, most wine labels now display the alcoholic content of the wine. Traditionally, the alcohol level was controlled by the Appellation, and so did not need to be shown on the label. In other words, to be classified AOC Bordeaux, the wine had to have between a 10-13 percent alcohol level, whereas an AOC Châteauneuf-du-Pape would be between 13-15 percent alcohol, and so there was no need to state this on the label.

Winemaker: At one extreme, we have the traditional winegrower who harvests his own grapes, ferments, ages, and bottles his own wine, which he then proudly sells under his own label, often with the words "Mis en bouteille à la Propriété" or "Mis en bouteille au Château." At the other extreme we have a vast tanker ship owned by a multinational corporation, transporting thousands of gallons of wine across the ocean in vast flexitank bladders to be bottled under a brand name at the country of destination before shipping in bulk to large retail chains around the nation.

Between these two extremes there are many other possibilities. In many wine areas, the farmers will sell their grapes to a local co-op to produce the wine. Traditionally, this was the way wine was produced in the Languedoc area of France, Argentina, South Africa, and California's Central Valley. The system is fine for producing low-quality table wine in bulk, but provides no incentive to produce wine of higher quality.

Because the landholdings in Burgundy are often too small for the individual growers to make their own wine, a tradition of wine merchants, or négociants, has developed over the centuries. négociants purchase grapes from select vineyards and produce the wine under their own labels. Most Burgundy négociant families reach back for generations and are highly respected for the quality of their wines. Well-known names from Burgundy include Maison Bouchard Père et

Fils (1731), Maison Louis Latour (1797), Maison Louis Jadot (1826), and Maison Joseph Drouhin (1880). A similar system is to be found in England, in which local wine merchants like Harveys (1796) or Berry Bros. & Rudd (1698) have been importing and bottling wine for generations and selling it under their own respected labels.

In some respects we see the négociant tradition continuing in the New World. A wine producer like Robert Mondavi, for example, grows and makes his own wine from his own grapes. But Mondavi also buys grapes from other growers and bottles that too under his own label. Just as with a négociant like Louis Jadot in Burgundy, as long as he maintains a reputation for high standards, consumers will have confidence in the wines carrying the Mondavi brand name. As globalization increases, this concept of branding becomes increasingly important. Many people would not think of buying a Bulgarian wine labeled Domaine Boyar Mavrud because they know nothing about it; however, if Costco chose to rebrand it under their own label, as Costco Bulgarian Red, people would be happy to try it because they have confidence in the Costco brand.

In addition to the date of the vintage and the name of the winemaker, the two most important items on a wine label relate to terroir and varietal, and these two terms need more detailed discussion and their own dedicated chapters.

Chapter

3

HISTORY OF WINE

Chapter Three: HISTORY OF WINE

"My books are like water; those of the great geniuses are wine. (Fortunately) everybody drinks water." — Mark Twain

---

Since the dawn of history, mankind's greatest quest has been to find not only food, but fresh, drinkable water. Many wars have been fought and lives lost in the struggle for access to fresh water. Because most available water has not been drinkable and carries disease, alternative liquids had to be found, and since the discovery of alcoholic fermentation some ten thousand years ago, beer and wine have been the most common safe alternatives to water.

Wine has always been consumed, not because it tasted particularly good, but because it was safer than water. Unless it came from a fresh spring, water often carried disease, and after a few days, most water was undrinkable. Because of the fermentation process, the alcohol in wine and beer kills many of the diseases found in untreated water. Wine will also store much longer than water, which made it invaluable for sailors on sea voyages; additionally, the grape juice in wine provided much needed nutrients to the human diet. Unfortunately, however, for most of its history wine has oxidized fairly rapidly, and thus has had (by modern standards) a thin, vinegary taste needing to be drunk as soon after fermentation as possible. For this reason wine was often flavored with resin, which made the wines sticky and thick. Even today the Greeks continue to make retsina wine, which is flavored with pine resin. Other additives included lead, lye-ash, marble dust, salt, pepper, and random assortments of herbs and spices. In addition to improving the taste of the wine, the additives provided valuable nutrients to the ancient diet. Rather than ferment the fresh grapes immediately after harvest, the grapes were allowed to dry in the sun, becoming like raisins prior to fermentation. This concentrated the sugar and resulted in a sweeter, more alcoholic wine which would preserve longer. When ready for drinking, ancient wines were cut with honey, dried fruit, and even salt water. In the first century BC, Pliny the Elder recommended that the seawater used to cut wine should come far away from shore because of all the human waste that contaminated the shoreline. Pliny was a great believer in resin, and was as much a connoisseur of the different types of tree resin as he was of wine.

Just as people today carry around their little plastic bottles to sip water throughout the day, so in the old days they used to carry their wineskins to sip from. The leather wineskin will have done little to improve the taste of the wine. It is probably no exaggeration to suggest that most people were slightly drunk most of the time—which certainly helps explain many otherwise strange historical decisions.

Ancient World

The earliest indications of wine production date back almost 9,000 years to the Southern Caucasus where the borders of Turkey, Iran, Iraq, Armenia, Georgia, and Azerbaijan meet in uneasy harmony. This is also the area where the Caucasus, the Taurus, and the Zagros mountains all come together, and where the ancestors of all our grains and vines are still to be found.

Vitus is the botanical name of the grapevine genus with the specific name vinifera (wine-bearing). Vitus vinifera of the subspecies silvestris is the original wild grape. The original wild vine, *Vitis vinifera silvestris,* still grows in the Zagros Mountains of Northwestern Iran and is thus the ancestor of all our modern wines.

This original vine, *Vitis vinifera silvestris,* is dioecious, which means that it has both male and female plants. At first, however, humans selected only the female plants, because only the females bear fruit.

Eventually, after centuries of human selection, a new hermaphrodite *sativa* subspecies emerged, which displayed both male and female flowers. Increasingly this new subspecies, *Vitis vinifera sativa*, was selected for human consumption. Thus today, *Vitis vinifera sativa* is the cultivated vine which has spread all over the globe and from which all wine is produced, while *Vitis vinifera silvestris* remains as a wild, woodland vine in the Transcaucasian Mountains.

Interestingly, because humans selected the hermaphrodite *Vitis sativa* to cultivate, this means its descendants have had very little sex in the subsequent ten thousand years. Recent DNA testing and genome scans reveal that Cabernet Sauvignon, Chardonnay, Merlot, and all the other varietals of *Vitis vinifera sativa* are all closely-related members of the same family. Forget "kissing cousins;" centuries of in-breeding means that all modern wines are increasingly susceptible to disease and will eventually need some sort of genetically engineered protection.

The oldest physical evidence of large scale wine production is at Hajji Firuz Tepe and Godin Tepe, Neolithic settlements in Iran's Zagros Mountains just south of the Bible's Mount Ararat. Indirect evidence of ancient winemaking is provided by the discovery of significant quantities of vinification residues (tartaric acid) with oak resin in clay jars, a wine press, fermentation vats, jars, and cups, dating back to the seventh millennium BC. Throughout the Near East, numerous archaeological grape seeds attributed to the cultivated grapevine, *Vitis vinifera sativa*, were found in Chalcolithic and mid-Bronze Age archaeological levels. This demonstrates the evolution of the cultivated *Vitis vinifera sativa* from the original wild grapevine, *Vitis vinifera silvestris*, which thus marks the beginning of civilized human development.

Because fermentation is a natural occurrence, the pleasing effects of alcoholic grape juice were probably discovered by a happy accident.

Interestingly, the Bible describes Noah as being the world's first viticulturist and as planting the first vineyard after the Great Flood had subsided: "And Noah began to be a husbandman, and he planted a vineyard. And he drank of the wine, and was drunken" *(Genesis 9:20)*. Tradition has always located the resting place of Noah's Ark on Mount Ararat in the Southern Caucuses—right in the center of the region where modern archeologists have located the earliest signs of *Vitis vinifera sativa* grape production and consumption. The oldest documented civilization in this region of Anatolia was the Hittites, who used wine primarily as a religious libation which they offered to the gods during royal ceremonies. Evidence exists to show that Hittite law protected winegrowers, and they would celebrate each successful harvest of grapes with a holiday and copious libations to the gods. Even today the Turkish government has a state-run vineyard, Buzbağ, growing the Boğazkere grape varietal near the town of Elazığ, west of Mount Ararat and between the source of the Tigris and Euphrates rivers—the cradle of civilization. Turkey is still the world's fourth largest producer of grapes, especially the widely-planted Sultaniye varietal.

The primitive method that Noah or any Neolithic winemaker near Mount Ararat would have used to make wine is still practiced in this region even in the twenty-first century. Wine is still made using a Kvevri, a large (800-3500 liters) earthenware vessel originally from Georgia in the Caucasus, and dating back to about 8000 BC. It has an inside coat of beeswax, resembles an amphorae without handles, and is used for the fermentation and storage of wine, often buried below ground level or set into the floors of large wine cellars. In the winemaking process, grapes are poured into the kvevri, crushed, and left to ferment and mature. Over a period of days, the grape skins are pushed down on the hour and the kvevri is finally covered with a suitable-sized stone cap, sealed with pine resin and clay and left undisturbed for up to two years. When the wine is ready, it is pumped out and bottled, after which the kvevri is sterilized with lime and sulphur, ready for re-use.

In many respects the deliberate cultivation of grapes and storage of wine in pots marks the switch from a nomadic to a settled society, and consequently, the birth of civilization. Thucydides wrote that "people only emerged from barbarism when they began to cultivate the olive and the vine." The potter's wheel, which was invented in Mesopotamia around the same time, 6,000 BC, is another indication of a settled, civilized society. Obviously, the simultaneous invention of pottery would assist the fermentation as well as the storage of wine. Because this was a period when writing was also invented, metals were being used, irrigated agriculture was first introduced, and urban living and complex social hierarchies were evolving, it has been argued that another reason people started to drink wine was to escape the growing urban pressures and stresses of Bronze Age life.

Professor Hans Barnard, one of the archeological team who in 2007 discovered the world's oldest wine production facility at the Areni-1 cave in Vayots Dzor in Armenia, about twenty miles east of Mt. Ararat, wrote: "Deliberate fermentation of carbohydrates into alcohol … prompted the domestication of wild plants and the development of ceramic technology." In other words: this carefully constructed and sophisticated site for the large-scale production of wine marks a significant step forward in the development of modern society.

Mesopotamia: The grape vine was widely-known in the ancient Mesopotamian world, and both the Babylonian and Sumerian civilizations used wine to mark special occasions. Because wine had to be floated on rafts down the Tigris and Euphrates river valleys from the Caucuses and Zagros mountains and was therefore expensive, its use was restricted to the ruling and religious classes, while the regular population tended to consume locally produced beer. The first written reference to wine drinking is found in the worlds's oldest written literature, the Sumerian *Epic of Gilgamesh,* written about 3,500 BC, in which the wild man, Enkidu, is seduced and tamed with wine by a lascivious temple-prostitute:

> "So he ate till he was full and drank strong wine, seven goblets. He became merry, his heart exulted and his face shone. He rubbed down the matted hair of his body and anointed himself with oil. Enkidu had become a man *(Epic of Gilgamesh, 1960: 65-6)."*

The drinking of wine had civilized him.

Egypt: The Egyptians, dating back to the First Dynasty, were the oldest civilization to make extensively documented use of wine. Excavation of 5,000 year old tombs in Abydos (Upper Egypt) reveals storage chambers for wine, which the dead were to carry with them on their journey to the afterlife. Spectral and mass molecular chromatographic analyses of amphorae found in Tutankhamun's tomb proved the presence of red wine as well as white wine. We also have 5th Dynasty written records of wine production which document six different wine-growing regions along the Nile River. Detailed paintings on the walls of Ancient Egyptian tombs illustrate a sophisticated and well-established winemaking culture. Thirty-six different amphorae found in the tomb of Tutankhamen, (ruled 1332 BC – 1323 BC), were each inscribed with the vintage and the terroir as well as the name of the producer. For example: "Year 5. Shedeh of very good quality of the estate of Aten of the Western River. Chief Vintner Rer."

Archaeologists have even found descriptions of the different styles of Egyptian wine:

Taenioticus: White to green, sweet, rich, aromatic, tart

Mareoticus: White, sweet, rigorous, with fine bouquet

Sebennyticum: According to Pliny, a type of wine produced with both Thasos grapes and another variety called Fuligem (sooty); pine resin was also added

Because of the importance of the annual Nile flood cycle to the whole of Egyptian culture and religion, the vine held a powerful significance throughout society. Starting the year like a piece of dead and discarded driftwood, the vine spontaneously begins weeping in early spring and, with its sudden profusion of buds, seems to epitomize the endless cycle of life, death, and rebirth. Osiris, the Egyptian God of Resurrection, was also the God of the Vine, and, like the vine, he died and was born again each year. Because wine was associated with divinity, it was drunk only by the royal families and the priestly elite; as in Mesopotamia, the common people would have drunk locally-produced beer.

Phoenicians: By 2,000 BC vine production had reached the shores of the Mediterranean where it was spread by the Phoenician traders from modern day Lebanon. Unlike the Greeks and the Romans after them, the Phoenicians were primarily traders, not colonists. They established trading posts all over the Mediterranean where they planted vines and produced wine for trade; vineyards planted in Sicily and Jerez (Cadiz) in 1100 BC are still in production today. The voluminous writings of Mago, a Phoenician wine expert from Carthage (Tunis), were studied for centuries by Greeks and Romans wishing to learn about wine cultivation.

Greeks: In order to cope with overcrowding in the small cities of the Greek mainland, the Greeks founded new city-states in other lands around the Mediterranean where they would try to reproduce the conditions and the culture of the city they had left behind. This included planting vines. When the Greeks first discovered Southern Italy and Sicily, they named it Oenetria—the Land of Vines—and they planted vineyards everywhere they settled. Further north, the Etruscans also planted vineyards, perhaps the oldest in Italy, in what is now Tuscany—the home of Chianti. The Tuscan vineyards continued to thrive under the Romans, and the wine was shipped down the coast from Pisa and up the coast from Pompeii for consumption in Rome.

Although some dry wines would have been produced, most of the wines made and drunk by the Greeks and Phoenicians were sweet, dark and aromatic—hence Homer's many references to "the wine-dark sea." Very often, herbs, spices, honey, and even pine resin were added to improve the taste and the wine was usually diluted with water, often seawater. The Greeks regarded the consumption of undiluted wine as being a sign of barbarism. The moderate drinking of diluted wine in a controlled setting, however, is what raised an educated man above the barbarian.

For Greeks, the embodiment of civilized life was the Symposium, when men gathered together to drink wine while talking and discussing politics and philosophy in Socratic dialogs as described by Plato and Xenophon. These were aristocratic and sophisticated gatherings, like a Georgetown dinner party, and wine was used to loosen tongues and create fellowship, not create drunkenness or violence. The drinking of wine in moderation was a recurring theme in Greek literature, and three cups of wine was commonly regarded as sufficient for any civilized person. The third century BC poet, Eubulus, described how Dionysis prepared a Symposium in *Semele or Dionysus*:

"Three bowls do I mix for the temperate: one to health, which they empty first; the second to love and pleasure; the third to sleep. When this bowl is drunk up, wise guests go home. The fourth bowl is ours no longer, but belongs to violence; it belongs to bad behavior; the fifth is for shouting; the sixth is for rudeness and insults; the seventh is for fights; the eighth is for breaking the furniture; the ninth is for depression; the tenth is for madness and *unconsciousness." (A modern version might conclude with "the midnight posting of inappropriate selfies on Facebook.")*

The first vines to be planted in France were around the Greek colony of Masalia (today's Marseilles) in 600 BC, and the whole of modern-day Provence and the lower Rhône valley were originally planted with Greek vines. Artifacts from Ancient Greece demonstrate the importance of wine not only to Greek culture but also to the economy, with images of grape clusters, vines, and wine cups decorating everything from pottery to coins. The Greeks founded colonies, traded wine, and planted vineyards, not only all around the Mediterranean coast but also all around the coast of the Black Sea. The importance of the Greek influence is demonstrated by the millions of amphora pieces bearing the unique seals of various city-states and Aegean islands, which are continuously uncovered by archaeologists all over these inland seas. As is discussed elsewhere, DNA testing of amphora as well as the potters' seal shows modern researchers not only the trading routes but also the volume of wine that was shipped by the Ancient Greeks. A single shipwreck off the coast of Marseilles contained almost ten thousand amphorae holding nearly eighty thousand gallons of Greek wine to be shipped up the Rhône valley into Gaul, and maybe as far as Germany or even England.

The original *Vitis vinifera* which had originated in the Southern Caucuses was thus transported, cloned, and replanted by each new civilization that discovered the joys of wine. From the Babylonians and Egyptians to the Phoenicians, Greeks and Romans—so the original hermaphroditic vine, over the centuries, developed new strains and varieties by cloning as it spread slowly westward through Europe—and eventually into the New World.

Roman World

By 200 BC the Romans had either defeated or assimilated the Phoenician, Etruscan, and Greek civilizations, and the history of wine cultivation moved onto a new level. Originally, the Romans had disdained wine as being a degenerate "Eastern" vice suitable only for Greeks and Carthaginians—"girlie men." An austere and militaristic people, the Romans preferred beer to wine and war to discourse. Eventually, however, after the defeat of Carthage in the Punic Wars, the Romans became enthusiastic wine consumers. By the time of Emperor Augustus, the Romans were consuming a bottle of wine per person, per day—or about fifty million US gallons annually. (These statistics include women, slaves, and children.)

Originally, the main source of wine for the Romans was from the old Phoenician vineyards around Naples, but after the eruption of Mount Vesuvius and the destruction of Pompeii in 79 AD, new vineyards had to be planted. As a result, so much of Roman land was dedicated to the growing of vines that just thirteen years later the Emperor Domitian ordered many of the vineyards to be dug up in order to grow food for the starving population.

The Romans were the first to really "industrialize" the production of wine with large vineyards, built and maintained by slaves, and using the principles first documented by the Phoenician writer Mago. Initially, as the Romans conquered and colonized the rest of the known world, they discouraged the planting of vineyards elsewhere in order to protect the export of their own wine from Italy. But following the destruction of the vineyards around Pompeii, with the rapid expansion of the empire and the growing demand from their own troops and colonies, the Romans started planting vineyards, initially in Provence and eventually all over the Empire—even in the British Isles.

From the earliest times in Mesopotamia and Egypt, wine had been associated with civilization. Unlike nomadic herdsmen, only a settled and organized society could cultivate and enjoy the pleasures of wine. With the rapid expansion of Roman power, wine became even more an indication of "civilization." As the uncouth, beer drinking barbarians of Gaul and Germany were assimilated into the growing Roman empire, wine—like roads, aqueducts and public baths— became yet one more indication of the civilized life.

Amphorae: The ancient Greeks stored their wine in large clay vessels called amphorae, which were used to transport wine all over the Mediterranean. Amphorae are shaped like long, tapered vases, with a pair of handles at the top. Their shape meant that they could be strung together by a rope through the handles and carried on ships in this manner, like bunches of grapes.

One reason we know so much about wine in the ancient world is that it was stored and transported in amphorae, which on average held about forty liters of wine (sixty modern bottles, or five cases). Since amphorae were always made from local clay in the region where the wine (or grain or olive oil) was being shipped from, scientists are able to use DNA testing to locate the origin of each amphorae, irrespective of where it was eventually found. Additionally, the handles of the amphorae acted like labels, and the potter would stamp a description of the contents into the clay handle, partly for taxation purposes and also to prevent fraud. Because amphorae were used for about four thousand years all around the Mediterranean and the Near East, we have been able to learn a lot about the wine trade of the ancient world by examining the thousands of amphorae remains. An amphorae made of Lebanese clay and found in a Phoenician shipwreck off the coast of Cornwall would indicate trade between Lebanon and England, for example.

There is a 150-foot-high mound in Rome, Monte Testaccio, about a mile in circumference, which was built entirely from fragments of discarded amphorae—a testament to the fact that Romans consumed some fifty million gallons of wine annually. The mound is located at one of the original entrances to the city, where the amphorae of wine from Naples and Greece were sailed up the River Tiber and unloaded. The wine would have been transferred into smaller containers for distribution throughout the city, and the original amphorae destroyed and discarded into a growing pile. Interestingly enough, the Monte Testaccio section of Rome is currently a fashionable night spot filled with nightclubs and wine bars—as though the original scent of wine still permeates the air.

Roman vineyards: It should be emphasized, yet again, that most wine was simply a healthier alternative to water and, by today's standards, was weak and tasted more like vinegar. The "vinegar" offered to Christ on the cross was not an insult or added torture; it was simply to quench his thirst with what the ordinary Roman soldiers themselves drank. The expensive wines that were sought after by the wealthier ruling classes were mostly white and sweet, raisinated wines with high alcohol content. The high sugar and alcohol levels meant they could be stored for much longer without oxidizing and turning to vinegar. Most of these wines were still imported from Greece and Lebanon, although the Romans produced their own Falernian wines from the slopes of Mt. Falernius not far from the city of Rome. Falernian wine was a white, raisinated wine made with the Aglianico vine which was brought to Italy by the Greeks. An inscription on the ruins of an ancient Roman bar says:

> For one coin you can drink wine.
> For two you can drink the best.
> For four you can drink Falernian.

The Romans, as with most things Greek, adopted the Greek Symposium and renamed it the Convivium. Unlike the Greeks, Romans permitted certain high-class females to attend their meetings, which were more like banquets, or even drinking parties. As the Falernian flowed, togas, gowns, and morals loosened; wine and dancing girls prevailed. The most famous example of such a Roman wine party is the description of Trimalchio's banquet in *The Satyricon* by Petronius:

Or again, as the Roman poet, Catullus enthusiastically sang:

> *"Come boy, and pour for me a cup Of old Falernian.*
> *Fill it up With wine, strong, sparkling, bright, and clear;*
> *Our host decrees no water here.*
> *Let dullards drink the Nymph's pale brew.*
> *The sluggish thin their blood with dew.*
> *For such pale stuff we have no use;*
> *For us the purple grape's rich juice.*
> *Begone, ye chilling water sprite;*
> *Here burning Bacchus rules tonight!"*
> —Gaius Valerius Catullus

There are few functioning vineyards in Europe today that were not first planted by the Romans almost two thousand years ago. In France alone, the Romans established all of today's major wine regions: Rhône valley, 100 BC; Loire valley, AD 100; Burgundy, AD 200; Bordeaux, AD 300; Champagne, AD 400. As the Empire expanded beyond Gaul, the Romans planted vineyards along most of Europe's river valleys, such as the Duoro, the Tagus, the Moselle, the Rhine, and the Danube.

The Romans displayed an uncanny ability to recognize the best places to plant vines. Some sites were obvious, like the Rhône valley and the hills of Burgundy, for example. Even planting vines in Bordeaux made sense as a way to supply wine to the armies in Britain and Spain. But what made the Romans think to plant vines on the remote, inhospitable reaches of the upper Douro River in Portugal, or even the steep, almost sheer slopes of Germany's Moselle Valley?

With the conquest of the thickly forested Gaul (modern-day France and Spain), oak barrels began to replace the clay amphorae which had been used to store wine since the time of the Egyptians, and it would have been around this time that the effect oak had on wine was first observed. Building upon the original observations and knowledge of the Phoenician writer Mago, the Romans carefully documented and recorded every aspect of winemaking. It seemed that every Latin writer from Cato, Cicero and Virgil, to Horace, Ovid and Pliny, among others, had their own opinions concerning wine, how it should be grown, aged, stored, and drunk. We even have copies of a correspondence dated AD 312 between the Emperor Constantine and the winegrowers of what are today the vineyards of Autun, near Beaune, discussing in the most remarkable detail exactly how to trim the roots of the local vine to maximize both the quality and the quantity of the wine. Emperor Constantine is, of course, famous for converting the Roman Empire to Christianity, and after the fall of Rome, it was the Christian church and monasteries, especially in places like Autun and Beaune, which kept the art of winemaking alive.

Religion and Wine

Wine has always been associated with religion. Because of its physical life-cycle, the vine has always been associated with death and rebirth. The Egyptian God Osiris was not only a god of rebirth but was also the God of Wine. In Greek mythology, the God Dionysus, who came from the East, was the God of Wine as well as God of Drama and the mysteries of Rebirth. Both Osiris and Dionysus were ceremonially killed and consumed by their followers in rituals involving the consumption of wine. "Dionysus' powers are manifold; he gave to men the vine to cure their sorrows," wrote Euripedes in *The Bacchae* in 405 BC.

The Romans renamed the Greek God Dionysus as Bacchus and his cult became one of the most important in the empire. When the early Christians appeared in Rome they were often mistaken for worshippers of Bacchus; not only did both Gods symbolize rebirth, but both were also strongly identified with wine. Dionysus/Bacchus was not only the God of Wine; he was also the god *in* wine, and so by consuming him, the drinker acquired all the power and mystery of the God: "Anyone who eats my flesh and drinks my blood remains in me, and I in him" (John 6:56).

Though celebrating wine as a symbol of rebirth as well as energy—the rising sap, the glorious flowering of the fruit, the rich and heavy bunches of grapes—the Greeks, the Romans, and the Christians have also recognized its dark side. Dionysus and Bacchus are both portrayed as beautiful young men but also as cloven-hoofed old Satyrs. Wine can inspire men to poetry and love but also violence and death. The gift of Dionysus can indeed bring joy and innocent gaiety, but when abused can result in pain and cruel madness. The Greek playwright Euripides best captured the dichotomy in his tragedy, *The Bacchae*, in which women, joyously celebrating the God with wine and dance, in their frenzy tear apart the male intruder with their bare hands, eat his flesh, and drink his blood. Rituals in Ancient Rome's private clubs, where the worshippers of Bacchus met to celebrate their Convivium, would involve eating the "flesh" of the God and, with wine, drinking his blood. The drinking of wine as a symbol of the blood of Christ and bread as his flesh is called the Eucharist, and represents the very heart of the traditional Christian ritual.

Following the fall of the Roman Empire around AD 400 and the invasion of the "barbarians" from the North, much of classical civilization was destroyed. Like reading and writing, the art of winemaking survived the Dark Ages only within the Christian monasteries. It was the monks and the friars who maintained the skills and learning of the Roman tradition.

Wine had always played an important role in the Jewish religion, and the Bible contains 280 references to wine (as well as forty-nine references to vine, seventy-two to vineyard, forty-nine to wine cup, and fifteen to winepress). Wine grown in what is today Israel, Jordan, and Lebanon, was highly-prized and widely-traded throughout the ancient world, from Babylon to Alexandria. Even during the Middle Ages, wines from the Middle East, Greece, and Cyprus were the most highly-prized and were shipped by the Venetian traders to markets as far away as England and the cities of the Baltic. These wines were white, sweet, high in alcohol, and made in the traditional manner with raisinated grapes—like the Falernian wines which the Romans prized above all others.

Religion also played an important role in the spread of wine beyond Europe during the later Middle Ages, and the Renaissance when Spanish Conquistadores planted vineyards all over South America and California in order to produce wine with which to perform the Catholic Mass. While the Protestant nations, especially in North America, had a more ambivalent attitude towards wine and alcohol, the spread of Catholicism across the Atlantic was extremely significant in the history of wine.

Middle Ages

Burgundy and Monasteries: Because of the importance that wine had always played in the Jewish-Christian tradition, it was primarily the Christian monasteries of Europe that kept the art of winemaking alive after the Fall of Rome. The extensive monasteries of Burgundy were especially important in the history of wine, because over the centuries, the monks maintained detailed records of temperatures, rainfall, soil types, harvests, and grape varieties. As readers of Chaucer, Rabelais and Boccaccio are well aware, the monks were not immune to the pleasures of wine themselves—among other pleasures of the flesh—and the monasteries were often the scenes of depravity inflamed by wine. It was in order to reform the excesses of the Benedictine monasteries that the Cistercian monasteries were established in AD 1112, deeper in the countryside and further away from the temptations of the town, but still surrounded by vineyards. Perhaps the best remaining example of a Cistercian vineyard is the Grand Cru Clos de Vougeot in the Côte de Nuits, which was first enclosed with a stone wall in 1336 and whose buildings can still be visited.

By the early Middle Ages, the wines of Burgundy had achieved such a reputation that they were sought after in the French royal courts in Paris and on the Loire, as well as in the Pope's palace in Avignon. Anxious to maintain the high-quality and reputation of his wines, Philippe the Bold, Duke of Burgundy in 1395, made it a hanging offense to make red wine with anything other than Pinot Noir on his territories. Offenders would be hanged from scaffolds out in their vineyards as a visual and swinging reminder to their neighbors. The Gamay grape was permitted further south to provide Beaujolais wine for the thirsty silk workers in Lyon, but for the red wines of Burgundy, only Pinot Noir was permitted.

Bordeaux and Britain: The development of wine in Bordeaux was influenced not by the Christian monks, but by the English and Dutch traders. The vineyards of Bordeaux and La Rochelle were originally planted to provide wine for the Roman Centurions in England, and this wine trade, between England and the Atlantic coast of France, continued even after the fall of Rome. Part of the reason for the

Hundred Years' War between the kings of France and England was for control of the vineyards of Aquitaine. As the wine trade with Bordeaux increased during the Middle Ages, many English and Dutch merchants established offices and warehouses along the banks of the Gironde outside Bordeaux's city walls.

The *Police des Vins* were a set of codes and business practices set up in the thirteenth and fourteenth century that governed the wine trade within the region of Bordeaux and the use of its port by neighboring areas. The codes were aimed at giving Bordeaux wine a position of dominance over other wine producers in the region and in the English wine market.

The codes had a particular effect on the winemakers from the inland areas, whose wines could not travel down the Garonne or Dordogne rivers to be sold in Bordeaux until after December 1st. This caused those growers to miss the busiest season for trade when prices were at a premium. This sharply disadvantaged the competition for Bordeaux wine. The wines of the Dordogne region are only now becoming recognized as having 'Premier Cru' potential.

Holding back the sale of wine until later in the year was a serious problem. With the exception of expensive sweet white wines, most wines would not be drinkable for more than a year. Already by the spring, the taste would have grown tart and bitter, and by the summer, when thirst was greatest, the heat would oxidize whatever wine remained. This is why the wine harvest was such a joyous affair and celebrated with such mirth and merrymaking.

Turgot, the Minister of Finance under Louis XVI, described the effect of this *Police des Vins'* arrangement in the eighteenth century:

"The conduct of this set of rules, most artfully devised to guarantee
to the bourgeois of Bordeaux, the owners of the local vineyards, the
highest price for their own wines, and to the disadvantage the growers
of all the other southern provinces."

Even the neighboring wines of the Right Bank, around the town of
Libourne, were excluded from the Bordeaux codes just as later they
were to be excluded from the classification of 1855. Ironically, in the
twenty-first century, some of those Right Bank wines from Pomerol and
Saint-Émilion have become among the most sought after in the world.

The history of the world would probably have evolved completely
differently if the English had been able to grow vines on their northern
offshore island. They might have stayed contentedly at home and left
the rest of the world in peace. Instead, the English were obliged to
cross the water and take other people's wine. For the past few hundred
years, the dominant names in the wine industry of Oporto in Portugal,
Jerez in Southern Spain, and Bordeaux in SouthWest France are all
British. The Hundred Years' War of the fourteenth century was in many
ways a struggle for control of the wine region of Bordeaux. Even
though they eventually lost possession of Bordeaux, British merchants
remained in the area, controlling the wine industry, with their counting
houses, their warehouses and eventually their châteaux. They also
made sure that the wines of Bordeaux (like the Sherry from Jerez and
the Port wine from Oporto) conformed to English taste.

Partly because of the difference in taste between the English and
French consumers, partly because of soil and climate differences, but
mainly because it had to survive a long sea voyage to England, the
wine of Bordeaux evolved differently from the wine of Burgundy. The
main grape varietal used for making wine in Bordeaux was Cabernet
Sauvignon, a grape with a skin so rich in tannins that it needs a long
time to mature, and thus ages well. This ability to age well continued

to be important long after the end of the Middle Ages, when the British Navy would stock up with Bordeaux wine for the long voyage to South Africa, India, and Australia.

Sweet White Wine: It should not be forgotten that long before even the Greeks and Romans, the most sought after and expensive wines were white and sweet. Red wines were for everyday drinking, but sweet white wines were what the wealthy classes drank for pleasure. Not only did the higher levels of alcohol and residual sugar satisfy the palette more than the thin and bitter red wines, but, more significantly, the sugar and alcohol meant that the wines would last much longer than the reds. Unlike the dry red wines from Western Europe which were made from fresh squeezed grapes, the traditional sweet white wines from the Eastern Mediterranean were made from raisinated grapes, which had been left to dry in the sun before fermentation. Drying out the grapes concentrated the sugars and resulted in more body and higher alcohol. Until the late eighteenth century, most red wines had turned to vinegar through oxidization within less than twelve months; it was only sweet white wines which would last a long time, which is why they were so valued by the European royalty. Today, with too much sucrose in our diets, we take sweetness for granted, but in the ancient world, access to sugar or even fresh fruit was limited, and sweetness was rare and greatly valued.

Even through the Middle Ages and much later, sweet whites still came from the East and were often referred to as Romneys, because these were the wines, like the legendary Falernian wine, which had been most preferred by the Romans. Sailing from Lebanon, Greece, Santorini, Cyprus, and the Levant, Venetian merchant galleys would deliver the wines as far away as London and Hamburg. It's worth noting that the only significant sweet wine still produced in Europe today using the traditional appassimento, or raisinating process,

Recioto della Valpolicella, comes from the shores of Lake Garda, just inland from Venice.

An indication of the relative value of different wines in the fourteenth century can be seen by comparing prices in shillings per gallon of various wines in England in 1362: dry reds from Bordeaux, eight shillings; Rhenish sweet whites, twelve shillings; Romneys from the Levant, sixteen shillings; Malvasia sweet white from Greece, twenty shillings; and, finally, the most expensive of all, Vernaccia from Venice, thirty-two shillings. Vernaccia is, of course, the infamous white wine in which, according to Dante's *Divine Comedy*, Pope Martin IV would drown a plateful of Bolsena eels before eating them and then drinking the wine—or maybe just swallowing them all down together.

As the European bourgeoisie and middle classes of the new towns and cities of the late Middle Ages grew in prosperity, they wanted to display their wealth and improve their living standards. Rather than drink the thin, sour local reds that the peasants drank, they wanted to drink the expensive sweet whites that previously only the aristocrats could afford. Thus the demand for sweet white wines in Europe increased dramatically.

By the eighteenth century, Cistercian monks in Germany had developed a reputation for strong sweet white wine made from Riesling grapes, which they stored in deep, cold cellars along the Rhine and Moselle river valleys. These German Cistercian wines (known as Rhenish in England) were stored and aged in huge oak barrels called tuns, which could hold fifty thousand gallons or more, and thus protected the wine from oxidization—meaning they aged well and improved.

Sweet white wine, known as Tokaji, began to be imported from Hungary in the late seventeenth century, and Louis XIV called it

"The King of Wines and the Wine of Kings." The demand for sweet white wine reached even as far as South Africa, whose sweet white Constantia was the favorite wine of both Frederick the Great and Napoleon. Legend has it that Constantia was the wine that Napoleon requested on his deathbed. By the end of the eighteenth century, the most sought after sweet white wines came from the Sauterne region of Bordeaux. Thomas Jefferson loved Sauternes, and while he was US president, George Washington, after just one taste, ordered thirty cases of Château d'Yquem. Prior to the Russian revolution in 1917, many Russian aristocrats would drink nothing but expensive Sauternes, and even today, the Russian oligarchs and mafia retain the same taste for Château d'Yquem.

Even though red wines have long since become the prestigious wines for serious drinkers and collectors, sweet white wines still command a loyal and wealthy following. As recently as 2012, a single bottle of 1811 Château d'Yquem sold for $115,000.

Age of Reason

Alternatives to wine as the drink of choice began to appear in the seventeenth century. Beer, of course, had always existed as an alternative, but until the discovery of hops, beer had an unpleasant taste and a very short shelf life. With the arrival of hops in England in the late sixteenth century, however, beer became much more popular. The hop vine is closely related to the cannabis plant, and adding hops to fermenting barley created a foaming beer with a pleasingly bitter taste and a much longer shelf life.

About the same time that the English and Germans were experimenting with beer, the Dutch were experimenting with distillation, a process that had first been developed by the Moors in Spain. The Dutch started distilling the rather bland Ugni Blanc grapes on the west coast of France in the regions of Cognac and Armagnac, and called it brandewijn (burnt wine) from which we get the name brandy. Three advantages of brandy over wine were immediately obvious. It was far less bulky and therefore cheaper to transport it was much stronger and more potent; and finally, it would last much longer—indeed it improved with age.

With the discovery and colonization of the New World, initially in the Caribbean, sugarcane provided another source of alcohol, and rum became a popular drink, especially with sailors. Further north, on the American mainland, the English and Dutch colonists started making their own alcohol from locally grown produce, such as wheat and rye to make beer, whisky, and gin.

The problem was that wine was expensive and bulky to transport from Europe and had a shelf life that would barely survive a long ocean voyage. Sloshing around with the roll of the ship, in often leaky barrels, much of the wine evaporated while the rest quickly oxidized and became even less pleasant to drink. Unfortunately, as we shall discuss below, vines proved impossible to grow in the North American colonies, and so the colonists were forced to develop home-grown alternatives to wine. This is one reason that North America never really evolved a wine drinking culture, and why whisky became the national drink.

Thomas Jefferson: One great champion of the consumption of wine as opposed to spirits was Thomas Jefferson, author of the American Declaration of Independence and US Ambassador to France. Jefferson was both a great connoisseur and consumer of wine, and he purchased large quantities of wine from all over France while he was ambassador. More importantly, he spent much of his life promoting the consumption of wine in America and trying, unsuccessfully, to plant vineyards in Virginia as the basis of an American wine industry. As we will discuss in more detail below, the European vine, *Vitis vinifera*, would simply not survive on the East Coast of America, and all Jefferson's dedicated efforts were doomed to failure. Consequently, all wine had to be imported from Europe, which made it accessible only to the wealthy. Jefferson's other doomed campaign was attempting to remove the duties on imported wine. Jefferson was concerned that because wine was so expensive, the citizens would prefer to drink gin and whisky, leading to public drunkenness. As he wrote in a letter to a friend in 1818, "No nation is drunken where wine is cheap; and none sober, where the dearness of wine substitutes ardent spirits as the common beverage."

What was especially galling and frustrating for Jefferson was that while the English on the East Coast and even the French in Louisiana had consistently failed to produce local wine, the Spanish had been successfully planting vineyards all over the West Coast of what is today California.

Coffee Houses: The seventeenth century also brought new competition to wine consumption from non-alcoholic sources. Coffee originally arrived in England from the Ottoman Empire via Venetian traders, and by 1675 there were three thousand coffee houses in London. Like wine, coffee provided a healthy alternative to water and with a pleasingly stimulating effect on the mind. Unlike wine, however, increased consumption did not lead to inebriated stupidity, but rather to increased intellectual acuity. This was the Age of Enlightenment, an era of rational thought and logical discourse, and it is a mystery that the taste for thin, vinegary, alcoholic wine ever survived the arrival of coffee. As though the competition from coffee were not enough, by the middle of the eighteenth century, tea had become the English national drink. Imported from China and then from India, mixed with sugar from the Caribbean colonies, tea was plentiful, cheap, and available to rich and poor alike.

With so many alternatives to choose from, wine consumption in the eighteenth century began to decline. We are seeing the same phenomenon at the start of the twenty-first century in traditional wine drinking countries, from France and Italy to Argentina, where young people regard wine drinking as old-fashioned and are switching to sodas, cocktails, and even recreational drugs instead of wine. After centuries of enjoying a monopolistic control of beverages for human consumption, the wine producers of Europe were suddenly overwhelmed with competition from beer, brandy, whisky, gin, coffee, and tea. If they were to survive, they would need to improve their product.

Quality control: The main challenges for wine producers were quality control and aging. Even the best of red wines turned to vinegar after about a year, and many wines turned bad and became undrinkable much sooner than that. There were many reasons for this. Wine merchants tended to mix wine from various sources, and so even an excellent wine could be degraded by being mixed with an inferior wine. Secondly, wine was stored and transported in barrels, and was thus increasingly exposed to air, resulting in oxidization. The main problem, of course, was ignorance; although Europeans had been successfully making wine for over two thousand years, nobody actually understood the chemical process involved. It was not until the mid-nineteenth century that Louis Pasteur discovered the existence of yeasts and explained the effects of oxygen and the importance of hygiene in the winemaking process. Consequently, most red wine was of inferior quality.

Faced with the threat of competition from other beverages in the eighteenth century, wine producers were already making improvements. The biggest change came with the growing use of glass bottles. Glass bottles prior to the eighteenth century were made in wood-fired furnaces and were thin and fragile, used only for carrying wine from the barrel to the table. But with the introduction of the coal-fired furnace, which could produce sufficient heat to melt sand (1,760 degrees Celsius or 3,200 degrees Fahrenheit); glass bottles became thicker and stronger and suitable for long-term transport and storage. At the same time, the use of corks as bottle stoppers was introduced, and the combination of the glass bottles and cork stoppers resulted in wines which could not only age but actually improve with aging. Unfortunately, it was illegal to sell wine in bottles until 1860, partly for political reasons, but mainly because there were no standard bottle sizes. Wine was therefore shipped in barrels, and then the wine merchant or the tavern owner would sell it by the jug. Customers were expected to provide their own jugs or bottles. The aristocracy, of course, could afford to purchase wine by the barrel and then have it bottled by the butler and stored in the cellar—which is what they increasingly did from the eighteenth century onwards.

Bordeaux Branding: Another improvement which had begun in the seventeenth century was the branding of certain vineyards. Rather than sell his wine to a wine merchant who might blend it with other, more mediocre wines, a Bordeaux aristocrat named Arnaud de Pontac insisted on marketing his own wines with the name of his country estate, Haut-Brion. A few years after inheriting the estate from his father, de Pontac began shipping the wines from Haut-Brion directly to London where King Charles II became a keen customer.

In a 1647 Bordeaux merchant's listing, wine was only classified as coming from large generic sources such as Medoc or Graves, and even on a listing in 1740, wine was still only classified by individual parish. Under this old system in which wines from various estates were blended together, there was no incentive for the individual producers to care much about quality. By putting his family name and the name of his château on his wines, de Pontac was making a statement about the quality of the wine which quickly resulted in name recognition, consistent quality, increased demand, and, of course, higher prices and profits.

In his diary, Samuel Pepys wrote in 1663 that while visiting Royal Oak Tavern, he "drank a sort of French wine called Ho Bryan that hath a good and most particular taste I never met with." Pepys was soon followed by the writer Jonathan Swift and the philosopher John Locke. One hundred years later, the American Ambassador to France, Thomas Jefferson, visited the Haut-Brion estate, analyzed the soil, and purchased six cases of the wine.

Other large Bordeaux estates, especially the major vineyards on the left bank of the Gironde river, north of the city, quickly followed de Pontac's lead, and wines from Château Margaux, Château La Tour, and Château La Fitte, soon became recognized and much sought after, especially by the English aristocracy and rapidly growing middle class. In the early eighteenth century, the Marquis de Ségur owned Château La Tour, Château Lafite, and Château Mouton, all of which he successfully marketed in London. Château Lafite in particular became a cult wine in London, and the British Prime Minister, Walpole, bought a new barrel of Lafite every three months. Even today, many of the billionaire wine buyers in China refuse to drink anything except Château Lafite. This emphasis on specific individual vineyards, promoted by men like de Pontac and Ségur, did much to improve the quality and thus the reputation of red wines in the market. A listing from 1745 not only matches individual vineyards to prices, but has also begun classifying them into first, second, and third "crus."

By the time Thomas Jefferson visited the region in 1787, just before the French Revolution, individual châteaux were marketing their wine under their own names and competing for market share. Already wines were being classified in different categories based on market price and demand, which obviously reflected quality. It is interesting that Jefferson's own evaluation of the Bordeaux wines in 1787 was almost the same as the official classification made sixty-eight years later in 1855, and which is still in use today. Jefferson's four top-rated wines were Margaux, de La Fit, La Tour and Haut-Brion, which are all still Premier Crus in the twenty-first century. The growing wealth of the English mercantile class, along with the aristocracy, created a demand for top-growth Bordeaux wines which remains unabated to this day. It became the mark of a true gentleman to purchase barrels direct from one of the Bordeaux vineyards (or via a reputable merchant such as Berry Bros. & Rudd), and have it bottled and stored in his own cellars. It was this dramatic improvement in the way Bordeaux wines were marketed, as well as stored, that began to increase the perceived value of dry red wines in comparison with sweet white wines, which had always been more highly valued.

Wines of the New World: As the European nations expanded their colonies into the New World, they took with them their thirst for wine. As we have seen, the English and French were unsuccessful in their attempts to establish vineyards on the East Coast of North America, but the Dutch were successful in South Africa as early as the mid-seventeenth century and by the early eighteenth century, the English were successfully growing wine in Australia. Although dry red wines were grown in these distant colonies for local consumption, the only wines that were considered worth exporting back to Europe were the sweet white wines, like Constantia from South Africa.

Unlike the English, the Spanish were successful in their attempts to grow wine in America, and were soon planting vineyards besides the Missions which they erected all along the coast of what is now California. Since most of the ships left Spain from the port of Cadiz, the missionaries probably took the local Palomino vines with them on the voyage, so the "Mission Grape" of the New World is the same grape that the Spanish today use for making Sherry.

Vineyards were successfully planted in Mexico, Peru, Chile, and Argentina—even as close to the equator as Bolivia. However, the rapacious Spanish monarchy saw this as a threat to their treasury, despite all the gold and silver they were importing. They did not want their colonies to be self-sufficient in wine; they wanted to continue exporting Spanish wine to South America. Wine production was therefore banned, and the colonists were obliged to purchase thin Spanish wine, which had become almost undrinkable after the long ocean crossing. Until they finally achieved independence from Spain, the colonists distilled their grapes to produce Pisco and Aguardiente, South American brandies.

Nineteenth Century

Classification of French Wine: By the middle of the nineteenth century, the importance of wine to the French economy had become obvious not only to the growers and landowners, but also to the government in Paris. In 1855, by order of Emperor Napoleon III, who wanted to promote French wines at the Exposition Universelle, the sixty-one major wines of Bordeaux were classified in rank based upon market prices for the previous one hundred years. There were five top ranks followed by various lower"Bourgeois" rankings (see Appendix B). The top rank, Premier Cru (First Growth), had only four wines: Châteaux Lafite, Latour, Margaux and Haut-Brion (the four wines favored by Jefferson). What is amazing is that despite further revolutions, foreign invasions, the scourge of Phylloxera, and two world wars—to say nothing of changes in ownership, dynastic upheavals, swings in public taste and dramatic shifts in the world economy—the Bordeaux ranking of

1855 remains unchanged to this day. The only change in the ranking over the past 160 years has been the elevation, in 1973, of Château Mouton from second to first growth status. It is interesting that Jefferson had judged Château Mouton as a third growth—not even a second.

Six years later in Burgundy, the Comité d'Agriculture de Beaune, introduced its own classification system based on an informal listing by Jules Lavalle, a French wine writer, who had divided the major vineyards into three classes, or crus, based on the climate or terroir of the different communes.

Where the Bordeaux classification is rigid and hierarchical (unchanged for 160 years), the Burgundian system is more democratic and fluid—and consequently more complex and difficult to understand. The 1861 Beaune classification (formalized in 1935) divided the region into different communes so that winemakers could market themselves by the name of their commune—some communes obviously being better known and valued than others. Within each commune, following the 1935 update, certain vineyards were classified as "Premier Crus," and their labels could show the name of the vineyard as well as the name of the commune. Out of these, usually no more than two or three per commune were classified as "Grand Crus," and these wines were allowed to show the name of the vineyard alone, with no reference to the commune. The Beaune classification is more fluid and democratic because it's in a constant state of re-evaluation. Almost like a restaurant fighting to maintain its Michelin four star status, so too the vineyards of Burgundy must constantly strive to maintain standards or risk losing their Premier or Grand Cru status (see Appendix B).

Louis Pasteur: By the middle of the nineteenth century, wine was France's second biggest export (after textiles), one-third of the population was employed in its production, and it represented almost a quarter of the nation's revenues. However, during the late

1840s, the industry had been almost destroyed by a disease called *oïdium*, which attacked most of the country's vineyards until it was eradicated by the widespread and determined application of sulphur. So important had wine become to the French economy that the government commissioned its most eminent scientist, Louis Pasteur, to study the scientific basis of wine and show how to improve and protect the industry. Pasteur's study, *Etudes sur le Vin*, was published in 1866 and had an immediate effect upon the scientific understanding of winemaking. It was Pasteur who first discovered the existence of yeast and its role in converting sugar to alcohol, but perhaps his most important legacy is his emphasis on sterilization and cleanliness in the winemaking process to avoid contamination and spoilage, which had previously been a major problem. But, if the correct procedures were followed, he concluded: "Wine is the most healthful and most hygienic of beverages."

Phylloxera: By the mid-1860s, therefore, the French wine industry was enjoying a healthy recovery. The two main regions, Bordeaux and Burgundy, had introduced classification systems and quality control, Napoleon III's government was showing active economic support, Louis Pasteur had established dramatically improved standards for the industry and, as a result of all this, the export market was growing rapidly to meet the insatiable demand by England's expanding middle classes for Bordeaux wines.

It was at this precise moment that the wine industry was presented with its worst crisis ever—Phylloxera—and even the genius of Pasteur was no match for this new disease.

One of the reasons that the English and French were unable to grow vines in their American colonies was the existence of Phylloxera vastatrix (*Daktulosphaira vitifoliae*), a local North American aphid with an extraordinary sex-life which feeds on the roots of the *Vitis vinifera*

123

and kills the vine. Phylloxera only existed east of the Sierra Nevadas, which is why the Spaniards had no problem growing wine on the West Coast in California. Native American vines had developed a resistance to Phylloxera over the centuries, but the European *Vitis vinifera* had no such resistance.

In 1862, a wine merchant named Borty in the southern Rhône valley planted ten experimental rows of some Native American grapevines within his walled garden in the small village of Roquemaure. The vines had been mailed to him by a friend in New York, and by the following summer, while the New American vines were thriving nicely, all M. Borty's Grenache and Alicante vines were showing symptoms of a mysterious infection. Very soon, all the vines in the surrounding villages were either dead or dying, and by the mid-1860s all the vineyards of the southern Rhône valley had mysteriously died. A few years later all the vineyards in Burgundy were dead, and by the 1870s all the vineyards of France were under attack. (Unfortunately, France itself was also under attack. France in 1871 had been defeated in the Franco-Prussian War; German troops occupied France, and Paris itself was under the violent control of the Commune.) The mysterious plague spread to Italy by 1875, Spain by 1878, Germany by 1881, and Greece by 1898. By the end of the nineteenth century, all the vineyards in Europe had been destroyed. When the vineyards of Bordeaux were destroyed in 1869, the wealthy vineyard owners moved to the Rioja area of Northern Spain, and were able to grow their vines there for several years until the Phylloxera aphid finally reached them, nine years later. Eventually, the Phylloxera blight travelled all over the world, as far as Australia and South Africa by the start of the twentieth century, and in the 1990s almost destroyed the Californian wine industry.

The demand for wine still needed to be satisfied, and Europe began importing wines from California and even from Chile. As we shall see later, Californian wines developed a poor reputation in the twentieth century following Prohibition, but previously, in the late nineteenth century, they had been highly regarded and won all sorts of international prizes.

The Phylloxera aphid was not identified as the cause of the problem until the late 1870s, and the solution to the problem was not widely accepted until the late 1880s. The solution was to replant all the vineyards in Europe with the Phylloxera-resistant American *Vitis riparia* rootstock, and then to graft whatever remaining European *Vitis vinifera* vines could be found onto the roots. The replacement of rootstock did not begin until the 1890s, with the result that almost every vine in Europe today is grown on American rootstock. A wonderful study of France's Phylloxera scourge and its eventual defeat can be found in Christy Campbell's compellingly fascinating book, *The Botanist and the Vintner – How Wine was Saved for the World*.

Small pockets of vineyards around the world managed to survive Phylloxera; for example, it never reached Chile, and there are individual vineyards in Southern Australia, Piedmont, Italy, and Southern Portugal which were not affected and still have the original un-grafted vines. In most cases, the vines appear to have been protected by sandy soils. The Champagne house Bollinger owns two unaffected vineyards with original, un-grafted Pinot Noir vines, which they use to produce one of the rarest and by most accounts greatest of all Champagnes, *Vieilles Vignes Françaises*.

Of course, many traditionalists complained that wine never tasted the same again and that the new vines grafted onto American rootstock have an inferior, if not "foxy," taste. Indeed, Benjamin Wallace's entertaining *The Billionaire's Vinegar* describes a whole culture of wealthy collectors who only drink wines bottled prior to the Phylloxera scourge.

Long-term effects of Phylloxera on the wine industry were mixed. Because every vineyard had to be laboriously and expensively replanted, more rational planning went into the layout of the vineyards and the choice of vines to be planted, resulting in greater efficiency. But many vineyards, and indeed many wine growing regions, lacked the financial ability to replant their vines, and so never recovered.

A good example is Chablis, which through much of its history had produced the most-valued and highly-regarded white wines in France. Grown in Yonne, in the northern reaches of Burgundy, the wines could be shipped down the Seine to the great markets of Paris. Unfortunately, the advent of the French railway system occurred the same time as the Phylloxera blight, and when it came time to replant the vineyards of Chablis, the winegrowers of the Yonne discovered that history had abandoned them beside the road. With direct rail links from Bordeaux, Dijon and Lyon, Paris had no further need for the wines of Chablis which, without a railway line, still needed to be transported the old-fashioned way by river.

An Interesting Decade: Altogether, the 1860s proved to be an eventful decade for French wine. To misquote Marcel Proust's Duchesse de Guermantes: "It started well but ended badly."

1855 – Napoleon III orders the classification of Bordeaux wines

1861 – Classification of Beaune

1862 – M. Borty plants some American vines in his garden in Provence

1866 – Pasteur's Etudes sur le Vin published

1867 – Most vineyards in Southern France appear to be dying

1870 – French government offers 30,000FR prize for a cure to Phylloxera

1871 – Proust born. France invaded and defeated by Prussia. Napoleon III abdicates. Phylloxera continues to destroy French vineyards

Twentieth Century

Prohibition: Founded by Puritans, the USA has always had a somewhat ambivalent attitude towards alcohol—and sex, too. It's a nation torn between cheap whiskey and rough whore-houses on one hand, and root beer and Mother's apple pie on the other. The long tradition of temperance movements finally culminated in the 1919 Volstead Act which, for the next fourteen years, banned the sale, production, and transportation of all intoxicating liquids. A minor loophole permitted some wineries, such the Christian Brothers, to continue making limited amounts of wine for Catholic priests to celebrate Mass, and a more significant and pernicious loophole allowed the production, sale, and consumption of unfermented grape juice.

Of the three major consequences of Prohibition, two are well-known and well-documented. Because the consumption of alcohol became illegal, people did their drinking in "speakeasies." Both for reasons of social ambience as well as economics, speakeasies encouraged the consumption of hard liquor rather than fine wines. Because the hard liquor was often of poor quality or worse, a tradition of cocktail-mixes arose to disguise the taste. During the fourteen years of Prohibition, therefore, Americans developed a taste for cocktails and spirits. It should not be forgotten that since the earliest colonial times, the inability to successfully produce local wine had encouraged Americans to drink locally produced hard liquor, rather than expensive, imported European wines.

Secondly, because alcohol became illegal, those Americans who were not strict teetotalers were forced to break the law and support an underground economy controlled by criminals, leading to the establishment and rapid expansion of organized crime, which remained entrenched in society even after the repeal of the 18th Amendment in 1933.

But a lesser known effect of Prohibition was the destruction of the highly-regarded Californian wine industry. California had been developing a wine industry since the Spanish missionaries started planting vineyards in the eighteenth century; by the late nineteenth century, Californian wines were competing successfully with the best European wines. Indeed, when the European vineyards were decimated by the Phylloxera plague in the latter half of the nineteenth century, it was Californian wines that saved the day. When Prohibition was introduced in 1920, California had a successful and sophisticated wine industry with well-tended vineyards planted with a wide variety of the best European *Vitis vinifera* vines.

Because of the loophole that allowed the production, sale, transportation, and consumption of grape juice, a large percentage of the population started making their own wine. Jugs of grape juice were soon being distributed all over America, with labels containing very detailed instructions of what NOT to do in case the juice began to ferment and turn into wine. Consumers were instructed at what temperature they should NOT store their juice, and for how long they should be careful NOT to store it at that temperature—least they should inadvertently turn their innocent juice into alcohol. Home winemaking became so big and blatant during Prohibition that it threatened the revenues of organized crime, and was banned by Al Capone in Chicago on pain of death (literally).

Ironically, the demand for crude grape juice became so high that the land value of vineyards sky-rocketed during Prohibition, but unfortunately the quality of the grape juice plummeted. Vineyards boasting the finest, most mature *Vitis vinifera* vines were torn up and replanted with crude but prolific varietals, such as Alicante-Bouschet, that produced the juice the market demanded; quality was replaced with quantity.

After the repeal of Prohibition in 1933, after thirteen years, ten months and eighteen days, Californian vineyards—which had been among the world's best—were capable of producing only the crudest of cheap jug wines for a national market that was interested only in hard liquor anyway. That is the real tragedy of Prohibition, and it took another forty years to recover.

Some of the effects of Prohibition unfortunately continue to haunt Americans even today. American wine drinkers in the twenty-first century are still constrained by the three-tier system of distribution. This system, which was introduced with the repeal of Prohibition, means that wineries can sell only to distributors, and distributors can sell only to retailers or restaurants. This means there are always two layers of price mark-up between producers and consumers. Part of the reason for this was to increase the retail price of alcohol to prevent public drunkenness, and another reason was to fragment the industry so that organized crime could not dominate it.

Although Prohibition has long been repealed, public drunkenness is no longer the social scourge it once was, and organized crime has moved onto more lucrative ventures, the three-tier system is probably here to stay. There are too many vested interests benefiting from its complex regulations, too many lobbyists campaigning for its continuance, and too many state and local politicians guzzling from the financial trough into which it pours. Each of the fifty states has complete control over the distribution of alcohol within the state, and it is difficult to imagine a day when a state's politicians would willingly relinquish control of so lucrative a system. Each state has its own conflicting set of regulations, most of which have not yet been tested in a court of law. There are many competing interests and players in the marketing of wine. With annual US sales of more than $21.6 billion from more than 3,700 wineries nationwide, wine is big business and lobbies on both sides have major interests at stake. Wholesalers want to retain the three-tier system for their livelihood, while wineries want all fifty states to open the door to direct shipping.

Despite the emergence of flash sale websites and the online marketplace with companies like Amazon offering price-saving possibilities, the archaic, Prohibition-era regulations will continue to make it difficult for a Florida resident from contacting her favorite Californian winery and ordering a case of her favorite wine at a fair market price. In any other business, if you found a way to effectively and profitably eliminate the middle distribution level, you'd be considered a business wizard. In the alcoholic beverage industry, you'll be considered a criminal.

Judgment of Paris: Although most Californian vineyards had been uprooted during Prohibition and the wine industry destroyed, a few dedicated vintners had enough faith in the region to try and revive its fortunes. With the assistance of the University of California at Davis, new, more scientific methods were introduced into the growing of vines and the winemaking process until, by the early 1970s, the improved reputation of Californian wines had even reached Europe.

In 1976, Steven Spurrier, a young Englishman who ran an extremely successful wine shop in Paris, decided to honor the bicentennial of US independence with a blind tasting of French and Californian wines. Spurrier made an astute and well-informed selection of hitherto unknown Californian Chardonnays and Cabernets, which he matched with the very best French wines from Burgundy (including two Grand Crus), and Bordeaux (including two Premier Crus). (The complete list is shown in Appendix C.)

The judges were not only all French; they were also the crème de la crème of the French wine industry. Everybody, including Spurrier, expected the French wines to win, and at best expected the Californians to get a condescending pat-on-the-head, be told their wine showed great promise, and maybe, in a couple of hundred years... The purpose of the event was to make a gallant, Gallic gesture in celebration of American Independence, and also to promote Spurrier's wine store and to cement his relations within the French wine establishment. In the event, Spurrier was almost drummed-out of France!

Not only did the Californian Stag's Leap Cabernet Sauvignon out-perform all the French red wines—including Haut-Brion and Mouton Rothschild—but out of the top four wines in the Chardonnay category, three were from California, including Château Montelena, which got first place. It was a complete and publicly humiliating disaster for the French wine establishment. Full details of the tasting are given in George Taber's wonderfully informative book, *The Judgment of Paris.*

The 1976 Paris tasting had significance and repercussions far beyond embarrassing the French wine establishment. By knocking France off its perch as the world's supreme terroir for producing quality wine, the '76 tasting opened up the rest of the world and conferred winemaking confidence on the other side of the Atlantic and on the other side of the equator. The lessons of the Paris tasting are best exemplified by Baron Philip de Rothschild.

Rothschild had inherited the Château Mouton estate in 1922. According to the 1855 classification, Château Mouton was rated as a Deuxieme Cru—a second growth. Rothschild's theory was that it was not included in the top first growths only because, in 1855, the estate was owned by an Englishman. For the next forty years, Rothschild dedicated his life to having Château Mouton Rothschild elevated from second growth to first growth, and finally this was accomplished in 1973. Rothschild celebrated the event by having the estate's motto changed from, "Premier ne puis, second ne daigne, Mouton suis" (First, I cannot be. Second, I do not deign to be. Mouton I am), and it was changed to, "Premier je suis, Second je fus, Mouton ne change" (First, I am. Second, I used to be. Mouton does not change).

Three years later, a panel of eminent French judges voted Château Mouton Rothschild second in the Paris wine tasting—second to Stag's Leap, a previously unknown wine from California. Baron Philip was understandably furious and devastated. "It has taken me forty years to become a first growth," he sobbed. But Rothschild was an extremely intelligent man, and he quickly learned his lesson. Within three years he had entered into an equal partnership with Robert Mondavi in California's Napa Valley to produce the very successful 1979 Opus One Cabernet Sauvignon. Not only did Rothschild continue to purchase vineyards in California, but he sent his daughter to Chile to partner with Concha y Toro, and now this French family has invested in vineyards all over the world. As George Tabor explains in his book, the Californians' success in the Judgment of Paris demonstrated that the quality of the grapes and the skill of the winemaker are far more important than the place where the wine is made—however venerated its historic traditions. (See Appendix C for list of wines tasted in Paris and final votes.)

British Influence: For such a small rainy island, off the coast of Northern Europe with no vineyards worth discussing, Great Britain has had, and still maintains, an extraordinary dominance in the world of wine. Since the time the Romans first planted vineyards in Southwest France around the city they called Burdigala on the wide Gironde River to supply its legions in Britannia, the British have maintained a very close relationship with this port city of Bordeaux.

The Hundred Years' War from 1337 to 1453 was essentially a struggle over the Bordeaux wine trade, and even after the French crown finally expelled the English armies and destroyed all English claims; the English trade, the English influence, and the English merchants still remained. Even today, British (and Irish) family names from that period still dominate the Bordeaux wine trade: Barton, Berry Bros, Johnston, Talbot, Lynch, Barges, Colks, and Lawtons, to name a few. As discussed elsewhere, even the distinctive Bordeaux style of wine—the claret—was developed to satisfy English tastes.

During those periods of war when English and French hostilities forced the English to look elsewhere for wine, the English developed close ties with Portugal, and even today, the wine trade in Oporto is still dominated by the English and Irish immigrants of the seventeenth century. The following list of current wine merchants in Portugal indicates this British heritage: Churchill, Cockburn Smithes, Croft, Dow, Gould Campbell, Graham's, Harris, Hutcheson, Burmester, Morgan Brothers, Forrester, Osborne, Richard Hooper & Sons, Sandeman, Smith Woodhouse, Symington, Taylor, Grahamn, and Warre.

In addition to Portugal as a "Plan B" backup supplier of wine, the British also developed close ties with Spain. Ever since 1587, when Sir Francis Drake "singed the King of Spain's beard" by stealing three thousand barrels of Sherry (or the equivalent of one million bottles) from the port of Cadiz, the English have been inordinately fond of Sherry, or "sac," as Shakespeare refers to it. In the nineteenth century, nearly 50 percent of the wine consumed in England was Sherry. Once again, as in Bordeaux and Oporto, the English merchants moved to Jerez in Southern Spain to keep an eye on business, and the names of their descendants can still be seen in any list of modern Spanish wine merchants: Garvey, Duff-Gordon, Wisdom & Warter, Byass, Harveys, Osborne, Sandman, Williams & Humbert. Even the quintessentially Spanish sounding Sherry, Tio Pepe, was originally founded by an Irish merchant called Murphy.

Indeed, wherever good wine is made, there turns out to be a British connection. In 1773, an Englishman named John Woodhouse decided that the decent local wine of Sicily could be improved by using the Solera process, and thus invented the powerful sweet wines of Marsala. It was another Englishman, Dr. James Busby, who first brought cuttings of the Syrah vine to Australia in 1832, and thus fathered the worldwide craze for Australian Shiraz. Despite French claims to the contrary, it was the English, not Dom Pérignon, who invented Champagne. In 1662, almost forty years before the monk reputedly claimed, "I am drinking stars," an English scientist, Christopher Merret, presented an eight page paper at London's Royal Society, in which he detailed what is now called *méthode Champenoise*, the secondary fermentation that makes wine "brisk and sparkling."

Even Argentina's most famous and prolific wine region has a British origin. In 1895, an English railway engineer, Edward James Palmer Norton, founded Bodega Norton, the very first winery in Mendoza Province. Thanks to the vision of this Englishman, Mendoza became the heart of the Argentinian wine industry and the fifth largest wine region in the world. As recently as 2007, Bodega Norton alone was exporting 1.5 million cases of Malbec wines annually. Even the world-famous Marlborough Sauvignon Blanc wines of New Zealand did not receive international recognition until they won the Sunday Times competition in London and were placed on the shelves of

English supermarkets. And of course, one of the most momentous and significant events in the history of modern wine, the 1976 Judgment of Paris, was organized by Stephen Spurrier, an Englishman.

And in the twenty-first century, the British domination of the international wine trade is stronger than ever. The center of the world's wine trade is not Bordeaux or Paris, not San Francisco or New York; it is Delamare Road, Cheshunt in Hertfordshire, a small village halfway between Potters Bar and Epping, a few miles north of London. Tesco House on Delamare Road is the world headquarters of Tesco, the world's biggest retailer of wine.

Perhaps the main explanation for the unparalleled influence of the English on the world of wine lies in the fact that the English, with minor exceptions, grow none of their own. As far back as 1760, an English Cellar Record Book that was a bestseller in London had specific sections devoted to Burgundy, Champagne, Claret, Madeira, Port, Rhenish, and Sack (Sherry). While the French King and his aristocracy had their own vast cellars, these would have been stocked almost exclusively with French wine. The English alone had such eclectic tastes that were limited to no specific producer, and the winemakers of France, Spain, Portugal, and Germany were all only too anxious to satisfy those tastes.

Because the English produce no significant wine of their own, all wine has to be imported. The English actually drink only 5 percent of the world's wine, but they import 17 percent of all the wine that is traded globally. The United Kingdom accounts for 20 percent of all money spent on wine in international markets, more than any other nation. Of every six bottles that ships around the world, one will end up on a supermarket shelf in England—usually a Tesco shelf. There are other big wine retailers in the UK, of course, such as Sainsbury's and Waitrose, for example, but Tesco is bigger—selling 320 million bottles of wine per year in England alone. Tesco is actually the biggest wine retailer in the world, operating 3,700 stores in fourteen countries in 2009. Sourcing its wine from producers all over the world, shipping it across the globe in vast containers, retailing the wine—often under its own Tesco brand label—in fourteen different countries, but most especially in England, means that the English market and English tastes continue to drive the international market for wine.

Wine in the Twenty-First Century

In the forty years since the Paris tasting of 1976, the world of wine has changed dramatically. No longer centered on France, the wine industry has become truly global. The average supermarket in America or England, for example, has a daunting Wall of Wine offering a choice of perhaps one thousand different bottles of wine from at least a dozen different countries. In my local store in South Florida, Sauvignon Blancs from their traditional home of Pouilly Fumé in the Loire Valley now compete with bottles from New Zealand's Wairau Valley, and Pinot Noirs from Burgundy's Côté de Nuits compete with Pinots from Oregon's Willamette Valley.

Partly to protect the consumer, partly to protect the reputation of the producer, and partly to promote wine exports, national and international rules and standards have eroded some local differences in wine, and in other ways emphasized those differences. Following the leads of Bordeaux and Burgundy, the French government introduced a wine classification for the whole country in 1935. In order to carry the AOC (Appellation d'Origin Controlée) designation on its label, the wine must be certified to have fulfilled certain conditions—primarily where it was grown and made. (See the chapter on France for more details.) As Italy, Spain, Portugal, and Germany all came together to form the European Union during the 1970s, each of the countries were obliged to introduce similar laws, dividing each country into individual wine regions and subregions which needed to be specified on the label.

Globalization: No longer designed to appeal just to a local taste, wines must increasingly satisfy a more universal standard dictated by wine critics like Robert Parker or Jancis Robinson, and magazines such as *Decanter* in the UK and *The Wine Spectator* in the USA. While boutique wineries still exist—and it's possible to find winemakers with their own unique taste and style—most of the world's wine is produced by a handful of huge international conglomerates that ship it around the world in standard twenty-four-foot shipping containers, holding twenty-four thousand liter disposable plastic bladders, and bottle it on arrival. The world of wine is not controlled by elite cabals in Bordeaux and Beaune, nor by Christies and Sotheby auction houses in Paris or New York. These days, the big decisions concerning the future of wine are being made on 999 Lake Drive, Issaquah, WA, and on Delamare Road, Cheshunt, just outside London—the respective head offices of Costco and Tesco, the world's two largest wine merchants.

Figure 3: World's top wine import and export nations

The following list from *BKWine Magazine* (www.bkwine.com) shows the world's top ten wine-exporting countries in 2013:

France: $10,441,798,000 (30.2% of total wine exports)

Italy: $6,696,378,000 (19.4%)

Spain: $3,429,986,000 (9.9%)

Chile: $1,889,985,000 (5.5%)

Australia: $1,779,479,000 (5.2%)

United States: $1,559,484,000 (4.5%)

Germany: $1,345,842,000 (3.9%)

New Zealand: $1,021,198,000 (3.0%)

Portugal: $962,321,000 (2.8%)

Argentina: $887,227,000 (2.6%)

The following list from *BKWine Magazine* shows the world's top ten wine-importing countries in 2012:

United Kingdom, 3,944 Million €uros

USA, 3,938 M €

Germany, 2,393 M €

Canada, 1,540 M €

China, 1,229 M €

Japan, 1,225 M €

Belgium, 964 M €

Switzerland, 925 M €

Netherlands, 872 M €

Russia, 817 M €

The US wine market is one of the fastest growing markets in the world, both in terms of production and consumption. It has expanded rapidly over the past few years on the back of increased consumption,

government support, online wine purchasing, and a growing
young population.

On the other hand, wine consumption is falling in all the traditional
wine-producing countries. Over the past thirty years, water quality
has improved dramatically throughout most of the Western world,
and is now safe to drink even in remote and rural areas. With stricter
drinking and driving laws, increased expectations of efficiency in the
workplace, and a decline in the café or pub as a center for social
life, wine is no longer the daily general beverage. Young people in
countries such as Argentina, Spain, Italy, and France are switching to
trendy cocktails, recreational drugs, or simple sodas instead of wine.
In Italy, for example, in the final fifty years of the twentieth century,
per capita wine consumption has dropped 45 percent from twenty-
nine gallons to fifteen. In France, over the same period, the drop is
even more extreme, from forty gallons to just sixteen—a decline of 60
percent. In Germany, wine consumption has dropped by a quarter,
and in Spain and Portugal, it has gone down by a third. It should be
noted, however, that the decline is limited to the cheap, poor-quality
wines, which, perhaps as a consequence, are vanishing from the
market. Over the past thirty or forty years, Europeans might be drinking
less wine, but they are drinking better wine; while Americans who
seldom drank any wine thirty years ago are now consuming more wine
than any other nation.

UK wine consumption has increased by 500 percent since 1970, and
the US wine market will continue growing at a rapid pace in coming
years. Although the UK imports more wine, the US now consumes more
wine, even surpassing France. In terms of value, the US wine market
achieved a value of around $33.5 billion with 871 million gallons of
wine sales in 2013. The economic recession had little impact on the
US wine industry, as consumers started enjoying low-priced bottles and
wines by the glass.

Wine Prices: In my wine classes, students are encouraged to ask questions and discuss everything about the wine we are tasting, except for its price. We never discuss price. Experience has taught me that if I say we are about to drink an expensive, $75 bottle of wine, half the class will like it, even before they taste it, just because it is expensive. The other half will either dislike it or be disappointed because it is over-priced. As explained in Mike Veseth's wonderful book *Money, Taste, and Wine,* the very concept of the price of wine physically affects how we respond to it. Veseth refers to a 2008 study by Antoine Rangel of CalTech, in which the test subjects tasted wine while their brains were scanned with an MRI. When they were told that the wine they were about to taste was expensive, those parts of the brain associated with pleasure lit up in anticipation. He also quotes many other studies, which show that in blind tastings, most people cannot tell the difference between expensive and cheap wines, and indeed very often prefer the cheaper one.

The following table shows the typical breakdown of a bottle of Californian wine retailing in Florida at $20 per bottle. These are rough but typical numbers based on fairly common assumptions. Most wineries work on a 50 percent gross margin, meaning they sell their wine for double the cost of goods. There is a traditional 1 percent rule of thumb that the retail price of a bottle of wine is 1 percent of the cost of a ton of grapes. So wine made from grapes that cost $2,000 per ton will retail at $20 per bottle. Since the repeal of Prohibition, the US has "enjoyed" a three-tier system of distribution, which means that the wine producer and the wine consumer are separated by the distributor and the retailer. Most distributors work on a 28-30 percent margin of their sell-price, and most distributors work on a 30-35 percent margin. As shown here, a bottle of wine which the winery sells for $10 per bottle will eventually retail for $20.

RETAIL COST OF US WINE, ANALYSIS

	Bottle	Case
Cost of grapes ($2,000 per ton and 60 cases per ton)	$2.78	$33.33
Cost of oak & fermenting	$0.64	$7.67
Cost of packaging & bottling	$1.17	$14.00
Total Cost of Goods	**$4.58**	**$55.00**
Winery admin/mktng/profit	$4.58	$55.00
Wholesale price by winery	**$9.17**	**$110.00**
FOB costs and taxes	$0.48	$5.76
Cost for distributor	**$9.65**	**$115.76**
Distributor's 28% of sell price	$3.75	$45.04
Cost for retailer	**$13.40**	**$160.80**
Retailer's 33% of sell price	$6.60	$79.20
Final retail cost	**$20.00**	**$240.00**

Figure 4: US Wine Sales by Retail Price

In 2016, US wine sales by retail bottle price were as follows, noted by Statista (www.statista.com):

$25 & above	4.8%
$20 - 24.99	4.0%
$15 - $19.99	8.5%
$11 - $14.99	18.7%
$8 - $10.99	27.3%
$4 - $7.99	30.1%
Less than $4	6.4%

I've observed in my local supermarket, which offers a selection of perhaps one thousand different wines, that the bottles in the $8 to $15 range are shelved at eye level where most people can find them, while the more expensive bottles are placed on the higher shelves and the cheaper selections are all on the lower shelves. Retailers recognize that most people shop for wine primarily by price category, rather than terroir or varietal. If you don't find what you were looking for initially, you can reach up for something better; or you can bend down for something less. In a 2012 paper presented to the American Association of Wine Economists, Dr. Elliot R. Morse quoted from a survey of six thousand blind tastings to argue that most people do not appreciate expensive wines: "Individuals who are unaware of the price do not derive more enjoyment from more expensive wine. ... we find that the correlation between price and overall rating is small and negative, suggesting that individuals on average enjoy more expensive wines slightly less." He went on to say that "Lecocq and Visser analyzed data from three data sets totaling 1387 observations on French Bordeaux's and Burgundies. They report similar findings: 'When non-experts blind-taste cheap and expensive wines they typically tend to prefer the cheaper ones.'"

Wine Today: Many people complain that we have created a world of "McWine" which has lost its individuality and local identity; the reds have less tannin and the whites less acid. To a certain extent this is true; although wine connoisseurs can still identify a Château Latour from a Château Lafite, I doubt that many could tell the difference between a selection of regular Cabernet Sauvignons from Australia, Chile, or California.

But most people have never been able to afford to drink a glass of Château Lafite or Château Latour. The wines that most people could afford, four hundred years ago or forty or even fourteen years ago were actually not very good; the selection was limited and the quality was poor. On the other hand, the expensive wines were not so impossibly out of reach. When I lived in France during the 1970s as a struggling writer and painter, I was by no means wealthy, but for special occasions, I remember buying a Cheval Blanc from Saint-Émilion, and I remember buying my father a Château Latour for his birthday. These were certainly extravagant gestures, and, I'm guessing, the equivalent of $40 or $50 in today's money. But these days, prices for these top wines have become impossible for ordinary folk, even as extravagant gestures. It's hard to find either of the two wines I mentioned for much less than $1,000 per bottle. (A single bottle of 1947 Cheval Blanc recently sold for more than $30,000.) However, while the price of the great wines has exploded through the roof, the price of decent wines has descended equally dramatically.

Today we live in a wine drinker's paradise; not only do we have a geographic selection that could not be imagined a couple of decades ago, but we also have consistently decent quality at affordable prices. Poor quality wine no longer sells, and people who make bad wine soon go out of business. The average person today has access to a wide selection of modestly priced and well-made wines from all over the world. Some purists complain that wine has become just another consumer commodity.

As a consumer I say, "Jolly good show! Let's enjoy it. Cheers!"

Chapter

4

TERROIR OF EUROPE

"Quickly, bring me a beaker of wine, so that
I may wet my mind and say something clever." —
Aristophanes

Terroir vs. Varietal

An American and a Frenchman attend a corporate dinner, and after returning home they tell their wives about the event. "We started the evening with a deliciously refreshing French Sauvignon Blanc," the American tells his wife. "Then we had a fabulous Pinot Noir and finished the meal with a sweet white Sémillon." Meantime, the Frenchman was telling his wife that the deliciously refreshing Pouilly Fumé was followed by a fabulous Chevrey-Chambertin, and that the evening concluded with a great Sauternes. Both men were describing the same wines, but the Frenchman, like most Europeans, was concerned with the provenance of the wine, where it came from—its "terroir." The American, however, like most non-Europeans, was primarily interested in the grape the wine was made from—its varietal. (The two wives, of course, were simply delighted that their husbands had had an enjoyable evening.)

Pouilly Fumé is an AOC from the village of Pouilly in the upper Loire valley, where the predominant variety of grape is the Sauvignon Blanc. The nearby village of Sancerre, like all the villages in that region, also only produces Sauvignon Blanc. The Frenchman was telling his wife what sort of Sauvignon Blanc had been served—not a Sancerre, but a Pouilly Fumé, which has more of a smoky, mineral taste than the Sancerre. Likewise, all red wines from Burgundy are made with Pinot Noir grapes, and the Frenchman's wife would have known that; what was significant was that it came from the commune of Gevrey-Chambertin, which produces some of the world's most famous wines.

Finally, the Frenchman and his wife both know that a wine from the Sauternes region of Bordeaux is sweet and made from the Sémillon grape. That it was a Sauternes was all she needed to know.

The American, on the other hand, was not being ignorant by ignoring the terroir or provenance of the wines; he simply had a different perspective. Coming from a country where Sauvignon Blanc, Pinot Noir, Sémillon, and a whole variety of different grapes could all be found growing within miles of each other, the type of grape is far more important than where it was grown.

Over the two thousand years that Europeans have been growing vines, they have learned which grape variety is best suited to each different geographic region. Sauvignon Blanc does best in the upper reaches of the Loire, while Chenin Blanc is better suited further down river in the Middle Loire. Towards the mouth and lower reaches of the Loire, the most suitable grape is the Muscadet. In the Americas, however, or Australia, New Zealand, and South Africa, where they do not have two thousand years of experience, wine growers are still experimenting to see which varietal works best in which terroir.

Perhaps the best example of the anti-terroir approach is Penfolds Grange wine from Australia. In 1952, Max Schubert, a winemaker employed by Penfolds winery in South Australia, decided to make a wonderful Australian wine that could compare with the best French Bordeaux. He chose not to use one of the usual Bordeaux varietals such as Cabernet Sauvignon, but to use a classic Australian grape, Shiraz. His focus was on extracting from the grape the essence of all the big-bodied fruit that it contained, and using his winemaking skill to produce one of the world's great wines. He succeeded—and since 1952, Penfolds Grange has been recognized as Australia's iconic wine and one of the world' greatest, with an average price of about $500 per bottle. What is so interesting is that Penfolds completely rejects the concept of terroir. They focus not on where the grape was grown but on what it tastes like. The grapes used to make Grange come from all over South Australia; there is no single vineyard that produces Penfolds Grange. It is the quality of the grape and the skill of the winemaker that counts, not where it was grown, not the terroir.

Varietal is a French term for grape-type or variety, and obviously different varieties of grapes have different characteristics. A wine made from a Pinot Noir grape, for example, will never look or taste the same as one made from a Pinot Grigio grape. We will discuss a selection of different grape varieties in the next chapter. First we will examine terroir.

Terroir: *Terre* is the French word for land, and *terroir* is the French term that refers to the characteristics of a specific geographic place where the grapes are grown and the wine is made. The concept includes not just the latitude of the vineyard and its specific geographical co-ordinates, such as the distance from the ocean, but also its elevation, whether it slopes north or south, the soil, the drainage, and even the microclimate. For example, within certain small vineyards in Burgundy which have been closely monitored and documented since Roman times, individual sections or *climats* are known to produce wines superior to others within the same vineyard. "Terroirists" will argue that the unique combination of soil, location, climate, and even the "air" make certain spots so unique that their superior wines can never be reproduced elsewhere. The French in particular have always argued that the unique blend of history, soil, and tradition has made French wines impossible to reproduce or even match in any other country.

A 2016 report by California's UC Davis suggests that another factor making each terroir unique is the local collection of bacteria and fungi, or "microbiome," on pressed grapes, which can help predict the flavor profile of the final product. By sequencing the local microbial

DNA, they showed that each individual vineyard, whether in France or California, has its own unique microbiome contributing to the distinctive taste detected in the finished wine.

The concept of terroir is not new; the Greeks and Romans, and even the Egyptians and Babylonians before them, paid great attention to the geographic origin of their wines. Ancient wine amphorae had the place of origin stamped into the clay, and Roman writers such as Cato, Pliny, Horace, and Virgil all wrote extensively about vintages from specific vineyards in various parts of the empire and beyond. However, it was the French who took the concept to almost mystical levels, with the underlying implication that wines of great quality could be grown only in France.

The tradition of terroir was most seriously developed in Burgundy, where, since the fall of the Roman Empire, vast areas of land were controlled by the Christian monasteries and abbeys, particularly the Benedictines and Cistercians. Because the monks were such dedicated record keepers they have documented hundreds of years' worth of data concerning rainfall, temperatures, and crop yield, for every individual plot of land within the region. Their observations and valuations of the wine produced are reflected in the Premier and Grand Cru classifications we still use today.

On the other hand, it is worth noting that it was a French wine historian, Roger Dion, who argued that the characteristics of the soil and the climate of the terroir in the making of a Grand Cru is of no greater importance than the quality of the paint and the canvas used in the creation of a great painting by Vermeer or Picasso.

Latitude: In the following pages we will examine many of the world's wine-producing regions: the Old World of Europe, the New World of North America, and the Southern Hemisphere. It is always interesting to compare the latitudes of wine-producing regions in Europe and North America. As the table of wine latitudes demonstrates *(Figure 5)*, North American wines are grown much further south than they are in Europe. On the other hand, the table also reminds us that Beirut was once one of the world's centers for fine wine, and a not insignificant portion of nineteenth and early twentieth century French wine was actually grown in Algeria.

WINE PRODUCING REGIONS OF THE NORTHERN HEMISPHERE		
North America	Degrees North	Europe
	49	Moselle, Germany
	48	Champagne & Alsace. France
Seattle, WA	47	Chablis, France
Quebec, Canada	46	Dijon, Burgundy, France
Willamette Valley, OR	45	Lyon, Burgundy, France
	44	Bordeaux, France
	43	Chianti, Italy
Finger Lakes, NY	42	Rioja, Spain
	41	Catalonia, Spain
New York	40	Madrid, Spain
Mendocino, CA	39	Puglia, Italy
	38	Palermo, Sicily, Italy
Napa Valley, CA	37	Seville, Spain
	36	Cadiz (Jerez), Spain
Paso Robles, CA	35	Algiers, Algeria
Santa Barbara, CA	34	Beirut, Lebanon

Figure 5: Latitude of Northern Vineyards

France

It is very possible that the original inhabitants of Gaul knew about growing grapes and fermenting wines, but the earliest documented cultivation of wine in France was by the Phoenicians, followed by the Greeks, who were planting vines around their colony of Masalia (Marseilles) as early as 600 BC. The Greeks planted vineyards all along the coast of modern Provence and up the Rhône river valley as far north as modern Lyon.

With the arrival of the Romans around 200 BC, we see the establishment of all the French wine regions that exist today. Initially, the Romans opposed the planting of vines in their new colonies as they were more interested in exporting their own "Italian" wine into new markets, but very rapidly the demand for and consumption of wine in the expanding empire outpaced supply and vineyards were planted throughout Gaul, from the rich river valley of the Rhône to the bare, chalky uplands of Champagne.

French Wine Classification

As explained in more detail in Chapter Three, the wine merchants of Bordeaux classified their wines in 1855 based on the previous hundred years' sales records. With a single exception, that classification remains unchanged 160 years later. The wine merchants of Burgundy followed suit by classifying their own wines in 1861, and then in 1935 the French government introduced a national classification, Appellation d'Origine Contrôlée (AOC), to cover every wine region in France. While the emphasis of the classification is on terroir—the geographic origin of the wine—the regulations can also specify what grape varietals are permitted, the alcohol or residual sugar level, as well as limiting the volume of wine produced per acre.

The following French wine regions will therefore all have their own AOC, as well as their own subregions. Bordeaux, for example, has about forty-five AOCs, while Burgundy has 106. President De Gaulle famously asked, "How can you govern a country which has 246 varieties of cheese?" He could well have added, "and 338 Appellations of wine."

Cru: Cru is a French term most closely translated as growth, being the past participle of the verb *croître* (to grow). Although widely used in relationship to wine, it has slightly different meanings in different regions. In Burgundy, the word is used to categorize the two highest levels of classified vineyards, Grand Cru being the best and Premier Cru being second best. In Bordeaux, the 1855 classification divided the wines between Premier Cru (First Growth) down to Cinquieme Cru (Fifth Growth), followed by various levels of Crus Bourgeoises (Bourgeois Growths). Premier Cru is therefore the very best of the best in Bordeaux, while in Burgundy it means only second best. Grand Cru is the very top-level for wines in Burgundy and Alsace, while in St.-Émilion the highest level is Premier Grand Cru Classé A. In Sauternes, on the other hand, the highest level is Premier Cru Supérieur—a level so prestigious that it includes only a single wine, Château d'Yquem.

Clos: Clos is a French term meaning enclosed. It was used primarily in Burgundy where the Cistercian Monasteries separated the small plots of land with walls made from the rocks in the soil—partly to clear the ground and divide the vineyards, and partly as protection from the Mistral wind. Many vineyards throughout France, not just in Burgundy, have incorporated the word into the name of the vineyard—even when the original wall no longer exists. Examples include:

Clos Haut-Peyraguey, Clos Fourtet, Clos des Jacobins, Clos de l'Oratoire, Clos Saint-Martin (Bordeaux); Clos Napoléon,

Chambertin-Clos de Bèze, Clos de Tart, Clos des Lambrays, Clos de la Roche, Clos Saint-Denis, Clos de Vougeot, Clos des Réas, Clos du Roi, Clos des Ursules, Clos des Mouches, Clos des Épeneaux, Clos du Val, Clos des Chênes (Burgundy); Clos des Goisses, Clos du Mesnil (Champagne); Clos Sainte-Hune, Clos Sainte-Odile, Clos Saint-Urbain (Alsace); Clos de la Coulée-de-Serrant, Clos du Papillon, Le Grand Clos (Loire); Clos des Papes, Clos du Mont-Olivet, Clos de l'Oratoire des Papes (Rhône).

The word has also been adopted in the New World, for example: Clos du Bois, Clos du Val, Clos LaChance (California); Clos Clare (Australia); and Clos Henri (New Zealand).

French Terroir

ALSACE: The wines of Alsace are unique among French, and most other European wines, in having the grape varietal named prominently on the label. Alsatian wines are bottled identically in tall, slender, green bottles, called *flûtes d'Alsace,* and made from one of the four white noble grapes of Alsace: Riesling, Gewürztraminer, Muscat, or Pinot Gris. Sylvaner is permitted under certain conditions, but it does not qualify as a "noble grape." Labeling the wines with the name of the varietal was unique to Alsace until the late twentieth century, when Californian wine experts like Frank Schoonmaker and Robert Mondavi adopted the same system.

Located at the edge of the Roman Empire, along the fault line between Mediterranean and Northern European civilizations, Alsace has passed back and forth between French and German cultures and has accrued influences from both. Surprisingly, for a region which has seen such political turmoil and warfare throughout its history, the major wine producers have been held by the same families for centuries. Hugel & Fils was founded by the Hugel family in 1639; Maison Trimbach was founded by the Trimbach family in

1626; Domaine Zind-Humbrecht was founded by the Humbrecht family in 1620; and the family of Lucian Albrecht has been producing wines in Alsace since 1425. These same families still dominate the Alsace wine trade today.

Because of their established reputations and ancient histories, the wine growers of Alsace never bothered to apply for any AOC classification status in 1935. It was not until 1975 that any Grand Cru classification was established. Currently there are fifty-one Alsace Grand Crus, each of which must come from a single vineyard and may produce no more than fifty-five hectoliters per hectare, which works out about 240 cases of wine per acre. Two Grand Cru vineyards are permitted to produce Grand Cru blends of the four noble grapes, and one vineyard, Zotzenberg, is permitted to include Sylvaner in the blend.

The wine region across the border from Alsace in Germany is called Pfalz—or Palatinate—and to all intents and purposes, the two regions share the same climate, the same soil, the same geographic features, similar history, and even grow the same grape varietals, especially Riesling, Gewürztraminer, and Sylvaner. However, the taste of the wines is totally different, which shows the importance of national taste and the winemakers' skills. A bottle of Riesling or Gewürztraminer in France or in Germany will both look the same—bottled in the tall, slim, green flûtes d'Alsace—but will taste dramatically different. The Alsace bottle is made to be drunk with a meal and will be floral, crisp and dry; the German bottle, however, is not necessarily designed for drinking with food, will be softer and distinctly sweeter than the French version. Germans tend to accompany their meals with beer and reserve wines for drinking alone, unaccompanied by food, as a refreshment.

BORDEAUX: Bordeaux is the largest fine wine area on earth; it is five times the size of Burgundy, and eight times the size of Napa Valley. It contains some nine thousand individual châteaux and forty-five different appellations. It should be noted that the definition of "château" is fairly vague, and while the Bordeaux châteaux include many splendid and imposing architectural gems, some are little more than garden sheds. In the 1855 classification, only five vineyards are listed as châteaux, but by the end of the century the number had increased to over 1,300, and today it is approaching ten thousand.

Compared to Burgundy, where many vineyards are too small to bottle their own wine and must sell to négociants, Bordeaux boasts many large estates that grow, bottle, and market their own wine on a financially sophisticated and international level. Many of the châteaux are owned by international business conglomerates, like Asian banks or American insurance corporations. Unfortunately, in the past few years, Bordeaux wines have become a status symbol for Chinese billionaires, and consequently the market prices for the wine have soared astronomically. Not content with buying the wine alone, the Chinese have started buying the actual vineyards. This new trend is admirably explored in the film *Red Obsession*. If Burgundy is terroir-driven with the emphasis being on the precise spot where the grapes were grown, Bordeaux is estate-driven with the emphasis being on the traditional taste of the individual château. In Bordeaux, it is the winemaker who blends the different grapes to create a specific house style, which distinguishes a Château Latour from a Château Lafite. In Burgundy, it is the patch of soil which distinguishes a Montrachet Grand Cru from a Bâtard Montrachet Grand Cru.

In Burgundy, only two grape varietals are permitted: Chardonnay for whites and Pinot Noir for reds. In Bordeaux, the six permitted grapes for red wine are Cabernet Sauvignon, Merlot, Malbec, Petit Verdot, Cabernet Franc, and Carménère, while white varietals include Sauvignon Blanc, Sémillon, and Muscatel. Again, the fact that a single grape varietal is permitted in Burgundy emphasizes the importance placed on the source of that grape, its terroir. That Bordeaux permits a variety of different grapes emphasizes the importance of the château's cellar master, or Maître de Chai, who blends them to achieve the distinctive estate taste.

The first vineyards in Bordeaux, which the Romans called Burdigila, were mentioned by Pliny the Elder in AD 71, and Château Ausone, in Saint-Émilion, is named after the famous Roman poet Ausonius who had a villa nearby. The original vineyards were probably planted to supply wine to the Roman legions in Britannia. Following the fall of Rome, the English reverted to beer, and all connection with Burdigala/Bordeaux was lost for many years.

However, when the French King Louis VII divorced Eleanor of Aquitaine in 1152, she married Henry, Duke of Anjou and Normandy, and included the port of Bordeaux as part of her dowry. Two years later, Henry became King of England, and Bordeaux thus became an English possession. Once again, Bordeaux became the cheapest source of wine for the British Isles, and a special relationship was established which continues into the twenty-first century. Because of preferential import tariffs granted by the English King John in 1203 and the *Police des Vins* granted by the French crown to benefit the wine growers of Bordeaux, there began an immense export boom of wine to England, with massive fleets of two hundred or more ships, sailing to England twice a year. To avoid loss to pirates, King Edward III insisted that the vast fleet of English ships sail together in the fall, carrying as much of the new harvest as possible, and then a second gigantic fleet should sail again in the spring, transporting the rest, the "reck," which had, in the meantime, been racked and transferred to clean barrels. In this way, 80 percent of the wine produced in Bordeaux, some thirty million modern-day wine bottles, was shipped to England. Thus Bordeaux established itself as a monopoly for the production, sale, and distribution of wine to Great Britain. For three centuries,

Aquitaine remained an English province, and Bordeaux and its wine became inextricably linked with the culture and fortunes of the British.

The British connection has continued ever since. As part of the Duchy of Aquitaine, Bordeaux was a British possession, and in many ways the Hundred Years' War was a struggle for control of the vineyards of Bordeaux. As discussed in the history chapter of this book, for a variety of reasons, the British markets had a strong and lasting effect not only on the history and development of Bordeaux, but also on the evolution and taste of its wine—originally called "clairet."

The original vineyards were close to the old city in the Pessac Leogran section of Graves, of which the two most-famous vineyards today are Château Haut-Brion and Château Pape Clement. Pape Clement was founded by Raymond Bertrand de Goth, Archbishop of Bordeaux, in 1297, before he became Pope Clement and moved to Avignon in 1308 to build his new château for the Popes, Châteauneuf-du-Pape. In 2016, the vineyards of Pape Clement celebrated their 710th consecutive harvest! Haut-Brion was founded in 1525, and was listed prominently in the cellar books of England's King Charles II and mentioned glowingly by Samuel Pepys and John Locke. In 1787, Thomas Jefferson purchased six cases which mysteriously vanished during the chaos of the French Revolution. (For further details, read *The Billionaire's Vinegar* by Benjamin Wallace).

Classification and En Primeur: As is discussed in detail elsewhere, all the major vineyards of the left bank were classified between first and fifth growths in 1855 based on the sale prices of the previous one hundred years and, with one exception, that classification has remained unchanged for 160 years. Ample documentary evidence shows that buyers have been ranking the various Bordeaux producers since 1647 when they first started selling Bordeaux wine *en primeur*.

En primeur means buying the wine before it is ready to drink. The wines are tasted and sold in barrels just a few months after harvest and long before they are bottled. The running of a Château and the storing of thousands of bottles of wine for maybe twenty years before they are ready to drink obviously requires a serious capital investment. Being paid in advance for future delivery of the wine is thus an important part of the Château owner's financial cash flow. At the same time, for the négociants and institutions (from Oxford University colleges, to the Ritz and other grand hotels), which purchase the wine en primeur; the discounted price is considered a worthwhile investment. Although there is also the risk of loss, depending on the skill and experience of the person tasting from the barrel and forecasting its taste twenty years in the future, the rewards can be considerable. For example, the 1982 vintage of Château Latour was sold at £250 a case en primeur in 1983, while valued twenty-four years later in 2007 at £9,000—which represents an annual rate of return of 16 percent compounded annually. Not too shabby!

As an indication of the incredible financial resources of Château Latour, and its owner François-Henri Pinault, since 2012 Château Latour no longer sells its wines en primeur. The Château will store and hold its future vintages at its own expense until they are ready for selling by the case.

Left Bank: These days the major Bordeaux wines come from the left bank of the Gironde estuary, north of the city in the area called the Medoc and drained by the Dutch in the seventeenth and eighteenth centuries. Medoc's location on the thin strip of gravel-filled land between the Atlantic Ocean and the wide estuary of the Gironde River combines with hot sunny days and cool but moderate nights to create the perfect environment for growing vines. The gravelly soil is perfect for drainage, and forces the roots of the vine to fight deep into the mineral-rich soil for water. The gravel beds get deeper moving south through the four main communes of the Medoc, from the crus Bourgeois of St.-Éstephe AOC, through the powerfully "masculine" premier crus of Paulliac AOC (Ch. Latour, Ch. Lafite and Ch. Mouton Rothschild), the secondary growths of St. Julian AOC (Ch. Léoville-Las Cases and Léoville-Barton), and finally to the most elegantly "feminine" wines of all from Margeaux AOC (Ch. Margeaux, Ch. Palmer), where the underlying gravel is deepest; it includes more vineyards from the 1855 classification than any of the other communes.

Right Bank: On the right bank, where the River Dordogne joins the Gironde Estuary at the town of Libourne, the soil contains more clay than gravel and, being slightly further from the ocean, the climate is harsher. Cabernet Sauvignon struggles here, so the wines are primarily Merlot with a high percentage of Cabernet Franc. The two most famous communes on the right bank are Pomerol and St.-Émilion, neither of which were included in the 1855 classification, and they were long regarded as secondary to the great wines of the Medoc. However, with the growing popularity of Merlot, which ages much faster than Cabernet Sauvignon, right bank wines such as Ch. Petrus (Pomerol) and Ch. Cheval Blanc (St.-Émilion) have become some of the most expensive wines on the international market.

Oddly enough it is here, in Pomerol and St.-Émilion, that the Garagistes movement was born. Jean-Luc Thunevin with his Mauvais Garçon (Bad Boy) wines in St.-Émilion, and Jacques

Thienpont with his Le Pin wines in Pomerol, both used their parents' garages to experiment with their own unconventional wine production. Both achieved great critical and financial success, and since then young garagistes have been moving to less regulated parts of the country, especially Languedoc, to experiment with new winemaking techniques. But it's here, in the highly regulated right bank of Bordeaux, that the movement was started.

Graves: The original vineyards of Bordeaux have been assimilated by the spreading city of Bordeaux, but some of the most famous remain, such as Ch. Haut-Brion and Ch. Pape Clément in the Pessac-Léognan AOC of the northern Graves region to the south of the city.

While the northern part of the Graves produces both excellent red and excellent white wines, the southern part is famous exclusively for its whites. The subregions of Sauternes and Barsac have long been renowned for their powerful, sweet white wines made from botrytized Sémillon and Sauvignon Blanc grapes. The intense sweetness is the result of the grapes being affected by *Botrytis cinerea*, a fungus commonly known as noble rot. In the autumn, the Ciron River produces an evening mist that descends upon the area and persists until after dawn. These conditions are conducive to the growth of the fungus, which desiccates the grape and concentrates the internal sugars. Harvesters pick individual grapes at dawn, when there is enough light to see but before the sun begins to warm the vines. This labor-intensive process is one of the reasons that the Sauternes and Barsac wines are so expensive. In July 2012, for example, an 1811 bottle of Château d'Yquem sold for £75,000 ($115,000). This is one of the reasons that Sauternes and Barsac wines are often sold in 375 ml half-bottles.

Dordogne and Sud-Ouest: The *Police des Vins* of the Middle Ages was a monopoly favoring the wines of Bordeaux and excluding the wines from the interior of South West France, all of which depended upon the port of Bordeaux for export. Consequently, the wines from along the Dordogne river and further south, from the river valleys of the Lot and the Garonne, have languished through the centuries and remained unknown outside their local markets. Even the wines of Pomerol and St.-Émilion across the river from Bordeaux were excluded from the 1855 classification of Bordeaux wines.

Finally, after centuries of being ignored, these wines are now receiving the international recognition they deserve. In the past couple of decades, Pomerol and St.-Émilion have become some of the most sought after wines in the world, competing with the best-known châteaux in the Medoc. The Merlot and Cabernet blended wines from the town of Bergerac on the Dordogne, such as Pécharmant, are being seen as a rich but economical alternative to high-priced Medocs, while the nearby sweet, botrytized wines from Château Monbazillac are building a reputation as a deliciously affordable alternative to expensive but comparable Sauternes such as Château d'Yquem. It is my fondest hope that Robert Parker never discovers the pleasures of Monbazilac or Pecharment.

Disclaimer: I have owned a house in the small Dordogne village of Molieres, near Bergerac, since 1971; I was married there and both my children were born there, so possibly I may be a little bit biased! We had a barrel of Monbazillac served at our wedding, and more than forty-two years later I am still savoring the memory of its sweet, delicious taste.

Further south, the wines of Agen and Cahors are becoming increasingly well-known, partly because of the success of the Malbec grape in Argentine. The wines of Cahors are made almost exclusively (70 percent minimum) with the Malbec grape varietal.

BURGUNDY: Burgundy (Bourgogne) is the area in central France which roughly follows the river Saone south from Dijon to Lyon, but also includes the Chablis region to the north. Burgundy has always been the rich "heart" of France. With its fertile farmlands, large white snails, Charolaise beef, Bresse chicken, and legendary wines, the Dukes of Burgundy were some of the most wealthy and powerful rulers throughout the Middle Ages; often more powerful than the Kings of France or England. The Romans probably planted the first vineyards in Burgundy, and even the Emperor Constantine was closely involved in their development. After the fall of the Roman Empire, many of the vineyards were maintained and developed by the spreading Christian monasteries, first the Benedictines and then the Cistercians. Wine production was important for the monks in order to celebrate the Eucharist. Monasteries were the centers of learning and civilization throughout the Dark Ages, and the monks kept meticulous records of rainfall and temperatures, soil condition, grape varieties, and viticulture techniques. Consequently, the vineyards of Burgundy have some of the most detailed documentation of any land on the planet.

The terrain of Burgundy is gently undulating with many hills, ridges, and valleys covered with rocks. In order to work the soil, the rocks have had to be moved out of the way, and since Roman times, have been used to build stone walls between the cultivated plots. In addition to clearing the ground of rocks and defining separate growing areas, the walls have also provided protection from the Mistral winds which pour down the Saone/Rhône valley from the north. After the French Revolution at the end of the eighteenth century, the monasteries were abolished and the lands given to the peasants. Because the average plot is small, it was simple to redistribute the vineyards of Burgundy among many different families, with very few of the large estates that we find in Bordeaux. For example, La Romanée is only 2.1 acres in size, and actually qualifies as both the smallest Grand Cru in Burgundy (smaller even than Romanée-Conti), and is also the smallest appellation in France!

So because the vineyards, divided into small individual plots, have been cultivated continuously for almost two thousand years, and because they have been studied in such detail, first by the Romans and later by the monks, and farmed since the Revolution often by the same peasant families, each individual vineyard has acquired its own special mystique. By its elevation, its angle to the sun, and the composition of its soil, each separate vineyard is subtly different from its close neighbors and produces a wine which is unique to that specific plot of land. The French call this *terroir,* and nowhere is the concept of terroir stronger than in Burgundy.

Already, by the fourteenth century, the Dukes of Burgundy had recognized the importance of their fine wines, both for the reputation and the economic wealth of the Duchy. Recognizing that quality of the wine was based on the superior Pinot Noir grape and feeling threatened by the popularity of the more prolific but inferior Gamay grape, Duke Phillip the Bold in 1395 banned Gamay grapes from his Dukedom and made the cultivation of any grape other than Pinot Noir a serious offense. One of his successors, Phillip the Good, reinforced the law, declaring, "The Dukes of Burgundy are known as the lords of the best wines in Christendom. We will maintain our reputation." This is why, even today in the twenty-first century, all red wines from Burgundy are made with Pinot Noir grapes. White wines in Burgundy are likewise all made from the Chardonnay grape. Labels of Burgundy wines do not show the varietal, there is no need. If it's a red wine, it must be Pinot Noir; if white, it must be Chardonnay.

Classification of Beaune: Following the classification of Bordeaux wines in 1855, the Beaune Committee of Agriculture created the classification of Beaune in 1861, which was a way to label and differentiate all the different Burgundy vineyards in terms of quality. This 1861 classification was the first official attempt to divide all the major Burgundy vineyards into three classes, but in fact it was just repeating and formalizing what was already long known and accepted. Since the time of the Roman Emperor Constantine, certain plots of land had always been venerated for the quality of the wine they produced. The same names of small stony fields resonate down through the centuries: Chambertain, Musigny, Vougeot, Romaneé, La Táche, Meursault, and Montrachet. All these names were included among the premier cru ratings of 1861, which in turn were based on what such nineteenth century researchers as Laval, Morelot, and Cavoleau had discovered from the records and catalogs of the Cistercian and Benedictine monks before them.

In 1935, the French government's *Institut National des Appellations d'Origine* (INAO) formalized the AOC system, which is still in force today throughout the country. In Burgundy, the ordering closely mirrored the classification of 1861. The INAO introduced four classes of wine for Burgundy: the Regional, the Village, Premier Cru, and rarest of all, Grand Cru. The easiest way to demonstrate the system is to pick an arbitrary Burgundy village and show how the different levels of classification apply. Chassagne Montrachet is a small village in the Côte de Beaune region of Burgundy, which is noted for its Chardonnay white wines.

Bourgogne AOC (Appellation d'Origine Contrôlée) is the generic classification and refers to any wine grown and produced anywhere in Burgundy.

Côte de Beaune Villages AOC is a regional classification and refers to any wine grown and produced in the Beaune region of Burgundy. This covers about sixteen miles between Aloxe-Corton in the north to the river Dheune in the south.

Chassagne Montrachet AOC is a village classification, and refers to any wine grown in one of about one hundred vineyards within the parish boundary of the village of Chassagne Montrachet. The AOC classification will also be stricter than the

Côte de Beaune Village's classification, and might also include minimum alcohol level or residual sugar and would specify that the grapes must be Chardonnay.

Chassagne Montrachet Premier Cru AOC refers to a wine grown in one of the fifty-one vineyards in the village that have earned Premier Cru status. The label will show the name of the specific vineyard in addition to the name of the village. Wine from Morgeot vineyard will therefore be labeled "Chassagne Montrachet, Morgeot, Premier Cru Contrôlée." Again, the rules will be stricter than for the regular village vineyards, and will include a limit on the quantity of grapes harvested per hectare or the number of cases of wine produced each year.

Grand Cru AOC indicates one of the three vineyards in the village that have earned Grand Cru status. In this case, the label does not even show the name of the village—just the vineyard itself. So the grand cru vineyard of Bâtard-Montrachet labels its wines "Bâtard-Montrachet Grand Cru Contrôlée." If you don't already know that this wine comes from the village of Chassagne Montrachet, then you shouldn't be drinking it!

Chassagne Montrachet has about one hundred vineyards in total; other villages may have more or less, but the same classification applies to them all: the village AOC, premier cru AOC, and finally the grand cru AOC. Chassagne Montrachet is unusual in that almost 50 percent of its vineyards qualify as premier cru. By contrast, the village of Santenay lies just a few miles south, but has only twelve Premier Crus and no Grand Crus. At the other extreme, in the Côte de Nuits, the village of Gevrey-Chambertin has nine grand crus and the village of Vosne-Romanée has six.

There are many hundreds of different wine labels from Burgundy, each with their own unique artwork. However, in order to clarify the different levels of AOC classification, three of the five labels shown above are deliberately selected from the same négociant, Louis Jadot, and thus display a consistency of design.

Five years after introducing the 1861 classification system, the wise men of Burgundy went even further and decided to add to each wine-producing village the name of its most famous vineyard. So, for example, the village of Gevrey became Gevrey-Chambertin; Chambolle became Chambolle Musigny; Vosne, Vosne-Romanee; and the village of Chassagne became Chassagne-Montrachet.

Unlike the large estates of Bordeaux which are often owned by American banks or Chinese adult toy manufacturers, the vineyards of Burgundy are usually small and owned by individual farmers. A very small number of winegrowers, known as Domaines, are large and wealthy enough to bottle their own wines, but most winegrowers are too small. Consequently, because few vineyards produce and bottle their own wine, over the centuries a system of négociants has evolved. Négociants are wine merchants who buy the grapes from smaller growers and bottle it to sell under their own label. Many négociants have built the family's reputation over several generations, and names such as Maison Louis Jadot and Joseph Drouhin are as well-known and respected as the famous vineyards from which they make their wine.

The major wine regions of Burgundy, from south to north, are as follows:

Beaujolais: The one place where the rules against Gamay were ignored was in the very south of Burgundy in the hills around the city of Lyon, where the rivers Saone and the Rhône are joined. So much Beaujolais wine was produced from the Gamay grape for the thirsty silk workers of the city that it was often called "the third river of Lyon."

Beaujolais is a light-red wine with few tannins, which is meant to be drunk when young. By French law, it may be sold and consumed on the third Thursday in November. In the early 1970s, a few restaurants in London, followed by more restaurants in New York, started racing each other to serve the Beaujolais Nouveau on the Thursday it was released or just a few days later. For several years, eccentric English hordes would race across northern France from Lyon, driving equally eccentric vehicles in an attempt to be the first to bring their bottle of Nouveau to London. Sometimes the Beaujolais was delivered across the English Channel by colorful hot air balloons, WWI biplanes, or even dropped in by parachute; across the Atlantic, of course, it was delivered by Concorde. This very rapidly became a marketing success and worldwide fad, and unfortunately many of the growers focused on producing vast quantities of the cheaper Beaujolais Nouveau to meet demand and discarding their better quality wines. Now that the Beaujolais

Nouveau vogue has run its course, the reputation for good Beaujolais wines that had been badly damaged by the craze for nasty Nouveau needs restoring. Serious growers in the communes of Brouilly, Morgon, Fleurie, and elsewhere in Beaujolais, are working hard to gradually reestablish the reputation of the Beaujolais appellation.

Maconnaise: Immediately north of Beaujolais, around the town of Macon, is the Chardonnay producing region of Maconnaise, of which the most famous appellation is Pouilly Fuissé. Unfortunately, when winegrowers of Burgundy were invited to Beaune to register for the classification, the arrogant winegrowers of Pouilly Fuissé were so confident that their Chardonnays were superior to all others, they did not even bother to attend. Consequently, there are no Pouilly Fuissé Premier or Grand Crus.

Côte Chalonnaise: Immediately north of the Maconnaise, the Côte Chalonnaise produces both red and white wines. Although some twenty-seven Premier Crus are produced, there are no Grand Crus.

Côte d'Or (the golden slope): This region is the glory of Burgundy and produces some of the most famous and expensive wines in the world.

Côte de Beaune: The southern section, close to the city of Beaune, is called Côte de Beaune, and produces mainly whites (Chardonnay). World-famous vineyards include Aloxe-Corton, Meursault, Puligny Montrachet, and Chassagne Montrachet, which we examined above.

Côte de Nuits: The northern section, close to Dijon, is called the Côte de Nuits, and produces mainly red wines (Pinot Noir obviously), such as Gevrey-Chambertin, Vosne-Romaneé, and Romanée-Conti—wines of almost mythical stature and unapproachable prices.

One of the best discussions of the rarity and pricing of the wines from these vineyards was given in a *Vanity Fair* article by Maximillian Potter in May 2011. The article was called "The Assassin in the Vineyard," and Potter has since expanded it into a gloriously fascinating book about Burgundy wine, called *Shadows in the Vineyard: The True Story of the Plot to Poison the World's Greatest Wine*:

"Indeed, whatever superlatives can be ascribed to a wine apply to the eponymous wine from the Romanée-Conti vineyard. It ranks among the very top of the most highly coveted, most expensive wines in the world. According to the Domaine de la Romanée-Conti's exclusive American distributor, Wilson Daniels, acquiring or purchasing a bottle is as simple as calling your local "fine-wine retailer." However, because D.R.C. is produced in such limited quantities, and because the high-end wine market is such an intricate and virtually impenetrable web of advance orders —futures—and aftermarket wheeling and dealing, it's not as simple as the distributor suggests. Wilson Daniels's own Web site points would-be D.R.C. buyers to wine-searcher.com, which is a worldwide marketplace for wine sales and online auctions. There, the average price for a single bottle from 2007 (excluding tax and the buyers' premium) is $6,455—and that's the most recent vintage available."

"A single bottle of 1945 Romanée-Conti would be a steal at $38,000. Last October, in Hong Kong, Sotheby's Sleigh staged a record-setting sale of Romanée-Conti. The 77 bottles, which included three magnums, were divided among 18 lots, spanned relatively recent vintages between 1990 and 2007, and fetched a total hammer price of $750,609. A single bottle of 1990 Romanée-Conti went for $10,953—which was a few hundred dollars more than the sale price that day for an entire 12-bottle lot of 1990 Château Lafite."

Chablis: Situated in the department of the Yonne in the northern part of Burgundy, Chablis has been famous throughout history for its white wines. Because of its colder climate and limestone soil, the Chardonnays of Chablis are known for their crisp acidity and flinty taste when compared to the more rounded and softer Chardonnays just sixty miles south in the Côte de Beaune.

Apart from the excellent quality of its wines, Chablis always had the major advantage of direct access to Paris by river, which made it a favorite at the royal court throughout the Middle Ages and beyond. However, the Phylloxera epidemic of the late nineteenth century coincided with the arrival of the railroads. Direct rail access to Paris from Bordeaux, Lyon, and Marseilles, left Chablis at a disadvantage. While there was money to pay for the replanting of vineyards in Bordeaux, Lyon, and Marseilles, the department of the Yonne was one of the poorest in France and, without a railroad to deliver the wine, there was little incentive or investment to replant the vineyards following the devastation of Phylloxera. A further blow came from the United States when, looking for a generic term for their bulk white jug wines, the Californians decided on the term "Chablis." For Americans, therefore, the word Chablis became synonymous with cheap and nasty.

Thankfully, the reputation of Chablis is gradually returning as local winemakers are restoring the old vineyards, and currently the Chablis region can boast forty premier cru vineyards. Additionally, although there is only one Chablis Grand Cru, it is divided between seven officially recognized vineyards, or grand cru climats. Despite the lack of railroads, the underlying quality of the terroir has never changed, and Chablis is being restored to its former glory.

BORDEAUX VS. BURGUNDY

The wines of Burgundy were developed by the monks and peasants for the Royal courts in Paris and Avignon; the wines of Bordeaux were developed by bourgeois merchants for the English aristocracy. The red wines of Burgundy are made from a single grape, while those of Bordeaux are a blend of many different grapes. The vineyards of Burgundy are usually small, owned by fifth generation farmers with dirt under their fingernails; the vineyards of Bordeaux are often vast estates owned by distant Chinese banks or transnational conglomerates. Even the shapes of the bottles are different. Burgundy bottles have gently sloping shoulders; they are slightly plumper with almost feminine curves. Bordeaux bottles are far more austere, with high masculine shoulders and straight upright sides. We associate Bordeaux with an ascetic English gentleman, rigidly slim, dignified and serious, as he cautiously pours, sniffs, and judges the taste of the wine which he has so carefully decanted. But our image of Burgundy is of a plump, good-natured monk, cheerfully washing down an excellent meal with yet another "beaker of the warm south."

If all red wines in Burgundy are made from the same grape, what makes the difference, then, between a bottle of Chevrey-Chambertan and, say, a Romanée-Conti? They are both made with Pinot Noir, and both vineyards are in the Côte de Nuits. The difference lies in the soil of the two different vineyards, the micro-climate, the elevation of the land, and the drainage; in short, the difference between individual Burgundy vineyards is their unique terroir. In Bordeaux, on the other hand, the wines are made with a blend of six possible different grapes, and so the difference between different bottles of Bordeaux depends to a large extent on how the winemaker chooses to blend them, rather than where they are grown. Châteaux Latour and Château Lafite are near neighbors in the commune of Pauliac, but both wines have a different and distinctive taste. It is not the terroir that distinguishes them, but the skill of the cellar master, the Maître de Chais, in maintaining the traditional house taste.

Victoria Moore, the splendidly entertaining and informative wine critic for *The Guardian, explained in her 2008 article "Clash of the Titans: Bordeaux vs Burgundy:"*

"One of my shameful wine secrets is that I crave good Bordeaux more than I do good Burgundy. Wine lore has it that Bordeaux is more for beginners; a drink you enjoy before your palate is quite fully mature and you learn to understand the exquisite beauty of Burgundy. Bordeaux is said to be cerebral: the algebra, the musical theory, the astrophysics and the essay; Burgundy, meanwhile, is a scintillating flare of emotion and pure being that eclipses thought like the sound of an operatic aria or the sight of the northern lights (without the technical explanation of why they appear). Roald Dahl once wrote that "to drink a Romanée-Conti is like having an orgasm in the mouth and nose at the same time," a sentence I cannot imagine being composed about Bordeaux, about which the words "distinguished" or "dignified" usually seem more apposite."

Another Pinot Noir fan quoted in Jean-Robert Pitte's excellent book *Bordeaux/Burgundy: A Vintage Rivalry,* said that "Bordeaux makes you pee while Burgundy makes you ejaculate."

The Romans first recognized Burdigila (Bordeaux) as one of Europe's strategically placed and protected natural deepwater harbors, and since that time it has always been important for trade and commerce. While the towns and the villages of Burgundy are rural and secluded, Bordeaux has always been an international trading center. Since the arrival of the English and Dutch in the early Middle Ages, Bordeaux has been affluent and attractive to outside investors. In recent years, it has become increasingly corporatized and preoccupied with hiking-up prices for Chinese billionaires. Burgundy, by contrast, is more pastoral and, might one say, innocent? It is a land of family-owned small-holdings where the owner works the fields himself, dirtying his hands and sampling the grapes daily until they are ready to pick. Where is the romance in drinking a wine owned by a New York or Hong Kong bank, compared to the romance of a wine made with love by a man whose family has been tending the soil and harvesting the grapes by hand for generations?

Many argue that the subtle mixture of the six grape varietals in a glass of Bordeaux creates a complexity that the mono-grape wines of Burgundy can never attain. Others argue that Bordeaux is for beginners learning to broaden their palate, pedestrian at best, while the mystic purity of a Pinot Noir from Burgundy offers a glimpse of the divine.

And so the debate continues into the twenty-first century—though perhaps it was already solved by the French writer Brillat-Savarin back in 1825, in his book *The Physiology of Taste*:

"'Your Honor,' an old marquise once asked, from her end of the table to the other, 'which do you prefer, a wine from Bordeaux or from Burgundy?'"

"'Madame,' the magistrate who was thus questioned answered in a druidic tone, 'that is a trial in which I so thoroughly enjoy weighing the evidence that I always put off my verdict until the next week.'"

The same writer also wrote: "Burgundy makes you think of silly things, Bordeaux makes you talk of them and Champagne makes you do them."

CHAMPAGNE

Although Chablis was politically considered part of Burgundy, geographically, with its flinty soil and colder climate, it is closer and more similar to Champagne. Champagne is the most northerly of France's wine regions, and like Burgundy, the grapes grown are either Pinot Noir or Chardonnay. Although Pinot Noir is a red wine grape, by removing the skin immediately before fermentation, the resulting juice will have no color. If the skins are left on for a short period during fermentation, the resulting juice will be pink or rosé. Champagne made from 100 percent Pinot Noir grapes (skins removed) is called Blanc de Noir; Champagne made from 100 percent Chardonnay is called Blanc de Blanc. Most champagne is made from a blend of the two varietals.

The Kimmeridgean chalk and limestone strata originates in Dorset, and characterizes the South Downs of England (most visibly at the White Cliffs of Dover), crosses the Channel to the white cliffs of Picardy (stained rosé with so much European tribal blood), and thence to Champagne, the upper-Loire, and finally Chablis, where it contributes to the distinctively crisp and mineral taste of all three wine regions. It is for this reason that French Champagne houses have recently begun planting vineyards in England, on the South Downs, as global warming pushes the vine-growing frontier ever northward.

Methode Champenoise: The "sparkle" in champagne is achieved by bottling the wine before it has finished fermenting so that it completes the process in the bottle. Sometimes extra yeast and rock sugar is added to the wine in order to continue this secondary fermentation. During this final fermentation, the bottles are placed neck down at a forty-five degree angle in a *pupitre,* a special riddling-rack for the *remuage,* or "riddling" process. Each day during remuage, the bottle is twisted gently in the pupitre by the riddler, a man whose job is to twist the bottles gently so that the dead yeast and lees fall like sediment into the neck while the carbon dioxide is absorbed under pressure by the wine. A professional remuer or riddler can twist forty thousand bottles each day in this fashion. When this secondary fermentation has finished, all the sediment will have collected in the neck of the bottle. The neck is then frozen, and the tube of ice containing the lees, or dead yeast, is disgorged from the bottle and topped-up with a dosage of old champagne before the bottle is sealed with a special mushroom shaped cork and secured with a wire-cage, or *muselet*. Because of the secondary fermentation and the carbonation inside the bottle, champagne bottles need to be made of extra-strong, thick glass, in order to withstand the internal pressure of ninety pounds per square inch.

By order of both United States and European courts, sparkling wines produced outside the Champagne region may not use the word Champagne. For a while, other regions were allowed to use the term *Methode Champenoise* if they used the secondary-fermentation process described above; however, since 2005, the only term that may be used for such wines is *méthode traditionnelle*.

Because Champagne is France's most northerly wine-producing region, the cold winters often caused the wine to stop fermenting until the spring, by which time the wine had often been bottled. Because French glass prior to the eighteenth century was so fragile, the bottles would often explode when the wine started fermenting again. Working in a Champagne cellar was considered a dangerous occupation. The story has it that because the bubbles in champagne were considered a hazard, rather than discard the wine, it was sold to the English who "know no better and will drink anything." Indeed, rather than complain, the English decided they liked the effect of the bubbles and asked for more.

In fact, the English were already experts in the manufacture of sparkling alcoholic beverages through years of experience with their local sparkling cider, which they stored in the newly developed strong glass bottles, or *verre anglais,* as the French called them. It was in fact the English who invented Champagne, not the French. On December 17, 1662, an English scientist, Dr. Christopher Merret, presented a paper at London's Royal Society, in which he detailed the bottling technique that is now called *méthode champenoise.* It was not until forty years later a Benedictine monk, Dom Pérignon, declared, "I am drinking stars," and began working tirelessly to improve and refine the methods of producing champagne. Very soon, after Madame de Pompadour claimed that Champagne is the only drink that left a woman still beautiful after drinking it, it became the most fashionable drink at the royal French court, and thence among European aristocracy. Ever since the eighteenth century, Champagne has been the most sought after and valued wine for all occasions. In terms of literary pairings, Champagne is the Oscar Wilde of wines. It is witty, deliciously naughty, and, like Oscar, it is sublime. It is hard to imagine Wilde's sparkling, high-spirited exchanges in the drawing rooms of Belle Epoch London and Paris without also thinking of champagne. Napoleon famously said, "In victory, you deserve Champagne. In defeat you need it." A hundred years later, Churchill rallied his troops by declaring, "Gentlemen, we fight not only for France, but for Champagne!"

Merry Widows: When the widowed Mme. Barbe-Nicole Clicquot inherited her husband's wine business in 1805, she introduced a number of lasting innovations, including pink (rosé) champagne and the modern strong champagne bottle shape—as well as her iconic yellow Veuve Clicquot label. A few years later, in 1860, when the widowed Louise Pommerey took over her husband's business, she was the first to create Brut, or dry champagne, and she was the first to discover and purchase the immense Roman chalk quarries beneath the city of Reims for storing her collection of over twenty million bottles of champagne. The third widow, or *veuve,* to inherit a champagne house was Lilly Bollinger. When a London newspaper reporter asked her when she drank Champagne she famously answered: "I drink it when I'm happy and when I'm sad. Sometimes, I drink it when I'm alone. When I have company I consider it obligatory. I trifle with it if I'm not hungry and drink it if I am; otherwise I never touch it— unless I'm thirsty."

It should not be forgotten that in addition to being a wine that can be drunk alone, Champagne also pairs well with just about every type of food, from sushi to lobster to grilled steak. The celebrated British economist, John Maynard Keynes, said that his single regret, looking back over his long life, is that he did not drink enough Champagne.

Depending on the amount of residual sugar, Champagne labels range from very dry (Extra Brut) to very sweet (Doux):

Extra Brut (less than 6 grams of residual sugar per litre)
Brut (less than 12 grams)
Extra Dry (between 12 and 17 grams)
Sec (between 17 and 32 grams)
Demi-sec (between 32 and 50 grams)
Doux (50 grams)

In addition to sweetness levels, Champagnes are also classified by bodyweight, from light to full. Some of the most famous brands are:

Light: Lanson, Taillevent
Light/Medium: Laurant-Perrier, Perrier-Jouet, Pommery, Taittinger
Medium: Heidsieck, Moet & Chandon, Mumm, Piper-Heidsieck,
Medium/Full: Ruinart, Veuve Clicquot
Full: Krug, Louis-Roederer

The various different sizes of Champagne bottles were discussed earlier in the chapter on bottle shapes. (Page 84.)

LANGUEDOC-ROUSSILLON

The Languedoc-Roussillon region refers to the southern French coast from the Spanish border to the Rhône Valley and Provence. The area is the single biggest wine-producing region in the world, being responsible for more than a third of France's total wine production. As recently as 2001, the region produced more wine than the entire United States. Traditionally, it has been the most unregulated wine growing area in France, producing vast quantities of unremarkable vin-de-table bulk wine. The most common grape varietal in the whole region, from northern Spain, east along the coast to France, is Grenache (known as Garnacha in Spain).

For much of its history, Roussillon has been more Spanish than French, being variously part of the Kingdoms of Aragon, Majorca, and Catalonia. Even today, the local patois is closer to Catalan than French. Roussillon enjoys more sunshine than any other part of France.

The Greeks and Phoenicians planted the first vineyards along the Mediterranean coast of Languedoc as early as 600 BC and, having the highest temperatures in France, the region has been mass-producing vin-ordinaire ever since. Because the wines of the region focused on quantity rather than quality, the stringent AOC regulations which applied elsewhere in France were not enforced in the Languedoc, which basically had little reputation to protect.

For much of the nineteenth and twentieth centuries, a significant amount of French wine was actually grown in Algeria and then shipped to France for blending into vin-de-table. Following Algerian independence in 1962, most of the French colonists, *pied-noirs*, moved back to France, where a great many settled in Languedoc and planted vineyards of Cinsaut grapes, the high-yielding, heat tolerant grapes they had grown in Algeria. The wines of Languedoc simply replaced the wines of Algeria for producing France's vin-de-table.

As a result of the change in philosophy following the 1976 Judgment of Paris (discussed elsewhere in this book), many young garagistes moved from elsewhere in France to experiment with new ideas and winemaking techniques in the Languedoc-Roussillon region. Garagistes is an expression used to describe young winemakers who experimented with new winemaking styles in their parents' garages—just as young Californians, like Steve Jobs, used their parents' garages in the 1980s to build prototype computers. These passionate young winemakers were attracted to the Languedoc-Roussillon region because land was cheap, the soil and climate were perfect for growing grapes, and the AOC restrictions were almost nonexistent. Instead of being limited by the restrictions, traditions, and AOC regulations of Bordeaux or Burgundy, young garagistes were free to grow vines and blend wine in whatever way they chose, using whatever varietal of grapes they wanted, and to experiment with total freedom. If they succeeded, their wine would sell based on their own reputation and brand, not on the land and traditions of where it was made. The success of the garagistes in the Languedoc-Roussillon has represented a rejection of the concept of terroir. The same phenomena can be observed across the border in the Penedes region of Spain, where young winemakers are abandoning the traditions and regulations of Ribera del Duero and Rioja, and moving to the less-regulated coast of Catalonia, east of Barcelona.

In addition to French garagistes, the flying winemakers from Australia also discovered the Languedoc in the 1980s and started buying land. With typical Australian disdain for French traditions and contempt for the old-fashioned, unhygienic methods of the

181

Pied-Noirs, the Australians replaced the high-yielding but flabby Cinsault, Airen, and Grenache vines with Cabernets, Shiraz, and Chardonnays. Even E.&J. Gallo, the vast Californian conglomerate, grows the Pinot Noir, Syrah, and Chardonnay grapes for their Red Bicyclette brand in the Languedoc, which they describe as "a verdant area of rolling hills and wildflowers bordering the Mediterranean Sea."

Some of the most interesting and competitively-priced wines in France are beginning to emerge from the Languedoc-Roussillon and onto world markets with a special focus on wines made from the Carignan and Grenache grapes. Lighter reds are being produced in the center of the region in St. Chinian, while more aromatic reds using Grenache are coming from neighboring Faugères. Corbières is the largest subregion, and has long been known for its fruity and juicy red wines made from Carignan, Syrah and Grenache. Languedoc also produces extremely good and bargain-priced sparkling wines, called Blanquette de Limoux, made with the Champagne method but using the local Mauzac grape. Banyuls, near the Spanish border in Roussillon, is famous for its powerful, sweet dessert wines.

LOIRE VALLEY

Apart from the breathtaking beauty of the royal châteaux which decorate the river, the Loire is also justly famous for its white wines. Although some red wine (Cabernet Franc) is produced in the Loire, especially in Chinon and Saumur, the region is mostly famous for its three white grape varietals.

Muscadet, the main varietal grown in the lower reaches of the river in the Pays-Nantes, is also referred to as "Melon de Bourgogne." Delicious with the region's plentiful seafood it has been described as "the perfect oyster wine."

Chenin Blanc, also known as "Pineau de la Loire," is the most common varietal in the central Loire area of Anjou-Saumur and Touraine, and has the unique quality of producing both sweet wines as well as dry or even sparkling wines from the same vine depending on the vintage and the winegrower's whim. Even when dry, Chenin Blanc still gives the impression of being sweeter than the Sauvignon Blancs further upriver. The small towns of Vouvray and Chinon have two of the most famous Chenin Blanc appellations.

Sauvignon Blanc is the varietal of the Upper or Eastern Loire, and although this section of the river lacks the châteaux and beauty of the lower reaches, its wines more than compensate. The same Kimmeridgean limestone ridge, which stretches from England's South Downs, across the White Cliffs of Dover, through the rolling hills of Champagne and Chablis, gives the same dry, flinty, mineral taste to the wines of the upper-Loire as it does to Champagne and Chablis. The two most famous appellations of the upper-Loire are based on the two communes of Sancerre and Pouilly-sur-Loire, which face each other across the river and have long been recognized as having the best Sauvignon Blanc in the world. That claim is now being challenged by the wines from Marlborough in New Zealand's South Island, which counter the Loire's more austere, mineral taste with a softer, fruitier flavor.

Chasselas. It should be noted that the commune of Pouilly-sur-Loire also permits a second varietal to be grown, Chasselas. Blended with Sauvignon Blanc, the resulting wine is known as Pouilly-sur-Loire. Only the unblended Sauvignon Blanc can be called Pouilly Fumé.

RHÔNE VALLEY

The Rhône valley contains about forty individual AOC Appellations. First planted by the Phoenicians, Greeks, and Romans, the Rhône valley has the oldest vineyards in France. Because of the marked difference in geography and climate, the region is divided between two regions, the North and the South. Though there is a marked difference between the wines of the two regions, the Côte-du-Rhône AOC is found in both.

Northern Rhône Valley: The northern Rhône valley which runs just forty miles from Lyon, south to Montélimar, has warm summers, harsh winters, and is plagued by the maddening Mistral wind, which brings cold air down from the mountains. The only red grape varietal permitted is the Syrah grape, and its most famous vineyards are around Hermitage. The Syrah grape is the exact same grape as Shiraz, which, of course, the Australians have made so popular during the past twenty years. Legend has it that a weary French knight, returning from the Crusades and sick of the bloodshed he had witnessed, became a hermit and retired to a stone hut on a hill where he planted a vine he had brought back from the town of Shiraz in Persia. We don't know if there is any truth to the legend, but we do know that an English doctor, James Busby, took some Syrah root stock when he immigrated to Australia and renamed the grape Shiraz. Busby later wrote, "according to the tradition of the neighborhood, the plant [Scyras] was originally brought from Shiraz in Persia, by one of the hermits of the mountain."

The white wines of the northern Rhône are mainly made from Viognier grapes, and also Marsanne and Roussanne. The most famous appellations are Condrieu and Château-Grillet.

Southern Rhône Valley: South of Montélimar the winters are mild, while the summers are hot; the river valley widens out and the range of permitted grape varietals also opens up. The main red grapes include Grenache, Syrah, Mourvèdre, and Carignan. One of the most-famous appellations is Châteauneuf-du-Pape which can be made from a selection of up to nineteen different grape varietals (ten red and nine white). White grapes include Viognier, Marsanne, Roussanne, and Picpoul.

Châteauneuf-du-Pape is the home of the Popes in Avignon, built by the Archbishop of Bordeaux, Bertrand de Goth, when he became Pope Clement V in 1309. As Archbishop of Bordeaux, he had already created the vineyard of Pape Clement, which celebrated its 710th consecutive harvest in 2016. As a puppet of the French King, Philip IV, Clement moved the papacy to Avignon from Rome and the popes remained in Avignon until 1377, when the papacy finally returned to Rome. In 1366, when the Italian poet Petrarch asked Pope Urban V why he remained in Avignon instead of returning to Rome, Urban explained that the quality of the wine of the Rhône valley was far superior to anything available in the Eternal City.

The southern Rhône and Provence are most famous for their refreshing rosé wines, long popular throughout France, and finally finding acceptance in the USA. Perhaps the most famous rosés come from the Tavel appellation, and usually include Grenache and Mourvèdre grapes. My personal favorite is Château Maime from the hills just north of Saint Tropez. Because of the power of the Mistral wind, not only are dust and pollen blown off the land and out over the Mediterranean, but also all the bugs and pests are blown away, leaving the vines disease-free. Like Argentina and Chile, the southern Rhône and Provence are excellent locations for organic or pesticide-free farming. Thanks to the Mistral, it is the pollution-free clarity of the air which has drawn so many painters to this part of France, for its enhanced palette of colors and unique clarity of light which enables the viewer to see for more than one hundred miles.

Spain

Spain has more land devoted to vines than any other country on Earth. However, because the summers are so hot and dry and the winters are so cold, vines must be spaced far apart to maximize the resources of the dry and infertile soil, resulting in very low yields. Nonetheless, Spain is the world's third largest producer of wine, after France and Italy.

Similar to the French AOC system of classifying and labeling wines, the Spanish have a DO system, Denominación de Origen, which shows the geographic source of the wine as well as controlling local regulations such as grape varietal and production methods. There is also a slightly-higher classification DOC, Denominación de Origen Calificada that is restricted to wines from Rioja and Priorat.

The earliest Spanish vineyards were planted over three thousand years ago by the Phoenicians in the far south of the country, in Jerez. They continued producing wine even during the seven hundred years of Moorish occupation, by arguing that the grapes were grown to feed the Sultan's armies and to make wine to poison the infidels. The Greeks followed the Phoenicians by planting vines along the Mediterranean coast, and then the Romans covered the rest of the country with vineyards as far inland as the Douro River of present day Portugal. Although the Spaniards have continued to produce and consume large quantities of wine since the time of the Romans, they never introduced any technological advances, and their methods were rustic and steeped in tradition. As recently as the late nineteenth century, they were still making and storing wine the way the Romans had shown them sixteen hundred years earlier, crushing the grapes by foot in stone troughs, or *lagars,* and storing the wine in badly sealed, underground amphora resulting in a highly oxidized taste. The taste was not improved by the Spanish tradition of storing and transporting wine in animal hides—usually freshly butchered hogs. Even today, many Spaniards retain a preference for oxidized wines. It was only in the late nineteenth century that the French persuaded them to use oak barrels in place of animal skins. This emphasis on oak can be seen in the traditional way Spanish wines are labeled:

Crianza red wines are aged for two years with at least six months in oak. Crianza whites and rosés must be aged for at least one year with at least six months in oak.

Reserva red wines are aged for at least three years with at least one year in oak. Reserva whites and rosés must be aged for at least two years with at least six months in oak.

Gran Reserva wines typically appear in above-average vintages with the red wines requiring at least five years aging, eighteen months of which in oak and a minimum of thirty-six months in the bottle. Gran Reserva whites and rosés must be aged for at least four years with at least six months in oak.

Spanish Varietals: Spain's classic grape varietal is the Tempranillo, which is used for most of its red wines. Another common red varietal is the Garnacha (Grenache) grape, which is found from Northeastern Spain all along the Mediterranean coast to Provence. White wines include the Albarino grape found north of Portugal in the Rais Baixas area of Galicia, the Verdejo grape found in the Rueda region, and the Viura grape of Rioja.

Spanish Wine Regions

Rioja: Between 1869 and 1901, in order to escape Phylloxera which was devastating France, wealthy Bordeaux winegrowers moved to the Rioja region of Northern Spain, which offered easy access back to France through the seaport of Bilbao. Either by buying their own vineyards or by educating and encouraging local Spanish farmers, the Bordeaux winemakers introduced modern French winemaking techniques to the Rioja during the twenty years before Phylloxera reached Spain. Most Spanish winegrowers resented or rejected these "foreign ideas," but two aristocrats adapted the new-fangled methods, and today the wineries of the Marques de Riscal (with its distinctive wire mesh on the bottle) and the Marques de Murrieta are two of the most successful wine producers in Spain. It was Murrieta who had lived in London for many years as a young man, tasting good wines in the gentleman's clubs of St. James, who was most horrified by the taste of dead pig in his local wines, and was determined to learn from the French. Rather than use the local Spanish grapes of Tempranillo and Garnacha (Grenache), the French replaced them with Cabernet Sauvignon, Merlot, and others to achieve the classic Bordeaux style. Following the harvest, the grapes were transported to Bilbao by train, fermented at the bodegas near the port, and then shipped back in barrels to Bordeaux for bottling. The winery of the Marques de Riscal was recently redesigned by the architect Frank Gehry to outshine even the nearby Guggenheim Art Museum in Bilbao.

Through much of the twentieth century, the only Spanish wines on the international market, other than Sherry, were from Rioja, and the highest praise that could be offered was to compare them to Bordeaux wines. Even today, Rioja wines are the most popular "foreign" wines in France. Since the fall of the Franco regime in 1975 and the subsequent modernization of the country, there has been a shift away from the Bordeaux style, and Rioja winemakers are returning to their Spanish roots and replanting traditional Tempranillo and Garnacha grapes. With a newfound local pride, they are promoting the unique tastes and traditions of Rioja while retaining the modern techniques introduced by the French. In addition to its famous red wines, Rioja also produces a light, refreshing white wine from the Viura grape, which is made to be consumed when young.

That the wines of Rioja still command the greatest respect is reflected in the fact that it's only Rioja (and some Priorat) wines which can earn the DOC - Denominacion de Origen Calificada classification on the label.

Duero River Valley: The Duero river, which runs from east to west across Northern Spain, changes its name to the Douro after crossing the border into Portugal, where it joins the Atlantic Ocean at the wine-center of Porto. For much of the Middle Ages, the river marked the boundary between the Christian North and the Moslem South, but fortunately most of the vineyards were located on the north side of the river, facing south. In Portugal, the Douro river is home to the country's most famous wine, Port, and in Spain the Duero river is home to three of Spain's most famous wine regions.

> *Toro:* In the harsh and inaccessible hills towards the Portuguese border, the summers of Castile and León are long and hot while the winters are extremely cold. Wine has been grown here since the first century BC, but it's only recently that the wines of Toro are being recognized internationally. Made primarily from the Tempranillo grape, Tinto de Toro, the wines are powerfully dark, fruity, and tannic, with high alcohol. Toro wines have been called the "rock star" version of the better-known Ribera Del Duero.

> *Rueda:* The white wines of Rueda—slightly upriver along the Duero from the Toro region—have been famous since the Middle Ages when the nearby city of Valladolid was the royal capital, and a labyrinth of deep cellars was dug to protect the wine from the brutal summer heat and the harsh winters. The wines are

189

made with the Verdejo grape, similar to Sauvignon Blanc, but with a blue-green bloom and a distinctive aroma of laurel.

Ribera Del Duero: Further up the River Duero from Rueda and due north of Madrid, the red wines of Ribera del Duero are experiencing a well-deserved popularity on the international market. Made from the Tempranillo grape, Tinto Fino, the red wines are often compared to the more famous wines of Rioja. The jewel of Ribera, of course, is Vega Sicilia, a mixture of Tinto Fino, Cabernet Sauvignon, and Merlot, which, because of its legendary exclusivity as much as its quality, is considered one of the greatest red wines in the world.

Catalonia: With its own distinct dialect, its capital in Barcelona, and bordering France, this historic province in Northeast Spain has always pursued its independence in politics, culture, literature, and winemaking.

The region was one of the first to introduce modern winemaking technologies and methods in Spain, and the subregion of Penedès is the most popular region for young winemakers to experiment with modern techniques, free from the limitations of tradition. Consequently, it is possible to find every type of wine produced in Catalonia and made from every selection of grape varietal.

Cava: The most popular and famous wine is of course Cava, the sparkling wine of the Penedès region. Cava has been produced here since the 1860s, when Josep Raventos visited France's Champagne region to promote his own Codorníu still wines and decided instead, on his return, to make Spanish "champagne." Although using the traditional Champagne methods including remuage and riddling, Cava is made from three local grapes, Macabéo, Parellada, and Xarel·lo, as well as Viura from the

Rioja region. Some Cava is made using the Chardonnay grape as in Champagne, but this is not common.

Priorat: This area has been producing high quality wines since the fourteenth century when the Carthusian monks first planted vineyards around their priory (hence the name). The unique quartz and slate soil, combined with extremely hot summers, produces a powerful wine of high alcoholic content. The wines really emerged on the international scene after a group of young winemakers—"the gang of five"—started producing their wines using two low-yielding local grapes, Carinyena and Garnatxa (Catalan for Carignan and Garnacha grapes). It is in recognition of the outstanding quality of these wines that, along with Rioja, they have been awarded the highest Spanish DOC certification (DOQ in Catalan).

Balearic Islands: Just off the coast of Catalonia, the Balearic Islands of Mallorca, Minorca, Ibiza, and Formentera have been producing wine since the Phoenicians planted the first vineyards around 1200 BC. Even during the Moorish occupation, the islanders continued to produce wine "for export to the infidels." Today, especially on Mallorca, there has been a recent expansion of "boutique wineries" focusing on the traditional Balearic varietals, such as Manto Negro, Montrasell (Mourvedre), and Callet. The best wines are full-bodied, long-lived, and powerfully high in tannins and alcohol—very similar to the wines from Priorat over on the Catalan mainland.

Jerez: Jerez is a small town close to Cadiz at the southern tip of Spain in Andalusia. The first vineyards here were planted by the Phoenicians three thousand years ago, and have been in continuous production ever since. The Palomino grape accounts for perhaps 80 percent of the vines grown in Jerez, while the other important varietal is the Pedro Ximénez grape used for sweetening.

The wines of Jerez are called Sherry and are unique in two major respects. Sherry is a fortified wine, and after fermentation is complete, a distilled portion of the wine is added to the blend, increasing the alcohol level from about 12 percent to about 18 or 20 percent. Secondly, the Sherry is aged in barrels using the Solera process developed by the English wine merchants. Barrels of Sherry are stacked in rows, one above the other, with the oldest barrels at the bottom. Wine for bottling is always taken from the bottom row of barrels, which are emptied by about one third. The bottom row is then topped-up with wine from the second row of barrels, and the second row in turn is topped-up from the row above it. The top row is topped-up with fresh wine from the new year's harvest. The wine, which is eventually bottled, will have passed through the different layer of barrels and will thus be a blend of many different vintages. Many soleras are over one hundred years old, and so their contents can include wines from the eighteenth and nineteenth centuries. Sherry is discussed in greater detail in Chapter Seven. It was the Palomino vines from Jerez which the Conquistadores took with them across the Atlantic in the sixteenth century, and which became the original vines of Chile, Argentina, and California.

Galicia: Galicia, in the northwest corner of Spain above Portugal, is not especially noted for its wines, partly due to its remoteness and also because of its extremely wet climate. For much of its history, Galicia's economy was based on the "Camino" of Santiago de Compostela and its Cathedral. Throughout the Middle Ages and even today, pilgrims travel from all over Europe to pray at the shrine of the Apostle St. James.

Some of those pilgrims included twelfth century Cistercian monks from Germany, who either carried seeds with them or actually planted the roots of the vine we know today as Albariño. The name actually means "white wine from the Rhine." Although grown all over Galicia, the best Albariño comes from the Rias Baixas region along the border with Portugal. Over the border, the Portuguese call the grape Alvarinho, and use it for making the highest quality Vinho Verde.

Albariño is fast becoming the most famous and popular white wine from Spain; refreshingly high in acidity, it also has a sweet floral nose, almost like Gewürztraminer, thus showing its German origins.

Portugal

Vines have been cultivated in Portugal for four thousand years, originally by the Tartessians (the original, possibly Celtic, inhabitants of Andalusia), followed by the Phoenicians, Greeks, and, of course, the Romans. Most of the early wine production during classical times was concentrated in Southern Portugal, but in modern times, the wines of Northern Portugal have proved more important.

Portugal is England's oldest ally, and the two countries have enjoyed a close relationship, cemented by wine, since the Treaty of Windsor, signed on May 9, 1386, and still valid in the twenty-first century. This *Aliança Luso-Britânica*, between England and Portugal, is the oldest alliance in the world that is still in force. Portugal has always been England's Plan B, and whenever, because of war or trade disputes, the English have been unable to import wine from France, they have traditionally turned to Portugal, and as a result Portuguese wines have always enjoyed favorable tariffs in England compared to the French.

The English market was so important to the Portuguese economy that when local wine fraud threatened to destroy that market in 1756, the Marquis of Pombal created the Douro Wine Company to control and regulate the wine trade with what was in effect the world's oldest wine appellation. In many respects, the controls introduced by the Marquis are still being enforced by the English, even today, as is discussed below in the section on Port wine.

Napoleon's invasion of Spain made strategic and economic sense, but the reasons for his invasion of Portugal in 1807 are less obvious. Since the British were unable to get wine from France because of the war, they had reverted to their usual Plan B and were shipping wine out of Porto. The reason that Napoleon wasted troops and energy to invade a relatively remote and unimportant country was simply to deprive the English of their source of wine. The invasion, however, had the unforeseen consequence of making the Portuguese royal family flee Lisbon and move the court to Rio de Janeiro. As a result, their hitherto ignored colony of Brazil subsequently became the preferred market for Portuguese wines. Nonetheless, the English market for Port wine from the Douro remains extremely important, even today.

As part of the European Community, Portuguese wines have the following classifications which are displayed on their labels:

IPR – merely indicates the source of the wine

DOC – much like the French AOC appellation for superior wines

VQPRD - *Vinhos de Qualidad Produzides em Regiao Determinada,* which is the highest-level possible and usually indicates Vinho Verde, Dao, or Port wines

Vinho Verde: Vinho Verde is a wine region in the northwest corner of Portugal between the Douro river and the Spanish border of Rias

Baixas in Galicia. Vinho Verde is the name of the wine produced
in this region from a variety of local grapes. The name translates as
"green wine" but actually means "young" wine, as it is bottled for
immediate consumption. The most common varietal for making Vinho
Verde is the Loueiro grape, but the best Vinho Verdes are made from
the Alvarinho grapes, which are grown on both sides of the frontier.

Vines in the Vinho Verde region are not laid out in vineyards, but
are typically grown on trellises, up the sides of houses, or even up
telephone poles. The wine typically goes through a secondary, or
malolactic, fermentation in the bottle, which creates minuscule bubbles
in the wine—not enough to make it a "sparkling" wine, but enough to
impart a pleasing tingle. Because of the relative lack of sunshine and
the heavy rain from the Atlantic, Vinho Verde wines do not have a
high alcoholic content, with 8 percent to 11 percent being the norm.
In order to qualify as an Alvarinho Vinho Verde, the wine must have a
minimum of 11 percent alcohol. Vinho Verde wines have traditionally
been grown by small family farmers for local consumption. In recent
years, it has been discovered by the international market as a light,
refreshing lunchtime drink.

Dao Wines: The Dao wine region is the large granite plateau in central
Portugal, which is also the country's oldest established wine-producing
area. The wine was already being officially classified and protected
for the English market as far back as 1390. The region is noted for its
powerful and tannic red wines made predominantly from the Touriga
Nacional grape. Most of the unfortified red wines exported from
Portugal come from this region.

Alentejo: Situated southeast of Lisbon, the hot parched region was
long known more for its cork forests and olive groves than for its wine.
Since 1991, however, following the arrival of the Rothschild family
investments, major international wine producers have been buying

up land and planting vines, and this has recently become the most expensive vineyard real estate in Portugal. Although some international varietals have been planted, most of the grapes are indigenous, such as Tempranillo, and the resulting wines are powerfully rich and luscious. Definitely a region to watch.

Mateus Rosé: I would be remiss while discussing Portugal not to mention Mateus Rosé, which is a medium-sweet, slightly-fizzy pink wine, similar to White Zinfandel, and especially popular with certain young women and elderly aunts. It was created in 1942 during a dark period of World War II as a way of marketing Portugal's embarrassing surplus of wine. Oz Clarke, in his wonderfully entertaining *The History of Wine in 100 Bottles*, tells the heartbreaking story of the owners of the elegantly baroque Mateus estate, which is featured on the label of every bottle. Apparently, they were given a choice between payment of a lump sum for the use of the name and image of the château, or a royalty of fifty cents for every bottle sold. With annual sales of more than three million cases per year, Mateus Rosé accounts for over 40 percent of Portuguese wine sales. The owners, in 1942, foolishly insisted on a one time, lump sum payment.

Port Wines: Port wines (Vinho do Porto) are fortified wines made from the Touriga Nacional grapes grown in picturesque quintas (vineyards) on the remote, steep slopes of the upper Douro river valley. The harvested grapes are pressed, often by human feet, to macerate the dark skins with the juice to create the desired dark color. The fermentation process is interrupted with the addition of distilled wine, *aguardente*, which raises the alcohol level, kills the yeast, and leaves residual sugar in the wine. The resulting sweet, alcoholic wine is brought downriver (originally in barrels in flat-bottomed boats, but now by road in tankers), where it is stored and aged in large oak casks for several years in deep cellars opposite the port city of Oporto.

Wine production of Port in the Douro has been controlled and regulated since 1756, making it the oldest defined and protected wine region in the world after Chianti (1716) and Tokai (1730). The controls were introduced by the Marquis of Pombal to protect the quality of the wine for the English market. The continuing power and influence of the English is best illustrated by a random selection of names of the leading Port houses operating in Portugal today, along with the year of their founding:

Churchill ,1981; Cockburn Smithes, 1815; Croft , 1678; Dow , 1798; Gould Campbell , 1797; Graham's, 1715; Harris, 1680; Hutcheson, 1881; J.W. Burmester, 1750; Morgan Brothers, 1715; Offley Forrester, 1737; Osborne, 1772; Richard Hooper & Sons, 1771; Sandeman, 1790; Smith Woodhouse, 1784; Symington, 1670; Taylor Fladgate, 1692; & J. Grahamn, 1820; Warre, 1670

Good English and Irish family names all!

Since the seventeenth century, these shippers' lodges—their offices and warehouses—have been located on a hillside rising up from the riverbank, in Vila Nova de Gaia, on the south side of the Douro facing Oporto, where the wine is aged, blended, bottled, and shipped. Each Wednesday at noon, members of these old English families meet at The Factory House (Feitoria Inglesa) across the river in Oporto, to make decisions concerning the international Port wine trade.

These Wednesday lunches are filled with English traditions; for example, a copy of *The London Times* is made available at the lunch—always a copy with the current day's date, but from the previous century. Another charming tradition is to refer to the Bishop of Norwich. Henry Bathurst, who was Bishop of Norwich from 1805 to 1837, lived to the age of ninety-three, by which time his eyesight was deteriorating and he had developed a tendency to fall asleep at the table towards the end of the meal. Consequently, he often failed to pass along the Port decanters, several of which would accumulate unnoticed beside him, to the mounting distress of those further along the table.

When Port wine is passed around during the meal, tradition dictates that a diner passes the decanter to the left immediately after pouring a glass for his neighbor on the right; the decanter should not stop its clockwise progress around the table until it is finished. If someone is seen to have failed to follow tradition, the failure is brought to their attention by asking, "Do you know the Bishop of Norwich?" Those aware of the tradition treat the question as a gentle reminder to pass the decanter of Port, while those who don't are told, "He's a terribly good chap, but he always forgets to pass the Port."

But among all this charming tradition, serious business decisions are still being made concerning vintages, pricing, and international distribution of this multi-million dollar industry, which continues to play an important role in the economies of England and Portugal. Although most English people do not drink Port with lunch, except in the Factory House, they do drink it after dinner, usually with stilton cheese, and the bottle is always passed to the left.

In the *Wine Spectator's* annual ranking of the world's Top 100 wines for 2014, three of the top four wines in the world were Portuguese, and the very top wine—best in the world—was a Dow Vintage Port.

Italy

When the Greeks first discovered the Italian peninsula, they named it Oenotria—the land of vines. It is probably the most perfect place on earth for wine production. It runs from the cool shelter of the Alps in the north to the hot coast of Africa in the south, and every vineyard in Italy is close to the shoreline and the moderating climate of the sea. The whole peninsula is bisected by the Apennine Mountains, a north-south backbone providing rainfall, shelter, and microclimates, with a mixture of volcanic, clay, limestone, and gravel soil—all perfect for the vine. It is not surprising that on average, Italy is the world's largest producer of wine, outperforming even France.

The Etruscans were planting vines, in today's Tuscany, long before the Romans arrived (as were the Greeks and Phoenicians), but it was the Romans who first turned winemaking into a vast, slave-supported, global industry. Initially, as the Roman Empire expanded, wine was exported from Italy, but demand very quickly outpaced supply, which is why the Romans began planting vineyards in all their conquered territories.

After the fall of the Roman Empire, however, we hear little of Italian wine. Unlike the French, Germans, and Portuguese, who could ship their wine to the thirsty English and Dutch markets by water, or the Spanish who had their vast empire to ship to, the Italians had no export market. Their immediate neighbors to the west, France and Spain, had no need of Italian wine; to the east, wine was forbidden by the Moslem rulers, while to the north, the Alps made the export of wine barrels an impossibility. Until the twentieth century, therefore, Italian wines were little known outside of Italy, and tended to be developed and drunk locally, with one Italian region having little knowledge or interest in the wines of another region.

Things changed when Italians began emigrating to the Americas in the nineteenth century. Italians moving to South America, especially Argentina, were able to satisfy their thirst for wine by growing it locally, but Italians in North America, especially in New York, had no choice but to import wine from the Old Country.

Unlike the French and Portuguese, who had for centuries developed regulations and high standards for their wines in order to compete in international markets, the Italians had no need to develop such standards. Consequently, when Italian wines began to appear on the international market, they were criticized both for their lack of quality as well as a lack of common standards. Following the Second World War, American soldiers returning from Italy had developed a taste for Chianti in its distinctive, straw-covered flasks, and its sudden international popularity led to over-production and eventually a declining reputation.

In 1963, the government introduced a classification system based upon the French AOC system, and in 1992, this was modified to match the more stringent European Union standards. Italian wines now have three basic levels of classification:

IGT: *Indicazione Geografica Tipica,* which merely confirms that the wine comes from a specific wine-growing area. There are about 120 IGTs in Italy.

DOC: *Denominazione di Origine Controllata,* which confirms that the wine conforms to the various standards and regulations of that specific wine region. There about three hundred DOCs in Italy.

DOCG: *Denominazione di Origine Controllata e Garantita,* which confirms that the government has inspected the wines and performed various analytical tests before bottling. DOCG bottles always have a numbered governmental seal across the cap or cork. There are about fifty DOCGs in Italy.

Italian Varietals: Although not quite as rigid as the French, different wine regions in Italy favor specific grape varietals. DOC and DOCG certification usually specify the grape to be used. Brunello di Montalcino, for example, must be made with 100 percent locally-grown Sangiovese grapes. Although international varietals such as Cabernet Sauvignon and Chardonnay are to be found in Italy, the following is a list of the most common Italian varietals, clockwise by region starting in the northeast:

Fruili-Venezia: (White) Pinot Grigio, Gewürztraminer.

Venice/Verona: (Red) Corvina, Molinara; (White) Pinot Grigio, Trebbiano, Glera/Prosécco

Abruzzo: (Red) Montepulciano; (White) Trebbiano

Puglia: (Red) Primitivo, Negroamaro; (White) Trebbiano, Malvasia

Sicily: (Red) Frappato Nero, Nerollo, Nero d'Avola; (White) Malvesia

Umbria: (Red) Sangiovese; (White) Trebbiano, Grechetto, Malvasia

Tuscany: (Red) Sangiovese; (White) Trebbiano, Malvasia

Piedmont: (Red): Nebbiolo, Barbera, Dolcetto; (White) Arneis, Moscato, Cortese.

North East Italy: The northeastern corner of Italy, encompassing the wine regions of Venice, Verona, and Friuli, is especially notable for three distinctly different types of wine.

Prosécco: Originally the name of a grape grown by the Romans in the village of Prosecco, over the border near Trieste, it has been renamed as Glera and is the principal grape used to make Prosecco. Prosecco is a currently fashionable sparkling wine, made using the Charmat method which is cheaper and faster than the traditional Method Champenoise. In 2008, Italy produced 150 million bottles of Prosécco, many of which were consumed in Miami Beach night clubs.

Pinot Grigio: Despite its international reputation as a bland and uninteresting wine, Pinot Grigio, from its home base north of Venice, warmed by the Italian sun and shielded by the Alps, is a refreshing and lively wine full of character and deserving of respect.

Valpolicella: Valpolicella is a wine region east of Lake Garda near the city of Verona. The name apparently comes from the Roman legions who stocked up with the local wine as they moved north into Central Europe. The soldiers called the region *vallis poly cellae* (valley of many cellars), and greatly valued its high alcohol wines, which they called *reticum.* The otherwise unremarkable Valpolicella wines are made primarily from the Corvina grape, and can be drunk young like Beaujolais. However, since the time of the Greeks, select Corvina grapes have been placed in baskets and allowed to dry in the sun, desiccating like raisins and concentrating the sugars in a process called *appassimento.* The grapes chosen for this process are selected from the outside, "the ears" of the grape cluster, which have received the most sun and thus have the highest level of sugar. This form of wine is called Recioto della Valpolicella. (Recioto means ears in the local dialect.) After fermentation has finished, the remaining residual sugar makes this a very alcoholic dessert wine. This form of raisinated sweet wine dates back to the earliest days of winemaking in the Holy Land, when the Greeks and Romans called it *Reticum* or *Recitium.* The tradition continued through the Middle Ages with the trading fleets of Venice, which continued to ship this sweet wine to the royal courts of Europe, as alluded to in John Masefield's poem "Cargoes:"

Quinquireme of Nineveh from distant Ophir,
Rowing home to haven in sunny Palestine,
With a cargo of ivory,
And apes and peacocks,
Sandalwood, cedar-wood, and sweet white wine.

A more modern form of Recioto was discovered in the 1950s, when producers started using strains of yeast that could consume all the residual sugars and thus increase the alcohol content to 18 percent or higher. This powerful dry red wine, which pairs perfectly with the local game and wild boar, is called Amarone della Valpolicella or more commonly, Amarone. The name Amarone means "the bitter one," in contrast to the traditional sweet Recioto. Obviously, such a powerful wine needs to be aged, five years minimum, and ideally for ten or more years. Amarone is the most powerful, full-bodied wine on the market, often compared to Port, but without the sweetness.

The lees, or residue, from the fermentation of both Recioto and Amarone can be used to produce Ripasso della Valpolicella by adding it to (or re-passing it through) regular Valpolicella wine to add extra alcohol and body. Ripasso is often referred to as a "poor man's Amarone."

Northwest Italy: Piedmont literally means "foot of the mountains," and protected by the Alps on three sides, it is a rich, agricultural area of hills leading down to the valley of the River Po. The wine industry is centered on the two towns of Asti and Alba, but the region is most known for two small villages which have given their names to the region's most famous wines made from the Nebbiolo grape—Barbaresco and Barolo. Barbaresco grows at a slightly lower altitude than Barolo, and therefore the grapes ripen sooner and the tannins are less harsh, which, under DOCG rules, allows the wine to age one year less and so can be drunk sooner. Barolo, being more concentrated and having more tannin, must stay in the barrel one year longer than Barbaresco. Both these powerful wines unfortunately have been discovered by Robert Parker, and therefore the increased prices in recent years have reflected his high approval rating. One particular wine from Barbaresco is called "Darmagi," which means "what a pity" in Italian. Apparently, this is what the winemaker's father said when he learned his son had planted Cabernet Sauvignon instead of the Nebbiolo grape to make his wine.

Though Nebbiolo is the most famous red grape varietal in Piedmont and Barolo is Italy's finest wine, Barbera is the most widely-planted, with Barbera d'Asti from the town of Asti being the most well-known. Not as tannic or structured as the Nebbiolo grape, Barbera has a light fruitiness, more like a Beaujolais.

Asti, of course, is also famous for the sparkling white wine Asti Spumante, made from the Moscato grape, which, if nothing else, has the distinction of making Prosécco taste better by comparison. In addition to the Moscato grape which is usually sweet, Asti is also known for the Cortese varietal, which is pale-lemon in color, fragrant, and steely, of which the best-known is Cortese del Monferrato. The white wine from the rival town of Alba is made from the Arneis grape, which means "little rascal" in Piemontese. Roera Arneis, from just north of Alba, is noted for its crisp and floral taste and is becoming popular in American restaurants.

Tuscany: Tuscany is the most famous wine region in Italy, noted for its Chianti, Brunello di Montalcino, and the Vino Nobile di Montepulciano, all of which are made with the Sangiovese grape. It is also, quite possibly, the oldest wine-producing region of Italy, as the Etruscans were producing wine here long before the emergence of Rome. It was the Romans who gave the grape its name—*sanguis Jovis*, or blood of Jove.

Chianti is the wine-producing region in central Tuscany roughly bounded by Florence to the north, Pisa to the west, and Sienna in the south. For a long time, Chianti was known for its straw-covered flasks (fiasco), but now the wine is usually sold in regular Bordeaux style bottles. The Chianti region encompasses seven subregions, each with its own regulations concerning the production of the wine, but all Chianti wine must include a minimum of 80 percent locally-grown Sangiovese grape. Originally, Chianti also had to include at least 10 percent of the local white grapes, Malvasia and Trebbiano, but for the past twenty years this is no longer the law. Chianti Classico, lying between Florence and Sienna, is the largest of the subregions and is the original home of Chianti. Chianti Classico is the only wine that can carry the logo of the black rooster on the neck of the bottle. To qualify for the black rooster, the vineyards must also restrict their yield of grapes to less than 52.5 hectoliters per hectare, or about 228 cases per acre. Chianti wines tend to be medium-bodied with medium tannins, and are not noted for high alcohol. However, because of the variations between the soils and the blending regulations of the different subregions, Chianti demonstrates a wide variety of different styles and tastes.

Super Tuscans: The DOCG regulations controlling the permitted varietals in Chianti used to be much stricter than they are now. During the 1970s and 80s, for a variety of reasons including overproduction to meet export demand, Chianti had developed a poor reputation and was perceived as thin and flabby. Many producers, therefore, rejected the DOCG regulations (and certification), and started blending the Sangiovese with more robust, locally-grown Cabernet Sauvignon grapes. Some growers even started producing a "Bordeaux" blend, using a locally-grown mix of the main varietals from Bordeaux. By the late 1980s, these "Super Tuscans, as they were known (and labeled only as IGTs), were fetching higher prices than the official DOCG Chiantis. During the 1990s, therefore, the regulatory Chianti DOC Board eased the restrictions so that Chiantis are now permitted to include such grape varietals as Cabernets and Merlots, and so many of the Super Tuscans are now being officially reclassified as Chiantis with DOCG certification.

Brunello di Montalcino: Brunellos are a Sangiovese wine from the village of Montalcino, just south of Sienna, in what would otherwise be the southern reach of the Chianti Classico subregion. The local clone of the Sangiovese grape was first identified by the Biondi-Santi family in the mid nineteenth century as being especially suited to the commune's soil, which is a mixture of limestone, clay, schist, volcanic earth, and a crumbly marl. The Montalcino terroir is higher and drier than the rest of Tuscany, and the wines have more tannins, more body, and a darker color than the regular Sangiovese wines of Chianti. Consequently, Brunellos, which must be 100 percent Sangiovese grapes, need to be aged for a minimum of two years in an oak barrel, and at least four months in a bottle, before being released to the market. Because Brunellos are some of the most expensive and sought after Italian wines, they have been the victims of major frauds which the Italian press refer to as "Brunellopoli." The US government currently blocks imports of Brunello that do not have proof that they are 100 percent Sangiovese. According to the novelist Richard Condon, a bottle of Brunello di Montalcino is the only acceptable wine to serve to a self-respecting New York Mafia Don.

Vino Nobile di Montepulciano: The Vino Nobile di Montepulciano received its DOCG status shortly after Brunello di Montalcino in 1980. The DOCG covers the Sangiovese wine of the Montepulciano area, which is the name of a village located in southeastern Tuscany. The wine received its name in the seventeenth century, when it was the favorite wine of the Tuscan nobility. The variety of Sangiovese in Montepulciano is known as Prugnolo Gentile, and is required to account for at least 80 percent of the wine. The wine should not be confused with another Italian wine, Montepulciano d'Abruzzo, which is the name of a varietal grown in the province of Abruzzo on the Adriatic coast of Italy facing Albania.

Pouilly Fumé and Pouilly Fuissé are often confused because they sound the same, but in fact, they are simply the names of two French villages—the first known for its Sauvignon Blanc and the second for its Chardonnay. In the same way, Montepulciano is the name of a grape grown in the province of Abruzzo, and it is also the name of a village in Tuscany where the wine is made from the local Sangiovese grape. Both these examples illustrate the possible confusion between terroir and varietal.

Vino Santo: The origin of the name "Holy Wine" is obscure. Possibly, the wines originally were brought from the island of Santorini by Venetian merchants, who labeled it San/Vin, or possibly it became associated with the Church because the priests preferred to use it during Mass.

Although Vino Santo wines are made in other regions of Italy, they are associated with Tuscany traditionally. Made from a blend of Trebbiano and Malvasia grape varietals, they are usually served as a sweet dessert wine—although sometimes they are produced in a version as dry as a Fino Sherry. The wines are often referred to as "straw wines" because, just like the Amarone and Recioto grapes of Valpolicella, the grapes are often left to dry and desiccate in straw baskets prior to fermentation, thus increasing their sugar content. The color of the wine also ranges from straw to a deep amber.

Vino Santo wines are aged for a minimum of three years in wooden barrels, and sometimes for five to ten years. The barrels for Vino Santo are often made of chestnut rather than oak, which causes the wine to evaporate more than usual. Rather than topping-up the ullage or air-space in the barrels to prevent oxidization, the "angels share" is left empty, and the resulting oxidization contributes to the unique taste as well as the deep amber color of the wine. Sometimes, if the oxidization is too extreme, the Vino Santo is sold as much sought after and expensive vinegar.

Other Italian Wine Regions

Orvieto: Orvieto is a city and wine region in Umbria, just south
of Tuscany, and like Tuscany, first developed by the Etruscans.
Although it produces some red wines, it is most noted—even before
the Romans—for its white wines made from a blend of Grechetto,
Malvasia, and Trebbiano grapes. Although today's Orvieto wines
are predominantly dry, full-bodied and fruity, traditionally they
were famous and much sought after for their sweetness. It was the
early Etruscans, who carved out cellar-like caves from volcanic and
limestone soil, which could house wine production with long, cool
fermentation, and produced the type of sweet wine that, as we have
discussed elsewhere, was so popular in the ancient world. From the
Middle Ages to the mid-twentieth century, the Orvieto region was
known for the sweet dessert wine made with the noble rot, Botrytis
cinerea. Unlike most botrytized wine, such as Sauternes, where
the grapes are introduced to the Botrytis cinerea fungus while they
are on the vine, the grapes of Orvieto were exposed to the fungus
after harvest, when they were packed into crates and barrels and
stored in humid grottoes carved out of the local volcanic limestone.
Made primarily from a Trebbiano sub-variety of grape, these sweet
wines were deep-gold in color, described by the poet Gabriele
d'Annunzio as "the sun of Italy in a bottle." Because of the high
labor costs, the production of fully botrytized wine is rare these
days, but in ideal vintage years, some producers, such as Marchesi
Antinori Castello della Sala Muffato, will make a sweet dessert wine
from partially botrytized grapes.

Puglia: Also referred to in English as "Apulia," Puglia is the
province on the "heel" of Italy facing the Adriatic. If Italy is the
largest producer of wine in the world, it is largely thanks to Puglia,
which produces more than any other Italian region; about 17
percent of the total. Since the time of the Phoenicians and Greeks,
wine-growing has been a local tradition, but until the dawn of the
twenty-first century, a large proportion of Puglia's grapes, sold to

co-ops, were used to add "substance" to wines produced in the rest of Italy and France. However, since the international discovery of Primitivo, this is no longer the case, and Puglia now boasts twenty-five different DOC areas and some excellent vintages of its own. At the end of the twentieth century, DNA testing showed that Californian Zinfandel, as well as Puglia's Primitivo, were both closely related to the Croatian varietal Crljenak Kaštelanski. Because of the Zinfandel connection, these two hitherto obscure and overlooked European wines became respectable, and for the first time were bottled under their own labels. It is the rise of Primitivo which has drawn attention to the rest of Puglia. The most-widely grown Apulian grape variety is Negroamaro (literally "black bitter"), which is used to produce some of the region's best wines, including Salice Salentino. The most famous grape, however, remains Primitivo, whose wines, including the Primitivo di Manduria, are generally high in alcohol content and full in body.

Sicily: The first vineyards in Sicily were planted by Mycenaean Greeks 3,500 years ago, and they have been in full production ever since. Unfortunately, like the wines of Puglia, Sicilian vines were prolific producers but not highly valued, and were used mainly for adding body and color to the more expensive wines further north.

The exception has always been the sweet wines from the city of Marsala in the far western tip of Sicily. In 1773, an Englishman John Woodhouse decided that the regular local wine could be transformed using in perpetuum techniques (similar to the solera system used to make Sherry in Spain). The addition of alcohol would not only fortify the wine, but also help it survive the sea journey back to England as was already being done by the English with Sherry and Port. It was an instant success with the British, and other entrepreneurs soon hurried out to exploit the wine's popularity. Towards the end of the nineteenth century, the English domination of Marsala-making was brought to an end by the arrival of Vincenzo Florio, one of Italy's first tycoons, who bought up much of the land around Marsala as well as Woodhouse's company. Florio and Pellegrino remain the leading producers of Marsala today, and their products sell all over the world.

A delightful alternative to Marsala are the Passito di Pantelleria dessert wines from the tiny, wind-swept island of Pantelleria, off the southern coast of Sicily. According to legend, Apollo was finally seduced by the goddess Tanit when she served him a cup of Pantelleria wine. Like Recioto and Amarone of Northeast Italy, the Passito di Pantelleria grapes are picked early and allowed to dry in the fierce Sicilian sun, thus concentrating the sugars before fermentation. This appassimento process results in very sweet wines which are high in alcohol.

Just as with Puglia, consumers began to discover the wines of Sicily at the turn of the twenty-first century. The Nero D'Avola grape in particular has achieved the same sort of international fame as Puglia's Primitivo. Both varietals are rich, fruit-forward, and full-bodied reds, with a dark-ruby color. The Nero D'Avola in particular thrives in the very hot and arid climate of Southern Sicily, almost within sight of the African coast. Sicily is definitely a region worth watching.

IGT: Indicazione Geografica Tipica is the lowest wine classification in Italy, and merely specifies the origin of the grape, much like the American AGA or the Australian AGIs. There are about 120 IGT regions in Italy, and many are in the south, in Puglia and Sicily.

Many young winegrowers, wishing to free themselves from the traditions and regulations of more established DOC regions, prefer to seek the IGT classification so they can experiment with different varietals and different viticultural techniques. Consequently, many young growers are moving to Sicily and Puglia, and interesting but competitively-priced wines are already emerging from these regions. For similar reasons, we are seeing the same thing happening in France's Languedoc-Roussillon region, and Spain's adjoining Penedès region.

When Chianti makers during the late 1980s first started adding Cabernet Sauvignon to make the Super Tuscans, they were forbidden from using the Chianti DOCG, and had to label their wines with the IGT classification. The young garagistes in Puglia are using the IGT label with pride.

Germany

Germany produces the most northerly wines in the world. It lies further from the Equator than any other wine-producing region, and is therefore most lacking in sunshine. As a result, most German vineyards are planted on the steep, south-facing slopes of river valleys to maximize the angle of the direct sunlight. Furthermore, lacking sunshine, most German wines are white and low in alcohol. German wines are also noticeably sweeter than other wines, partly because chaptalization (the adding of sugar) is permitted, and partly as a reflection of the national taste. Germans on the whole prefer to drink beer with their meals and to drink wine by itself, and compared to their French neighbors, they prefer their wine to be sweeter.

At their best, German wines include some of the most expensive and sought-after white wines in the world. Rieslings from the Rhine and from the Moselle can combine a uniquely delicate balance of a velvety sweetness with a sharp refreshing acidity which few other wines can match. Unfortunately, and certainly since the Second World War, the vast bulk of German wine has been undistinguished, if not downright awful. The reasons for this are partly historical and partly administrative or political.

History: Although the Romans planted vineyards along the northern boundary of their Empire, little is known about German wine till the Middle Ages, when the Benedictine and later the Cistercian monasteries brought winemaking to an art form.

Known by the English as "Rhenish," the sweet white wines were stored and aged in massive oak barrels, or tuns, holding as much as fifty thousand gallons in the Cistercian monasteries along the Rhine and Moselle river valleys. By 1500 AD, these Rhenish wines were much in-demand in all the courts of Europe—including the French. After the discovery of noble rot and late-harvest (Spatlese) wines in 1775, these sweet white wines became some of the most expensive in the world.

Unfortunately, the devastation of the Thirty Years War of the seventeenth century damaged much of the German wine infrastructure, and this was further harmed in the 1800s after Napoleon secularized the remaining vineyards belonging to the monasteries. The final blow to the German wine culture came with the wars of the twentieth century, which devastated the whole country. During the allied occupation following World War II, the winegrowers were influenced by the unsophisticated taste of the occupying English and American soldiers, and so sweet, bulk wines such as Blue Nun and Liebfraumilch became the norm in Germany, thus, unfairly, harming the reputation of German wine.

Classification: Further damage to the reputation of German wine is due to the continuing political administration of German wine laws and labeling regulations, which are not only complex, but also confusing and unhelpful to the consumer. As the English writer, Kingsly Amis, famously observed, "A German wine label is one of the things that life is too short for."

Geographic Classification: German geographic classification is the complete opposite of the French concept of terroir. While the French narrow-down in search of the smallest plot of land to display its own unique characteristics, the Germans lump together a whole group of neighboring plots into a single vineyard that is called an *Einzellagen*. While an appellation in Burgundy can be as small as two acres, the very smallest Einzellagen permitted under German law is five hectares (12.5 acres—or 8.5 American football fields). Back in the 1960s, there were thirty thousand individual vineyards in Germany, but in 1971, in order to "avoid confusion," these were reduced to 2,600 by raising the minimum size to five hectares. The new laws of 1994 made the situation even worse by including the "Grosslage," which is the collection of Einzellagens in a village or commune onto the label. The average consumer has no way of telling if the name on the label is from a single vineyard— Einzellagen—or from a large group of vineyards—a Grosslage. Because of political pressure from co-ops and large bottlers of inferior wines, the laws regulating German wine labels can be deliberately misleading and make it difficult to know exactly where a specific wine comes from.

At first glance, the German system resembles the French system, descending from a general region such as Burgundy, to a more defined region such as Côtes-de-Beaune, to an actual village such as Chassagne-Montrachet, and finally to the individual vineyard of Montrachet Grand Cru. The Germans appear to have a similar system:

The Anbaugebeite describes the whole region, such as Mosel-Saar-Ruwer

The Bereich is a subregion such as Mosel

The Grosslage is a group of vineyards in the same village or commune, such as Piesporter

The Einzellagen is the individual vineyard, which has a minimum size of five hectares.

Unfortunately, it is seldom clear from the label whether the name of the wine refers to the Einzellagen or the Grosslage. In other words, the system is tilted towards the producers of inferior wines, who wish to benefit from the confusion with the names and reputations of superior wines.

For example, the best wines in the Mosel village of Piesporter come from the very steep, granite slopes facing south behind the village of which the two best einzellagen are called Goldtropfchen and Schubertslay, both of which are responsible for the excellent international reputation of Piesporter wines. However, all the bland, inferior wines grown within the Piesporter Grosselage are also sold with the Piesporter name on the label. Without knowing the names, it's impossible for the average consumer to differentiate between an Einzellage (e.g., Piesporter Goldtröpfchen) and a Grosslage (e.g., Piesporter Michelsberg). As can be imagined, the vines grown on the steep granite slopes above the village produce small quantities of a crisp, robust Riesling, while the vines grown in the flat alluvial fields in the bend of the river below the village (which could be excellent for strawberries, tulips, or roses) produce vast quantities of sweet, flabby juice completely lacking in taste or character. Both wines, however, enjoy the Piesporter classification on the label.

Matters are not helped by the German habit of also including the name of the large geographic region, the Anbaugebeite, on all the labels. Thus, a bottle of wine from the town of Piesporter will also be labeled with the Anbaugebeite "Mosel/Saar/Ruwer."

Prädikatswein

All German wines of high quality are known as Prädikatswein, which translates as "quality wine with specific attributes," and they are graded at the time of harvest into the following categories, depending on their sweetness level. Because Germany has such a cold climate for growing vines and so little sunlight to ripen them, the emphasis understandably has always been on the sweetness of the grape when it was picked, rather than the location where it was picked.

Kabinett - literally "cabinet," meaning wine of reserve quality to be kept in the vintner's cabinet or wine-rack; fully ripened light wines from the main harvest, typically semi-sweet with crisp acidity, but can be dry if designated so.

Spätlese - meaning "late harvest;" typically semi-sweet, often (but not always) sweeter and fruitier than Kabinett. The grapes are picked at least seven days after normal harvest, so they are riper. While waiting to pick the grapes carries a risk of the crop being ruined by rain, in warm years and from good sites much of the harvest can reach Spätlese level. Spätlese can be a relatively full-bodied dry wine if designated so. While Spätlese means late harvest, the wine is not as sweet as a dessert wine, which the term "late harvest" usually implies in the USA.

Auslese - meaning "select harvest;" made from very ripe, hand-selected bunches, typically semi-sweet or sweet, sometimes with some noble rot character. Sometimes Auslese is also made into a powerful dry wine. Auslese is the Prädikatswein, which covers the widest range of wine styles, and can even be a dessert wine.

Beerenauslese - meaning "select berry harvest;" made from overripe grapes individually selected from bunches and often affected by noble rot, making rich, sweet dessert wine.

Eiswein -meaning "ice-wine;" made from grapes that have been naturally frozen on the vine. Making a very concentrated wine, they must reach at least the same level of sugar content in the freshly pressed juice as a Beerenauslese. The most classic Eiswein style is to use only grapes that are not affected by noble rot.

Until the 1980s, the Eiswein designation was used in conjunction with another Prädikatswein (which indicated the ripeness level of the grapes before they had frozen), but is now considered a Prädikatswein of its own. These wines are similar to the ice wines produced in Northern New York State, Michigan, and Southern Canada—brought to the New World by German immigrants.

Trockenbeerenauslese (TBA) - meaning "select dry berry harvest" or "dry berry selection;" made from selected overripe shriveled grapes often affected by noble rot, making extremely rich, sweet wines. "Trocken," in this phrase, refers to the grapes being dried on the vine rather than the resulting wine being a dry style. TBA wines are extremely rare and expensive, much sweeter even than Bordeaux's Sauternes wines, but with a much lower alcohol content.

As with most things German, this all appears logical and well-organized, and the consumer should, by reading the label, have a clear idea of what style of wine to expect from the bottle. However, the difference between a Spätlese and an Auslese, for example, is established at the time of harvest—before the wine has been fermented and bottled. Depending on the winemaking process or the preference of the individual winemaker, the Auslese can actually end up to be a drier wine than the Spätlese. This is rather like selecting the correct bus to return home from the NYC Grand Central Bus Terminal based on the direction it is facing.

V.D.P.: The Verband Deutscher Prädikatsweingüter (the Association of German Prädikat Wine Estates, abbreviated VDP), is a group of some two hundred quality-oriented German vintners who are committed to terroir-driven viticulture at the highest level. Recognizing the various deficiencies in the German Wine laws, as previously described, this group of winegrowers have established and enforce their own much stricter and terroir-focused standards. All their approved wines carry the VDP logo on the neck of the bottle. More information can be found on the group's website at www.vdp.de/en/home/

German varietals

Riesling is the most-planted grape varietal and is used for the production of all the top-quality German wines. Because of its high acidity, top-quality Rieslings can age for hundreds of years. The town hall in Bremen contains barrels of Riesling dating back to 1653, and the Wurzburg Burgerspital has one remaining Steinwein bottle of the 1540 vintage. Even today, if you have the money, it is possible to buy a bottle of Bremen's 1727 Rudesheimer Apostelwein.

Because it needs over four months of sun in order to ripen, a poor growing season can negate a whole harvest. In the small river valleys of the Saar and the Ruwer leading into the Moselle, they enjoy a decent harvest of Riesling only three out of every ten years.

Muller Thurgau is the second most-planted German varietal. It is easier to grow than Riesling, with a much shorter growing season, but is bland and neutral in taste. Along with Sylvaner, it is the main grape in the production of Blue Nun and Liebfraumilch.

Sylvaner: Once this was Germany's most planted grape, but since the 1960s, has been replaced either by Riesling for quality or by Muller Thurgau for quantity.

Spätburgunder (Pinot Noir): Because of its northern location and lack of sunshine, there is little red wine produced in Germany. Most red wine is made from the Spätburgunder grape, which, as the name suggests, is similar to the red wines from Burgundy—like a Pinot Noir.

German wine regions

The main German wine regions were initially planted by the Romans, and are almost all planted on the south facing riverbanks of the Rhine or its tributaries.

Rheingau: This has been a classic German wine-producing region throughout the Middle Ages. Located in the center of Rheingau, where the river Main joins the Rhine, the small town of Hochheim has historically been the center of the wine trade and was the first German village to exclusively plant Riesling vines. The English word Hock, a generic term for Rhine wine, is derived from Hochheim, as are the distinctive tall, brown bottles, also called hock bottles, by the English. The best vineyards are located on the steep granite slopes on the north side of the Rhine, facing south across the wide river, so that in addition to the direct sun on the plants, sunlight is also reflected off the surface of the river, reaching up into the lower clusters of grapes.

The heart of the Rheingau is the village of Johannisberg, about twenty-five miles west of Hochheim, which produces fruity and spicy Rieslings in vineyards first planted by Charlemagne in the eighth century. It was at Schloss Johanisberg in 1775 that the concept of Spätlese, or late harvest wine, was first discovered and eventually codified. However, once again the single good-quality Einzellagen in the village has given its name to whole Grosslage of indifferent producers, thus diluting the quality and value of the name.

Nahe: This is a small tributary of the Rhine with vineyards on south-facing slopes. These wines are valued as being especially "clean" and "grapey."'

Pfalz (Palentine): Pfalz lies due north and is almost a continuation of Alsace in France, and almost identical in terms of soil, climate, and varietals. However, the wines from Pflaz are always markedly sweeter than the equivalent wines from Alsace. The only difference between the wines of Alsace and Pfalz is one of national taste and preference; otherwise, they could be almost identical. Lots of young experimental wineries have started to relocate to this region.

Rheinhessen: A large bulk-winegrowing area north of Pfalz growing mainly Muller Thurgau or Sylvaner grapes. Much of it is sold as Liebfraumilch or Blue Nun. The village of Nierstein produces great whites—but, as always, the Grosslage name has been abused by overuse.

Baden & Wurtenburg: With a warmer southern German climate, Baden & Wurtenburg produces mainly dry (Troken) wines which go better with food than most German wines. Ninety percent is grown by co-ops and sold to négociants, like the conglomerate Badisher Winzerkeller.

Franken: A very unique area, different from the rest of Germany. The region is well-known for its mainly Sylvaner grapes to make Burgundy-style whites. These wines, which have been compared with the great Burgundies, are very dry and age well—a vintage from 1540 was drunk in 1960 and was very well-received.

Mosel-Saar-Ruwer: The Anbaugebeite of the Mosel–Saar–Ruwer encompasses three river valleys: the Moselle, which runs from the French and Luxembourg frontier in the west to the river Rhine at Koblenz, and its two small tributaries, the Saar and the Ruwer. These Moselle vineyards are among the most northerly in the world; even in a good summer they receive little sunshine and never experience the high temperatures needed to produce high sugar content. Consequently, the Riesling wines, though deliciously delicate and refreshing, are pale in color and low in alcohol.

Because much of the land is composed of slate and granite, the river twists and bends around the granite ridges as it flows northeast to the Rhine. The combination of poor topsoil with slate and granite creates the perfect well-drained mineral environment for the crisp Riesling, and the spot where the river twists away from a granite outcrop leaves a perfect south-facing slope to plant the vines. In order to maximize their exposure to the sun, vineyards are planted on extremely steep, south facing slopes. Some slopes are angled at an incline of sixty-five degrees, which makes mechanical harvesting impossible and manual harvesting physically draining as well as extremely dangerous.

Mid-Mosel: The best Mosels come from the middle of the district, especially from two famous villages, Piesporter and Bernkastel, both located where the river bends sharply beneath a south-facing granite outcrop. As we saw previously, Piesport's reputation was built upon two specific vineyards, or einzellagen, Goldtropfchen and Schubertslay, but because of lax labeling laws, the identity of the two has been lost in the vagueness of the Piesporter Grosslage.

Bernkastel is commonly recognized as having some of the best vineyards in Germany. Pale-whites offer a gleam of green, and pale-gold which coats the mouth with sharpness and scent. Bernkastel has ten single vineyard sites: Lay, Riesenberg, Bratehoefchen, Matheisbildchen, Schlossberg, Kurfuerstlay, Johannisbruenchen, Rosengaertchen, Sephaus, and Doctor, of which Doctor is the most famous of all. Unfortunately the Bernkastel Grosslage on the label makes it difficult to know what quality wine you will actually find in the bottle.

Saar: Saar is a small north-flowing tributary of the Mosel near the Luxembourg frontier. Planted by the Romans, all the Riesling vineyards are on steep, south-facing slopes of slate soil. Since the early Middle Ages, most of the vineyards and estates have been owned by the Catholic Church, monasteries, or mysterious and anonymous anstalts headquartered in Liechtenstein. Since most harvests fail due to poor weather, only three or four years in a decade will produce a decent wine, which means that only the extremely wealthy can afford to maintain vineyards in the Saar and Ruwer river valleys. However, when the conditions are good, then the Rieslings of these two rivers produce some of the rarest and most expensive wines in the world. They are famous for being lush, fragrant, and fruity, combining the most delicate balance of high acidity and rich sweetness. The most famous vineyard is Scharzhofberg, which dates back at least as far as 1037 and, as part of the Weingut Egon Müller estate, is widely considered to be among the greatest white wines in the world. They offer a subtle combination of intensity and elegance that is simply incomparable.

In 2006, Egon Müller eisweins were selling at €1,550 per bottle, and in 2001, twenty-four bottles of Egon Müller 1994 Scharzhofberg Trockenbeerenauslese sold for €4,718 each! The legendary 1959 vintage is priceless, but impossible to find.

Ruwer: The Ruwer is another north-flowing tributary of the Mosel, very similar to Saar but much smaller. In good years the wines produced are much more perfumed than Saar wines and are equally sought after. The Karthäuserhof vineyard, for example, was officially founded in 1335 (although its origins go back to Roman times), and today is famous for its dry Rieslings. Nearly all the vineyards in the valley have been owned directly or indirectly by Catholic abbeys or monasteries—which might explain why the Vatican City has by far the highest per-capita wine consumption in the world:—seventy-four liters per annum, per priest, or nun.

Eastern Europe

During the Roman Empire, Eastern Europe had far more vineyards than the Western Empire. East European wines were considered some of the best in the known world. Following the collapse of Roman rule, however, with the lack of any political stability, the wine industry fell into disrepair. The arrival of Islam during the Middle Ages, followed by communism in the twentieth century, completely demolished all memory of the region's glorious winemaking traditions.

But the glory will return, and already some of the old names are returning to the world stage.

Greece: As discussed elsewhere, Greece has been producing great wines for over 6,500 years. The reputation of, and demand for, Greek wines continued through the Middle Ages and beyond, traded by the Venetians and always commanding high prices in Northern Europe for its sweet white wines. The Islamic, Ottoman Turks controlled Greece for about four hundred years, and unfortunately destroyed the ancient culture of wine production until Greek independence in 1821. However, some wine cultivation survived in the more remote regions, especially on the islands such as Santorini. Since the late 1980s, serious wine production has moved Greek wines beyond the level of the resin-taste of Retsina wine. Wine grapes are now grown throughout the Greek mainland as well as the islands. Top regions include the Cyclades, especially Santorini, where Assyrtiko and other vines are tied into a basket shape to protect the fruit against the continuous wind, and the Peloponnese peninsula, particularly Neméa, which produces full-bodied, juicy reds like Agiorgitiko.

Greek Varietals:

Assyrtiko *(White):* Perhaps the most famous of Greek varietals, this wine is always associated with the island of Santorini, whose relentless winds and dry, desert like volcanic soil create both dry and sweet white wines with a powerfully acidic and mineral finish. The vines are traditionally woven into a nest-like protection against the winds, which ensures a long, slow, and full ripening. Some of the vines on Santorini are reputed to be over five hundred years old. The Greek Gods created this wine to be drunk with fresh seafood—especially octopus.

Moschofilero (*White*): This pink-skinned grape from the high plateau of the central Peloponnesian peninsula produces notably aromatic white and rose wines, which are light, crisp, and low in alcohol. With fresh scents of limes and roses, this makes the perfect al fresco wine for summer picnics.

Agiorgtiko (*Red*): This is the most-widely grown of Greek varietals, and its thick-skinned berries are capable of a wide range of styles, from light-reds to Robert Parker-style fruit bombs. Grown most notably in the northeastern Peloponnesian region of Nemea, the wines have succulent tannins which enable the wines to age well in oak. Delicious with goat roasted over an open flame.

Xinomavro (*Red*): The most famous wines made with the Xinomavro grape come from Naoussa in the Macedonian region of northern Greece. Xinomavro means acid-black in Greek, which aptly describes both the color of the grapes and the resulting wine. The wines, with their lingering taste of olives, are high in both tannins and acid, which means they can be aged for a very long time. Perfect with Greek salad and feta cheese.

With lush velvety reds made from the Agiorgitiko grape and minerally, crisp, and bone-dry whites made from the Assyrtiko grape, the serious wines of Greece are once again asserting their classic heritage.

Hungary: Described by Louis XIV as "Vinum Regum, Rex Vinorum" (the King of Wines and the Wine of Kings), Tokaji Aszú, the unctuous, honeyed wine made from super-concentrated, botrytized grapes, has long been the archetypical Hungarian wine since it was first documented in 1571. Beloved by Thomas Jefferson and Russian czars alike, Emperor Franz Josef (who was also King of Hungary) had a tradition of sending Queen Victoria Tokaji wine as a gift every year on her birthday—one bottle for every month she had lived, twelve for each year. On her eighty-first and final birthday (1900), this totaled an enviable 972 bottles. As sought after and expensive in the twenty-first century as it was in the eighteenth, these ebulliently floral, lusciously fruity wines are traditionally a blend of local grapes including varieties of Muscat, the world's oldest varietal. Even under Ottoman and then Soviet rule, Hungary still managed to somehow produce Tokaji wines, which have never lost their international appeal. Following the collapse of the Hungarian Communist regime in 1989, Hugh Johnson, the great English wine writer, founded a winery to revive the fortunes of this "Vinum Regum," which he called "Royal Tokaji." This sweet golden wine, tasting of ripe peaches, apricots, pears, and mandarin oranges, is made from three local varietals: Furmint, Hárslevelü, and Muscat de Lunel. The other famous wine from Hungary is Egri Bikavér—Bull's Blood—which, although weakened under Soviet rule, is now once more being made in the traditional manner:dark, strong and powerful.

Georgia: As discussed elsewhere, Georgia's border with Turkey, Armenia, and Azerbaijan is the site of the world's oldest winemaking activity. This is where wine has been made and drunk longer than anywhere else in history. Even today, the Neolithic winemaking techniques dating back to Noah are still in use. The vast, underground amphorae called *kvevri* are still being used to produce wine in the traditional manner. Through most of the twentieth century, almost all of Georgian wine was exported to the Soviet Union, where quality was not a priority and individual winemakers were not incentivized to excel. Switching to the competitive international markets after the 2006 break with President Putin's Russia, Georgian winemakers are now starting to focus on quality. With nine thousand years of tradition behind it, Georgian wine is ready for a comeback.

Romania: Proud of its Roman wine-producing past, Romania is now the sixth largest wine producer in the European Union. If not yet famous for its quality wines, it is already a best-seller in America's Sam's Club, with a wide selection of red and white wines at less than $7.00 per bottle.

Slovenia: Emerging from decades of communist atrophy followed by the horrors of the late twentieth century Bosnian wars, Slovenia is now home to some of the most exciting wines in Central Europe. Following the deadening effect of state-owned co-operatives, much of Slovenia's wine production has returned to small, family-owned operations where individualism and experimentation have taken center stage. Long recognized for its oak trees, which make some of the world's finest wine barrels, Slovenia is increasingly being recognized for its wines.

Croatia: I hitchhiked down the Dalmatian Coast through Croatia during the 1960s when it was still part of communist Yugoslavia and fell in love with its wines. On the dramatic and beautiful Adriatic coast, facing Italy, Croatia has been producing wines since even before the Romans arrived. I was a young man in the '60s, but still vividly recall the heady taste of freshly-grilled goat meat washed down with generous glasses of the local Crljenak Kaštelanski (Zinfandel), sitting on a moonlit beach beside the wine-dark sea. Croatian émigrés in the twentieth century were very influential in the development of the Californian, Australian, and New Zealand wine industries, and now, following the end of the Bosnian conflict, they are returning home and promise to make Croatian wine a major player once again on the world stage.

Chapter

5

THE NEW WORLD

Chapter Five: THE NEW WORLD

"Nothing makes the future look so rosy as to contemplate it through a glass of Gevrey Chambertin." — Napoleon Bonaparte

---

The *Vitis vinifera* vine finally expanded beyond the bounds of Europe in 1492 when Columbus sailed the ocean blue. Two peoples are primarily responsible for the spread of wine production in the New World: the Spanish, who needed an abundant supply of wine to celebrate the Catholic Mass in all the lands they conquered, and the English, who needed wine to assuage the thirst of their sailors and soldiers in the Empire on which the sun never set.

The Spanish took vines, probably from the locality of Cadiz from which they set sail across the Atlantic, and which themselves were the vines first planted by the Phoenicians in 1100 BC. They were known as "Mission Vines," and planted all over the New World in the fifteenth and sixteenth centuries. The first vineyards were planted on Hispaniola, and later in Mexico (1549) and Peru (possibly as early as 1540).

Spanish colonization of the Americas occurred primarily on the West Coast, first in South America moving south from Peru to Chile, and eventually north from Mexico into what is today California, where each new Mission along the Pacific Coast planted its own vineyard. In all cases, the motivation was to supply wine for the Eucharist during the celebration of the Catholic Mass. At the same time, there was a continuing but often ignored prohibition from the Spanish authorities, who wanted to export Spanish wine and did not want the colonies to be self-sufficient. The problems were that wine from Spain had usually oxidized by the time it had crossed the ocean, it was expensive, and the locally produced wine simply tasted better.

While the Spanish controlled the west coast of both North and South America, the English and French struggled to control the East and Center of North America. Part of the English desire for a colony in North America was to have an independent source of wine so they would not be dependent on other European suppliers. Unfortunately, neither the French nor the English realized that because of the vine disease Phylloxera, vines would not grow, either on the English controlled East Coast or in the French colonies of Louisiana and New France.

Moving in the other direction, however, both the English and the Dutch realized that the Cape Colony of South Africa was the perfect base to grow wine and resupply their navies sailing to their Empires in the Far East. Very soon, by 1685, the South African wines of Constantia were actually being shipped back to Europe for consumption by Frederick the Great in Prussia and Catherine the Great in Russia.

From South Africa, the English started to transplant South African vines to the new colonies in Australia as early as 1788, and the exercise was so successful that by 1822, Australia, referred to as England's vineyard, was exporting its wines to Europe, and by the 1880s was winning international prizes.

New World vs Old World Wines

Most of the vineyards in the New World are in hotter climates than their European homeland; consequently, with more dependable sunshine, the grapes are riper, resulting in wines which have a higher alcohol level and which are more full-bodied and fruitier. It has been argued, not without a certain level of Eurocentric snobbery as well as a certain level of truth, that New World wines reflect their culture—being more "loud" and "brash" than their more subtle and discreet European counterparts. In some ways, this has been exacerbated by Robert Parker, the American wine critic who has encouraged more full-bodied and fruit-forward wines in the New World.

Fruit Bombs: As discussed elsewhere, I have mixed feelings concerning Robert Parker. Initially, many Californian winemakers were striving to reproduce French wines and to recreate the same tastes. It was Parker who told them to be true to their terroir and to make wines which reflected the local conditions. "If you want to make French wines," he said, "go to France." This is most clearly shown in the difference between Chardonnay wines from Burgundy and California. The Californian Chardonnays are much more oaky, alcoholic, fruitier, and full-bodied. The Burgundies are far more subtle and lighter-bodied, exhibiting more herb, earth, mineral, and floral components. Parker is correct in encouraging the Californians to be themselves and not slavishly copy the French; it is just that his opinion is so influential that the pendulum has now swung the other way, and all Chardonnays are becoming the "hedonistic fruit bombs" that Parker so enjoys. The average alcohol content for European reds is about 12.5 percent while in the New World, 14 percent is more common.

Many Europeans argue that New World fruit-bombs overwhelm food, and that the lack of acidity and tannins fails to cleanse the palette while eating. However, while Europeans have always associated wine with food, a 2011 survey by Wine Opinions (www.wineopinions. com), found that most of the wine consumed by Americans is not drunk as part of a meal but rather alone as a cocktail, before or after a meal. So the harmonious balance of acid, tannins, and fruit, which pairs so well with food, is less important when the wines are to be enjoyed by themselves and the soft-rounded pleasures of the fruit can stand alone.

Annual variations and vintages: One of the big differences between annual vintages in Europe is rainfall. Lack of rain or too much rain, or rain falling at the wrong time, can destroy a whole year's crop. This is why the quality of the wine from major European regions varies from year to year, and why the vintage of a European wine is of such importance. This is much less of a problem in the New World, where seasons are much more predictable and consistent. Much of Europe's wine country is in the Mediterranean climate zone, with unpredictable rainfall and climate fluctuations. Much of California, however, like Australia and Chile, is desert. As early as 1962, Professor Albert J. Winkler at UC Berkeley had analyzed the temperature and climate of California's grape-producing regions, and divided them into what are still referred to as the five Winkler Zones. Within those five zones, the annual rainfall and temperatures are fairly consistent, and thus predictable, by the winegrower. Rain does not usually fall during the growing season, and so water is provided, through irrigation, by the farmers. This means that the farmer has much more control over the growth and development of the vine, and it also means that his wines can be consistent from year to year. The only potential downside to this is drought. As this book is being written, California is introducing drastic laws to restrict car washing and lawn watering in order to adjust to the fourth year of severe drought; but so far, in late 2017, Californian winegrowers have not yet been affected.

Varietals: With over two thousand years of experimentation and experience, Europeans had learned which grape varietals grew best in which region, and thus the concept of terroir and regional styles developed, most especially in France. Consumers were aware of the difference between Burgundy and Bordeaux, for example, or Champagne and Chablis. New World winegrowers, however, had to learn by trial and error, and so would plant a wide variety of different vines in the same geographic area. There was no concept of terroir, and the difference between a Napa and Sonoma red wine was a meaningless concept. Nobody had heard of either place; there was no tradition or reputation behind either name. Winegrowers, therefore, referred back to the French classics, and would label their red wines "Burgundy" and their white wines "Chablis," for example. Initially, most New World wines were simply imitations of Old World wines, and so in addition to Californian Burgundy and Chablis, there was Australian Sherry and South African Port.

The formation of the European Union in the 1970s gave increased legal power to European winemakers who objected to the indiscriminate use of regional names like Champagne and Burgundy. At the same time, wine writers like Frank Schoonmaker and winemakers like Robert Mondavi encouraged the Alsace tradition of classifying and labeling the wines by their constituent grape. Consequently, for the past forty years, all New World wines have been identified by their grape varietal rather than their terroir. Today, even some French wines are identifying the varietal on the label in order to compete in the US market.

Marketing: While many European vineyards, especially in Burgundy, remain small family-owned affairs, many of the New World vineyards are owned by large corporations. The recent international increase in wine consumption leading to the dramatic globalization of the wine industry has led to vast economies of scale. In order to secure a contract with Costco or Tesco—who will need to stock the shelves of hundreds of their retailers—the wine producer needs to guarantee the delivery of thousands of bottles of consistently identical and dependable wine. This means that small independent wineries cannot compete with giant corporations. Consequently, especially in the New World, there has been rapid consolidation in the industry, with large international conglomerates owning lots of different brands in many different countries. Constellation Brands, for example, owns ninety-one different wine brands, including Mondavi in California, Kim Crawford in New Zealand, and Ruffino in Italy. The quintessential French company Pernod owns the quintessential Australian Shiraz producer,

Jacob's Creek, and the quintessential Australian beer producer, Fosters (through its Treasury Estates subsidiary) owns that jewel of Napa Valley wineries, Beringer. The consumer may believe that he is getting a cute bottle of French artisanal wine from the Languedoc when he buys a bottle of Red Bicyclette, but the winery is actually owned, controlled, and marketed by E&J Gallo, California's largest producer of jug-wines.

Figure 6: Selection of major wine brands sold in the USA by owner

Constellation Brands (91 brands), including: Woodbridge, Rex Goliath, Kim Crawford, Blackstone, Simi, Estancia, Covey Run, Ste. Chapelle, Mondavi, Ruffino

E&J Gallo (50 brands), including: Alamos, Ecco Domani, Black Swan, Indigo Hills, Turning Leaf, Canyon Road, Martini, Barefoot, Carlo Rossi, Red Bicyclette

Foster's Treasury Wine Estates (50 brands), including: Beringer, Château St. Jean, Greg Norman, Lindeman's, Matua Valley, Penfolds, Rosémount, Souverain, Stags' Leap, Wolf Blass

Trinchero Estates (26 brands), including: Sutter Home, Ménage à Trois, Trinity Oaks, The Bandit, The Show, Napa Cellars, Reynolds, Little Boomey, Terra D'Oro, Three Thieves

Bronco (110 Brands), including: Charles Shaw, Two Buck Chuck, Estrella, Rutherford Vintners, Fox Hollow, Fat Cat, Crane Lake, Forest Glen, JW Morris, Red Truck

Ste Michelle (15 brands), including: Château Ste. Michelle, Stag's Leap, Colombia Crest, Snoqualmie, Northstar, Red Diamond, Col Solare, Villa Mt. Eden, Red Diamond, 14 Hands, Ethos Reserve

In his fascinating book *Wine Politics,* Tyler Colman quotes a senior French wine industry official in 2000, saying, "We don't make wine to please consumers. We make wines that are typical of their terroirs. Fortunately for us, consumers like them." Unfortunately for that arrogant official, the times are a-changing, and consumers are no longer dependent on the dictates of French bureaucrats. The Aussies have joined the game. While the winemakers of Burgundy fine tune their Appellation laws and wine labels to differentiate one side of a hill from another, and German winemakers create consumer confusion with labels mixing Grosslage with Einzellagen, the Australians cut straight to the chase with pictures of sweet, cuddly animals.

In 2005, the Old World conglomerate LVMH (Louis Vuitton Moet Hennessey) sold six hundred thousand cases of wine at an average price of $44, making $26 million. However, in the same year, the New World newcomer, Yellowtail, sold seven million cases of wine at an average cost of $6, making $42 million.

Yellowtail is a family owned Australian wine company that only began exporting to the United States in 2000, and which branded itself with brightly colored images of a cute Wallaby. In 2001, it sold 112,000 cases, a number that jumped to 7.5 million in 2005, helped by distribution through Costco. Yellow Tail has enjoyed similar success in the UK, which, in 2000, began importing more wine from Australia than from France. And in 2005, Yellowtail sold more wine to the US than all the French producers combined. Both research and experience demonstrates that most consumers today, especially when buying New World wines, want to buy wine by grape variety and brand name. Young consumers in particular tend to avoid what they consider to be confusing and pretentious wine labels, characteristic of some Old World wine bottles. Terroir and provenance have been surpassed by cute and cuddly.

Argentina

Both Chile and Argentina were colonized in the sixteenth century
by Spanish Conquistadores and Catholic missionaries who planted
Spanish vines from the region of Cadiz. In Chile, the vine was called
the Pais while in Argentina, the vine was called Criolla Chica. But
apart from sharing this same original vine, the history and the wine
culture of the two nations have nothing more in common. In Chile,
there was always a focus on good-quality wines for the aristocratic
landowners, and the winemaking methods were dominated by French,
especially Bordeaux, traditions. In Argentina, with a large population
of wine drinking workers from Spain and Italy, the focus was always
on quantity rather than quality, and the winemaking traditions were
traditionally Spanish. In Chile, the earliest vineyards were close to the
capital city of Santiago, but in Argentina the capital of Buenos Aires is
at least seven hundred miles from the nearest vineyards, on the far west
of the country in Mendoza Province, high in the Andes.

As a result, the Argentinean wine industry was fragmented between
those who grew the grapes in the Andes, those who transported the
grapes across the pampas to the East Coast, and those in Buenos Aires
who turned the grapes into wine. The farmers had no motivation to
strive for quality; they were paid a fixed amount per ton of grapes, and
the grapes of all the neighboring farmers would be mixed together.
The farmers' only motivation was to grow as much Criolla Chica
grapes as possible. The Criolla vine is very vigorous and prolific, and
can produce many clusters weighing as much as nine pounds each. If
a few leaves or twigs, or even a dead field mouse was added to the
mix, then that would simply add to the weight that the farmer delivered
and was paid for. The transporters initially used horse-drawn wagons
to cross the pampas, and later trains and trucks; they too had no
interest in quality. They too were paid by the ton when they delivered
their loads to the wineries of Buenos Aires.

Finally, the wine producers themselves had no motivation to focus
on quality. They had a vast domestic market of thirsty workers who
would drink whatever they were offered. There was no export market,
as the domestic market was insatiable, if not unquenchable. Rather
than worry about quality, the wineries focused on size and quantity.
In the early twentieth century, for example, the Giol winery, covering
260 hectares, was proudly known as the largest winery in the world,
and boasted huge tile-covered pools to store the grape juice and vast,
monumental barrels to store the wine. During its time of glory, the
winery would produce almost three hundred thousand hectoliters of
wine annually; it had eight basements, a thousand oak barrels, giant
casks, two enormous sinks for mixing four thousand bottle blends,
and 270 fermentation casks. Four hundred workers and operators
were employed there and built their houses around the winery. In all
Argentinian wineries of this period, the emphasis was never on taste or
quality, but always on size and quantity. And the thirsty gauchos out
on the plains and the immigrant workers in the vast factories around
Buenos Aires happily drank it all up, with an average per capita
consumption of twenty-four gallons, or 120 bottles per head. If the
Europeans and North Americans disdained Argentinian wine, who
cared? Let them buy Chilean wine.

This happy state of affairs came to an end towards the close of
the twentieth century. Not only had Argentina suffered decades of
political, social, and economic turmoil, but in the final decade of
the century, an even worse disaster struck. Young people stopped
drinking wine.

This was not just an Argentinian phenomenon. It was occurring
worldwide, especially in traditional wine-consuming countries. Young
people were finding alternatives to wine drinking, switching to fancy
cocktails, recreational drugs, craft beers, or simple caffeinated-
sodas like Coca-Cola. But while the French and Italians could export

their wines to make up for the declining domestic youth market, the Argentinians were unable to export. Their wine was awful, and nobody outside the country wanted to drink it.

But the wine Gods move in mysterious ways, and the fortuitous timing of this disaster could not have been better. As the wine industry in Chile expanded with astonishing speed, the price of land for vineyards in Chile increased even more so. With their own domestic wine market suddenly collapsing, Argentine wineries and winegrowers were more than happy to sell to foreign investors who'd been priced out of Chile. The injection of foreign capital and the introduction of the latest winemaking technologies from around the world completely revolutionized the Argentine wine industry.

Led by visionaries such as Nicolás Catena, an isolated and inward-looking nation producing jug wine for the domestic market almost overnight became an export-driven producer of top-quality vintages. Once again, the Rothschilds are leading the way, just as they did in California, Chile, and China. Domaine Baron de Rothschild (Lafite) formed an alliance with Nicolás Catena to produce the award-winning Caro blend of French Cabernet and Argentinian Malbec. By the end of the 1990s, Argentina was exporting more than 3.3 million gallons (12.5 million liters) to the United States, with exports to the UK also strong. Wine experts, such as Karen MacNeil, wrote that the Argentine wine industry had been considered a "sleeping giant" that by the end of the twentieth century was finally waking up.

Argentinian Varietals: Until recently the most common grape in Argentina was the **Criolla Chica**, the original grape imported from Spain by the Conquistadores. Following the twenty-first century rebirth of the Argentinian wine industry, Criolla Chica is being replaced with the usual international varieties: Cabernet Sauvignon, Chardonnay, and Shiraz, as well as Tempranillo from Spain.

However, the crowning glory of Argentinian wine is **Malbec**. Malbec is one of the six official varietals used to make Bordeaux's claret, but, except in the region of Cahors in Southwest France, Malbec was never bottled unblended. Malbec was traditionally a blending grape used for its inky-dark color and pronounced tannins. However, in the dry air and high altitudes of the Andes Mountains, in some of the world's highest vineyards, Malbec has come into its own, and is now the most widely planted varietal in the country. Argentinean Malbecs have a deep color, intense fruity flavors, and a velvety texture but less tannins than the wines of Cahors, which makes them uniquely drinkable at a young age.

The other splendid wine for which Argentina is justly famous is its white wine, **Torrontes**. Probably descended from a hybrid of the original Criolla Grande vine of the Conquistadores and the Muscat grape, Torrontes is a deliciously refreshing wine with hints of peaches and nectarines mainly grown in the northern Salta province near the Bolivian border.

Argentinian Wine Regions: All the Argentinian wine regions are located in the west of the country, in the foothills of the Andes. Because the Andes mountain range forms a rain shadow, the vineyards tend to be dry and receive water from the annual spring snow-melt. Unfortunately, at those rare times when there is rainfall, it tends to come in the form of hailstorms, and a pounding of large hailstones can destroy a whole crop. A combination of the dry air and the high altitude of the vineyards appear to leave the vineyards of Argentina, as in Chile, free of pests and disease. Both countries are thus able to excel in organic farming. Phylloxera never reached Chile, and the form that arrived in Argentina was much weaker than the blight which destroyed the vineyards of Europe.

By far the largest, most important region is the province of **Mendoza**, which produces over two-thirds of Argentina's wine. As of the beginning of the twenty-first century, the vineyard acreage in Mendoza alone was slightly less than half of the entire planted acreage in the United States, and more than the acreage of New Zealand and Australia combined. The first vines were planted in Mendoza by Edmund James Palmer Norton, an English engineer who had helped construct the Transandine Railroad, linking Argentina and Chile over a twelve thousand foot mountain pass. Recognizing the potential of Mendoza for wine, Norton founded the Bodega Norton winery in 1895, and planted it with Malbec vines which he had imported from Bordeaux. Bodega Norton now exports over 1.5 million cases annually. Since Norton's time, the vineyards have been planted at ever higher altitudes in Mendoza's Luján de Cuyo and the Uco Valley, and local vintners are studying the effects of increased altitude on the Malbec clones. In 1994, Nicolás Catena was the first to plant a Malbec vineyard in excess of five thousand feet.

The second-largest producing region is **San Juan**, which, being much hotter and drier than Mendoza, mainly produces fortified wines, brandy, and vermouth.

In the far north of the country, closer to the equator, is the province of **Salta**. Salta is home to the highest vineyards in the world, higher even than in Mendoza. Vineyards in Europe are seldom planted higher than sixteen hundred feet, and even in Mendoza are seldom much higher than five thousand feet, but in Salta, vineyards are planted as high as ten thousand feet. Planted at such high altitudes but close to the equator means that the vines are subject to daytime temperatures as high as 100°F, while dropping at night to 50°F. This has the effect of creating extra acidity, while adding complexity, body, and depth to its wines. The most famous wine from Salta and its subregion of Cafayate is Torrontes, a full-bodied but refreshing white wine which has recently started earning well-deserved international recognition and accolades.

Bolivia: The wine industry in Bolivia is still small but growing, and there is not yet any export infrastructure, which is why it does not have its own chapter in this book. However, it is worth noting that despite its proximity to the equator, the high altitude of its vineyards in the Andes enables it to produce some excellent wines. The high altitude and extreme daily temperature swings have a chemical effect on the wines which cannot be reproduced elsewhere. Even a wine made from the humble Trebbiano grape has been compared to a Puligny-Montrachet, and the Malbecs can be compared with those from Argentina. Certainly a country to watch.

In 2010, the Argentine government officially declared wine to be the country's National Drink.

Australia

Most English and American introductions to Australian wine came through the classic 1972 Monty Python sketch called "Australian Wines," with an Australian accented voice-over by Eric Idle:

> *"A lot of people in this country pooh-pooh Australian table wines. This is a pity as many fine Australian wines appeal not only to the Australian palate but also to the cognoscenti of Great Britain.*
>
> ***Black Stump Bordeaux:*** *Black Stump Bordeaux is rightly praised as a peppermint flavoured Burgundy, whilst a good Sydney Syrup can rank with any of the world's best sugary wines.*
>
> ***Château Blue:*** *Château Blue, too, has won many prizes; not least for its taste, and its lingering after burn.*

Old Smokey 1968: *Old Smokey 1968 has been compared favourably to a Welsh claret, whilst the Australian Wino Society thoroughly recommends a 1970 Coq du Rod Laver, which, believe me, has a kick on it like a mule: 8 bottles of this and you're really finished. At the opening of the Sydney Bridge Club, they were fishing them out of the main sewers every half an hour.*

Perth Pink: *Of the sparkling wines, the most famous is Perth Pink. This is a bottle with a message in, and the message is 'beware'. This is not a wine for drinking; this is a wine for laying down and avoiding.*

Melbourne Old-and-Yellow: *Another good fighting wine is Melbourne Old-and-Yellow, which is particularly heavy and should be used only for hand-to-hand combat.*

Château Chunder: *Quite the reverse is true of Château Chunder, which is an appellation contrôlée, specially grown for those keen on regurgitation; a fine wine which really opens up the sluices at both ends.*

Hobart Muddy: *Real emetic fans will also go for a Hobart Muddy, and a prize winning Cuivre Reserve Château Bottled Nuit San Wogga Wogga, which has a bouquet like an aborigine's armpit."*

Possibly the Australian wines of the early '70s deserved this mockery, but unfortunately the image of loud, ignorant, convict-pee persisted well into the 1990s when it was no longer deserved. Somehow, during those twenty-some years, Australian wine switched from sugar-laced, fortified plonk to some of the most drinkable and successful wines in the world.

A number of factors brought about this change; following the Second World War, European immigration to Australia increased dramatically and many of these new arrivals, especially from the Mediterranean regions, brought their wine-producing skills with them. At the same time, following the inaugural flight from London to Sydney by BOAC in 1967 (which I happened to be on), young Australians began visiting Europe and becoming exposed to a culture of wine drinking which they brought back home with them. Also in 1967, public licensing hours were extended to 10:00 p.m., thus ending the heavy-drinking culture of Australia's six o'clock swill. Simultaneously, like UC Davis in California, the Australian Wine Research Institute at the University of Adelaide was fast becoming recognized as one of the world's leading centers for wine research.

Finally, the success of the Californian winegrowers in the 1976 Judgment of Paris gave Australian winemakers the confidence to ignore French conventions and to aggressively compete on the world market. In fact, as early as 1952, ignoring a culture of six o'clock swill, pioneers such as Max Schubert at Penfolds were already producing some of the world's greatest wines, unabashedly celebrating the unique and powerful qualities of Australian Shiraz. By 1985, Lindeman's Bin 65 set the new standard for Chardonnay wines worldwide. Thanks to these pioneers, it was the Australian wine producers, not Monty Python, who would have the last laugh.

While only half a million cases of Australian wine were shipped to the US in 1990, within fourteen years that number had increased to twenty million cases. By the year 2000, for the first time in history, the UK was importing more wine from Australia than from France. Australia is now the world's fifth largest exporter of wine, and its winemaking results have been impressive, establishing benchmarks for a number of varietals such as Chardonnay and Shiraz. The University of Adelaide has researched and innovated canopy management and other viticultural and winemaking techniques with an emphasis on super-hygienic, ultra-modern, stainless steel efficiency. Australian winemakers have a general attitude toward their work that sets them apart from producers in Europe whom they regard as hide-bound and constrained by tradition. Australian winemakers travel the wine world as highly-skilled seasonal workers, relocating to the northern hemisphere during the off-season at home. They are an important resource in the globalization of wine, and wine critic Matt Kramer notes that "the most powerful influence in wine today" comes from Australia.

Australian Varietals: With no native vines of its own, all Australian wines are made with the strains of *Vitis vinifera* imported by the Europeans since the 18th century. In addition to the normal top four international varietals—Cabernet Sauvignon, Merlot, Pinot Noir, and Chardonnay—Australia has also focused on wines from the Southern Rhône Valley—Shiraz (Syrah), Grenache, and Mourvedre. In fact, Australia has become a rival to the Rhône in the production of what are known as GSM wines (Grenache, Syrah, and Mourvedre). This is a traditional Southern Rhône blend, most famously found in Châteauneuf-du-Pape, in which the Grenache provides the alcohol, warmth, and fruitiness; the Syrah provides the full-body, dark color and tannins, while the Mourvedre contributes elegance, structure, and acidity to the final blend.

Syrah is by far the most widely-grown varietal in Australia but, for whatever reason, the Australians call it Shiraz. In many ways Shiraz became emblematic of Australian wines as they so dramatically burst onto the world stage at the end of the twentieth century, and the extraordinary success of Shiraz has encouraged many Syrah producers around the world, even in Europe, to relabel their wine as "Shiraz."

Because there is such a wide variety of climate and soil conditions in Australia, and because there are so many recent immigrants from Southern European wine regions including France, Italy, Spain, Greece, Slovenia, and Croatia, it is inevitable that Australians are experimenting and will find eventual success with many other varietals, such as Sauvignon Blanc, Riesling, Viognier, Sangiovese, and Tempranillo, among others.

Australian Wine Regions

Western Australia: Although long known for the Chenin Blanc wines of the Margaret River area among other fine wines, Western Australia is so remote from the rest of the country—let alone the world—that most of its wines are consumed locally.

Victoria: Used to be the largest wine producer in the nineteenth century, but never recovered from the Phylloxera epidemic at the turn of the century.

New South Wales: Originally this was an important wine-producing region, and the lower Hunter Valley, two hours out of Sydney, is still famous for its Chardonnays and Shiraz wines, while the upper Hunter Valley is becoming known for its Sémillon wines; the region as a whole has long since been eclipsed by South Australia.

South Australia: Known as the "California" of Australian wines, South Australia produces almost 50 percent of the nation's wine. Centered around the city of Adelaide with its University and the Australian Wine Research Institute, the area is known as a wine "superzone." The Adelaide Superzone includes the following G.I. subregions (Geographic Indicators) many of which will be recognized by English and American consumers (the subregions are listed from north to south, to the east of Adelaide):

> *Clare Valley:* Poor irrigation – reduces yields but concentrates flavor. Famous for Chardonnays, Sémillons, and Rieslings

> *Barossa Valley:* Oldest and most prestigious wine-producing region. Hot and dry. Famous for Shiraz originally planted by refugees from Silesia in 1842, which miraculously survived

Phylloxera. Increasingly developing Rhône style Grenache and Mourvedre.

Eden Valley: Henschke Hill of Grace—130 year old Shiraz vines (which also escaped the Phylloxera blight). Also world-famous for limestone flavored Rieslings

Langhorne Creek: Vines grow along Bremer River for the famous (French-owned) Jacob's Creek Shiraz.

Currency Creek: Cooler temperatures – Whites. Riesling Chardonnay, Sauvignon-Blanc, Sémillon.

McLaren Vale: Wet climate. Soil varies from sand to clay to limestone, therefore offers widest selection of varietals in South Australia, including Sangiovese and Zinfandel.

S. Fleurieu: Gravelly soil similar to Bordeaux; Cabernet Sauvignon, Malbec, Riesling and Viognier.

Kangaroo Island: Bordeaux style reds. Sandy loam and gravelly soil.

McLaren Vale is also the home of Mollydocker, a family-owned winery that produces some of the most powerful red wines in the world. Their most famous wine is The Boxer followed by Two Left Feet, both of which offer alcohol levels well in excess of 15 percent. *The Wine Spectator* and Robert Parker gave their Carnival of Love an almost unheard of ninety-nine points, though another critic described it as "Amarone gone off the rails." In any event, for people who enjoy big, swaggering, broad-shouldered reds— the Mollydocker wines are well worth searching for. In the *Wine*

Spectator's listing of the Top 100 Wines of 2014, a Mollydocker Shiraz won second place.

Chile

The earliest Chilean vineyards were planted by the Spanish Conquistadores and missionaries in the sixteenth century, probably with Spanish vines, known as Pais, brought down via Mexico and Peru. Vineyards in the New World were prohibited by the Spanish Crown who wanted the colonists to drink imported Spanish wines, even though the wines were old and oxidized by the time they crossed the Atlantic. While the Peruvians and Mexicans largely complied—turning their wine into pisco and aguardiente brandy—the Chileans, being more remote from Spain, continued growing their own grapes. As early as the eighteenth century, wealthy Chilean landowners were being influenced by French rather than Spanish winemaking techniques, and would often stopover in Bordeaux on their visits to Europe.

Influenced heavily, like most Chilean vineyards, by Bordeaux winemaking styles, Don Silvestre Errázuriz was the first to import French varietals: Cabernet Sauvignon, Merlot, Cabernet Franc, Carménère, Malbec, Sauvignon Blanc, and Sémillon. He hired a French oenologist to oversee his vineyard planting and to produce wine in the Bordeaux style. The Phylloxera epidemic of the mid-nineteenth century, while destroying nearly all French vineyards and decimating the French wine industry, was a boon to Chile's emerging wine trade, as many French winemakers traveled to South America, bringing their experience and techniques with them. During the latter half of the nineteenth century, when all the European vineyards were suffering from the Phylloxera blight, it was the vineyards of Chile and California that actually supplied the wines for the Europeans to drink. Phylloxera never reached Chile.

Chile is a long, narrow country running from the hot, dry deserts of the north to the cold wet valleys of the south, constantly irrigated by the snow run-off from the Andes and cooled by the cold water of the Pacific Ocean. The valleys of Chile enjoy an ideal combination of soil, sunlight, temperature, and humidity, and Chilean wines are among the most organic in the world. Due to the dry summer season, Chilean vineyards resist infestation and natural geographic barriers have protected the country from the arrival of Phylloxera and other diseases. The absence of these threats allows producers to grow their vineyards with reduced dependence on chemical agents. For whatever reason, the sandy soil or the dry air, the Phylloxera aphid seems never to have crossed the Andes, and thus Chile boasts some of the oldest and "purest" vines in the world, since they never needed to be grafted and replanted.

Chile has always focused more on fine wines for the wealthy local market, unlike neighboring Argentina, which focused on bulk wines for the working class. Chilean wines long had a good reputation internationally until the Second World War, when the industry entered a period of decline which lasted until the late 1980s. During this period, the wine industry was affected dramatically by the tax levied on wine and social uncertainties due to political instability and change. It was not until the restoration of democracy that, with an influx of foreign investment, the Chilean wine industry really started to expand. International interest increased following the 1976 Judgment of Paris. As soon as Baron Phillippe de Rothschild had accepted that his flagship wine had been defeated by an unknown Californian wine, he sent his daughter down to Chile, where she formed a significant and successful fifty-fifty partnership with Concha y Toro, the country's leading wine producer. In the 1990s, flying winemakers from Australia and California introduced new technology and styles that helped Chilean wineries produce more internationally-recognized wine styles. Gradually, the wineries began to convert to French and American oak or stainless steel tanks for aging. Financial investment resulted in the form of European and American winemakers opening up their own wineries, or collaborating with existing Chilean wineries to produce new brands. These include:

Robert Mondavi, collaboration with Viña Errázuriz to produce Seña

Château Lafite Rothschild, collaboration with Los Vascos

Bruno Prats and Paul Pontallier of Château Margaux, opened Domaine Paul Bruno

Château Mouton Rothschild, partnered with Concha y Toro Winery to produce Almaviva

Because the modern Chilean wine industry has been treated as a well-funded, long-term serious business venture with big players and international goals, it has always invested in the best and most modern equipment and employed the world's leading experts. Most importantly, the Chilean wine-producers made an important, early decision: to endure financial losses for several years while they established their wines in the international markets. For more than a decade, Chilean wines have been noted for their high quality and low price. Now that the excellent quality of their wines has been clearly established, Chilean producers are able to gradually raise prices. Such a strategy is only possible when the investors have the patience and financial resources to maintain it. Brazil is an example of a country taking the opposite approach. The Brazilian winegrowers appear to think that by charging high prices for their product, consumers will automatically assume that the quality is good. It is not.

The only problem with Chile's strategy was that it was dominated by bankers and investors, limited to the tried and true, not by passionate visionaries willing to take risks. Chilean wines were accepted as solid and dependable, but also as dull. An English writer, Tim Atkin, had famously described Chilean wine as "the Volvo of the wine world ... safe but boring."

In 2004, winemaker Eduardo Chadwick of Viña Errázuriz made history in Berlin. His Viñedo Chadwick 2000 took first place in a blind tasting of sixteen wines from France, Italy, and Chile. Second place went to another Chilean wine, Mondavi and Errázuriz's Seña 2001. Following in third place was Rothschild's fabled Château Lafite 2000 from Bordeaux, and forth place Château Margaux 2001. Finally, it was recognized that Chilean wines were not only about value, but about true quality and excitement as well. The Volvo had become a Ferrari!

Chilean Varietals: For most of its history prior to the twenty-first century, the most widely-planted grape in Chile was the **Pais** grape, the same grape known in California as 'Mission'. This was the grape first brought to the Americas by the Conquistadores in the sixteenth century, and is a direct descendant of the Andalusian Palomino grape used to make Sherry.

Otherwise, the varietals in Chile reflect French Bordeaux, rather than a Spanish influence, and the most-widely planted vine is Cabernet Sauvignon, followed by Merlot and Carménère. The most common white grape is Sauvignon Blanc, followed by Sémillon. Most wines are made in the "New World" style, and it would take an expert to tell the difference between a Chilean varietal and one from California or Australia, though the Cabernets show more of a distinctive "Chilean" style than the other varietals, having softer tannins and being designed for easier drinking.

The most unique Chilean varietal, however, is **Carménère**, which was originally grown in the Bordeaux region and was part of the traditional six-grape blend for making Bordeaux's claret. Following the Phylloxera blight of the late nineteenth century, it was believed that the Carménère grape had become extinct, and so it was never replanted. Recent DNA testing of what was thought to be Chilean Merlot has shown it, in fact, to be the long-lost Carménère varietal. Because Chile is unique in never having suffered from Phylloxera, the original vines imported from France by Don Silvestre Errázuriz in the nineteenth century, including Carménère, are still surviving. Recognizing a good marketing, opportunity, Chilean wine producers are promoting Carménère as a unique Chilean varietal. Another way that Chileans are seeking to develop a unique national style is by blending their original varietal of Pais with other varietals to create a distinctive Chilean flavor and taste.

Chilean Wine Regions: The first vineyards in Chile were planted around the capital of Santiago. To the east they climbed into the foothills of the Andes, and to the west they reached the Pacific port of Valparaiso.

Maipo: This Central Valley around Santiago is still the heart of the Chilean wine industry and has been compared to California's Napa Valley; it is famous for its Cabernet Sauvignons, such as the well-known Santa Rita. The Maipo region's flagship wine, Almaviva, comes from the Puente Alto vineyard, and is a joint venture between Concha y Toro and Bordeaux's Château Mouton Rothschild. Almaviva has been one of the country's most important benchmark reds since its first successful vintage in 1996—exactly twenty years after Mouton Rothschild's defeat in the Judgment of Paris!

Casablanca Valley: Running east-west from Valparaiso, Casablanca is famous for its Sauvignon Blancs and Pinot Noirs due to the cooling effects of the Pacific Coast fog and the thick cloud cover— similar to conditions in Oregon's Willamette Valley and also New Zealand, which are both famous for the same two varietals. The first vineyards were only planted here after the restoration of democracy in the 1990s, when the wine industry started to expand.

Rapel/Colchagua: As new vineyards are planted, they open new regions, moving south towards cooler climates. The reds of Colchagua are all made in the Bordeaux style—not surprisingly, since one of the most famous vineyards, Viña Los Vascos, is owned by Bordeaux's Rothschild family.

Since the start of the twenty-first century, the number of wineries in Chile has grown from twelve to over seventy. Chile is now the ninth-largest wine producer in the world, and the fourth largest exporter. Although the price of Chilean wines is starting to rise, they still offer a high-quality for a very reasonable price.

China

Strictly speaking, China is not part of the "New World." Indeed, it is one of the oldest wine-producing countries on the planet. However, wine has not been an important aspect of Chinese culture until very recently. Already within the first two decades of the new century, China has become not only a major producer but also a major consumer of wine. Within the next decade, China could prove itself one of the leading players in the world of wine.

Although grape wine has been consumed in China for at least 4,600 years, a stronger version containing up to 20 percent alcohol, called *Huangjiu,* or "yellow-wine," made from fermented rice and cereals, has always been more popular. Additionally, the Chinese have always consumed a distilled version called *Baijiu,* which has a 40-60 percent alcohol content. Alcohol in China is typically consumed in the form of toasts, drunk in small shot glasses and tossed to the back of the throat—the complete opposite of everything described in Chapter One of this book.

Modern *Vitis vinifera* grapes were probably first introduced by the Greeks, led by Alexander the Great in the third century BC, and planted in the extreme west of China in what is today's Xinjiang Autonomous Region. Marco Polo referred to the local wines when he passed through this area in the thirteenth century. This Uighur populated province (ironically the most Islamic part of China) is still the major wine-producing region in the nation, even though it clings to the edge of the Gobi Desert. One of the vineyards covers twenty-five thousand acres at 262 feet below sea level!

Following Deng Xiaoping's Economic Reforms in the early 1980s, agricultural land was de-collectivized, private entrepreneurs were permitted to develop vineyards, and foreign investment was encouraged. At the same time, a growing middle class was becoming exposed to the outside world, traveling to Europe and bringing back knowledge about foreign cultures—including wine.

The French brandy house, Remy Martin/Cointreau, established a joint venture in 1980 which eventually became Dynasty Wines, producing over one hundred types of wine products in China. Initially, Chinese wines were limited to the export market, but with the growing wealth of the domestic market in the twenty-first century and a fast evolving appreciation for wine, 90 percent of Chinese wine is now consumed domestically. While the disposable income of the growing middle class accounts for the consumption of home-grown Chinese wine, it is only the extreme wealth of the Chinese billionaire class that can account for an obsessive consumption of French, especially Bordeaux, wines. The Chinese love of Bordeaux wine is delightfully explored in the 2013 movie *Red Obsession*.

Although most Chinese wine comes from the Xinjiang Autonomous Region on the border with Pakistan, Afghanistan, Tajikistan, and Kazakhstan, a new northern area, Ningxia Province, also bordering the Gobi Desert, is rapidly becoming the center of China's fine-wine industry. With 160,000 acres of vineyards planned by 2020, Ningxia will be three times the size of Napa. The French luxury goods giant LVMH has recently invested $28 million in a state-of-the-art winery called Chandon. An international competition named "Bordeaux Against Ningxia" was held in Beijing in December 2011, when experts from China and France tasted five wines from each region. Ningxia was the clear winner, with four out of five of the top wines. The best wine in the whole competition was the 2009 Chairman's Reserve, a Cabernet Sauvignon which even Robert Parker rated as "not bad." It is unclear whether the name referred to Chairman Mao and his Little Red Book.

Another rapidly expanding wine-growing area is Shandong Province on the coast of the Yellow Sea, which, with 140 wineries, already produces 40 percent of Chinese wine. The latest company to invest in Shandong is Bordeaux's Domains Barons de Rothschild, which harvested its third vintage in 2015. Based on Rothschild's previous successes in California and Chile, Shandong Province is a region to keep an eye on.

In just the past decade, China has become one of the world's top ten wine markets, and is actually the largest consumer of red wine in the world, as well as being the sixth largest producer of wine. Between 2006 and 2015, China's wine consumption grew by 54 percent. According to Sotheby's, it is no longer London or New York but Hong Kong which is now the world's largest market for fine wines at auction. Furthermore, China is one of the world's biggest consumers of Bordeaux's Premier Cru wines, and has had a significant effect on the price structure. Chinese billionaires have long had a predilection for Château Lafite (like the English aristocracy before them), followed by Château Latour, Château Mouton-Rothschild, Château Margaux and finally by Château Haut-Brion. This preference for Lafite has had the unfortunate consequence of making Lafite the most popular target of international wine-fraud, resulting in a number of recent scandals and uncertainty in the Chinese market. There is a growing tendency among Chinese billionaires, therefore, to focus on the previously overlooked Château Haut-Brion wines (Jefferson's favorite), because its unique bottle shape makes it more difficult for criminals to reproduce.

But despite China's seeming integration into the international wine market, it retains certain Chinese idiosyncrasies. For example, the reason that Chinese are almost exclusively red wine drinkers has less to do with their appreciation of tannins and more to do with red being a lucky color traditionally associated with good fortune and good health. The Chinese still serve wine in small, shot-sized wine glasses, and, although it is a sign of progress that wine is replacing strong baijiu spirits at business banquets, it means that when that priceless 1959 Château Lafite is being poured, all the guests can toss it back in a hearty group toast without even needing to taste it.

New Zealand

Wine was not traditionally part of New Zealand culture, which was more centered on beer, rugby, and sheep. Indeed, alcoholic consumption in New Zealand was focused on the six o'clock swill, which was the hour between the end of work at 5:00 p.m. and the closing of public bars at 6:00 p.m., during which time men would desperately try to consume as much beer as physically possible. John Cleese, of Monty Python fame, visited New Zealand on tour in 1964, and even he was impressed by the level of desperate public intoxication demonstrated during that one short hour. Introduced during the First World War, the swill was part of New Zealand culture until the late 1960s, when bar closing time was finally extended till 10:00 p.m.

As a valued member of the British Commonwealth, New Zealand was able to export all its agricultural produce —especially sheep and lamb—into England, which happily consumed as much lamb as the New Zealanders were able to ship. So with a week spent rearing sheep, some rugby at the weekend, and as much beer as the swill would allow, life was good and there was little demand for wine. Furthermore, New Zealand was so isolated from the rest of the world that there was little international travel, and thus little exposure to other cultures—especially those that drank wine. The only vines grown in New Zealand were planted by some mid-century Croatian immigrants from Dalmatia, and the resulting wine was known as Dally-Plonk.

This idyllic state of affairs came to a sudden end in 1973, when the United Kingdom joined the European Economic Community and suddenly import duties were imposed on products from the Commonwealth. Overnight the British stopped importing New Zealand lamb, and so the Kiwi government needed to find an alternative to sheep-rearing to support the national economy. Bravely, they decided to switch to viniculture, and seeing a geographic and climate similarity with Germany, the government paid farmers to replace their sheep pastures with Muller Thurgau grapes. Ten years later, supported by yet more government money, the farmers ripped up their Muller Thurgau vineyards and replanted them with more fashionable grapes, like Chardonnay and Sauvignon Blanc.

With the abolition of the six o'clock swill in 1967 and the growing exposure of young New Zealanders to European culture following the arrival of passenger jets in the late 1960s, a developing local market for wine began to replace the culture of beer. Following the success of the Californians at the 1976 Judgment of Paris, winemakers around the world received a boost of confidence and were encouraged to experiment with their own wine styles instead of slavishly copying the French.

The big breakthrough came in 1985, when a winemaker called Ernie Hunter entered his Sauvignon Blanc wines in the *Sunday Times* international wine competition in London. His wines won and were voted top Sauvignon Blancs in 1986, 1987, 1988, 1992 and 2001. Very soon, other Sauvignon Blanc wines, also from Cloudy Bay in Marlborough, on the northern tip of South Island, won attention in London. Because of the unrivaled importance of the London wine market and unparalleled influence of the English wine magazines, Marlborough wines have ever since been hailed as among the best Sauvignon Blancs in the world. Indeed, some critics claim they are superior to France's more austere and acidic Sancerre and Pouilly Fumé wines from the Loire Valley. Others have described the fruit-forward Marlborough Sauvignon-Blanc as tasting like cat's-pee on a gooseberry bush, though it's unclear how familiar New Zealanders are with the taste of gooseberries. In any event, Marlborough is now firmly established as one of the world's leading producers of Sauvignon Blanc. Across the strait from Marlborough, in Martinborough at the southern tip of North Island, the region is becoming world-famous for its Pinot Noirs and Chardonnays. Obviously, the powerfully dangerous and unpredictable waters surging between the two islands of New Zealand, joining the Tasmanian Sea to the Pacific Ocean, must have a powerfully benign effect on grape production.

Hawkes Bay on North Island, being closer to the equator and thus receiving more sun, produces decent red wines—some Cabernet Sauvignon, but mainly Merlot. At the other extreme, Central Otego at the southern end of South Island, has the most southerly vineyards on earth and, despite the fury of the Antarctic waters and winters, wine writer Jancis Robinson considers it one of the five top wine-growing areas in the world—especially noted for its Burgundy-like Pinot Noir, Pinot Gris, and Riesling.

In a period of about just forty years, New Zealand has changed its culture from one of beer-swilling rugby players to one of the world's major cultivators of fine wine. For a small remote country on the edge of the world, it has managed to install a most impressive selection of excellent wines on the shelves of wine stores everywhere.

South Africa

With its Mediterranean climate, well-drained soils of clay, shale, and limestone, proximity to the waters of the Atlantic and Indian Oceans, and warm growing climate, South Africa is the ideal place to grow top-quality wines. Hugh Johnson wrote, "The most dramatically beautiful wine country in the world is surely South Africa." Geographically, it was ideally located for the Dutch and English fleets to restock with fresh wine en route to their empires and colonies further to the east.

The first vineyards were planted by the Dutch in 1654, initially just to supply the Dutch sailors heading to the Orient, but by the end of the seventeenth century, the sweet white wines of Constantia were so highly-regarded that they were being shipped back to Europe for the Royal courts. Both Frederick the Great of Prussia and Catherine the Great of Russia praised the dessert wines of Constantia, and Napoleon Bonaparte had as much as 1,126 liters (297 gallons) of Constantia wine shipped in wooden casks each year to Longwood House, his home in exile on St. Helena, from 1815 until his death in 1821. The Count de las Cases reported that, on his deathbed, after consuming thirty bottles each month, Napoleon refused everything offered to him but a glass of Constantia wine. Even Jane Austen recommended Constantia wine's healing powers for a disappointed heart, and other writers, from Charles Dickens to Charles Baudelaire, spoke glowingly of its charms and pleasures.

The sudden influx of French Huguenots starting in 1688 added French winemaking skills to the well-established viticultural skill of the Dutch farmers, and South African wines were soon in great demand throughout Europe, especially in England, where they benefited until 1860 from favorable Empire import tariffs.

This happy situation came to an end at the close of the nineteenth century with the double-whammy of Phylloxera and the Boer War (1899-1902). The Boer War not only badly damaged England's international reputation and the South African economy, but also introduced institutionalized racial discrimination, leading eventually to apartheid. Phylloxera, as it did everywhere, destroyed all the vineyards, forcing winegrowers out of business, or causing them eventually to replant with new vines. Unfortunately, most farmers chose to replant with low-quality but high-yielding grapes like Cinsaut, which was the bulk wine grape of French North Africa and Languedoc.

The widespread replanting of high-yielding Cinsaut quickly resulted in a national wine glut, and to combat desperate scenes of surplus wine being poured into rivers and wells, the government in 1918 established a co-op to control the wine industry, Koöperatieve Wijnbouwers Vereniging van Zuid-Afrika Bpkt (KWV). Through most of the twentieth century, as South Africa became increasingly isolated due to its apartheid policies, the rigid bureaucracy of the KWV slowly strangled the wine industry, and most South African wine was used for the production of cheap brandy and cooking Sherry.

With the release of Nelson Mandela and the end of apartheid in 1990, the dead hand of the KWV was removed, and South Africa finally began the renaissance of its wine industry. With private, international investment, modern technologies, and flying winemakers from around the world, South African wines are once again becoming respected and sought after.

South African Varietals: As noted, following the Phylloxera epidemic, most vineyards were replanted with the high-yielding Cinsaut grape from the Languedoc, which was renamed Hermitage. This was cloned with Pinot Noir to produce Pinotage, which is a varietal unique to South Africa.

The most widely-planted grape in South Africa is Chenin Blanc, locally referred to as "Steen," which is more acidic and crisp than the more usual style from the Loire Valley. The most popular red grape is Cabernet Sauvignon.

South African Wine Regions: Most South African wine is grown and produced on the southern tip of the continent within one hundred miles of Cape Town. The three most important regions are almost suburbs of the city: Constantia, Paarl, and Stellenbosch.

Constantia was, of course, famous from the seventeenth through nineteenth century for producing some of the world's best white wine. In recent years, the winery Klein Constantia has been scrupulously reproducing the original wine using the same natural methods and the same Muscat vine as was used in the eighteenth century. The resulting wine, Vin de Constance, is the wine that Nelson Mandela drank to celebrate his release from prison in 1990.

Paarl, because it housed the offices of the KWV, was the center of the wine industry for most of the twentieth century; however, the real center of South African wine today is the region of Stellenbosch. Stellenbosch is especially noted for its Sauvignon Blanc, which ranks with the world's best and also for its Bordeaux-style reds. The University of Stellenbosch has a reputation similar to Adelaide's Wine Research Institute and UC Davis for research into wine production, and the Stellenbosch Vine-Hopper railway wine tour is perhaps the world's most delightful way to explore a wine region.

After a century of bad fortune and mismanagement, South African wines are emerging to claim their rightful place on the world market. These wines have great potential.

USA/North America

The first Europeans to discover America called it Vineland. In the year AD 1000, the Viking explorer Leif Erikson, exploring the coast of Newfoundland, was excited to discover native vines growing wild, thus starting a European obsession with producing wine in America.

Five hundred years later, when the second wave of Europeans arrived, the English, Spanish, and French colonists were determined to plant vines and make American wine. In 1570, the Spanish Missionary Father Juan de la Carrera wrote back to the king about some beautiful vineyards he had discovered in today's South Carolina, "so beautiful and well plotted as any in Spain." A few years later Sir Walter Raleigh founded an ill-fated colony in Roanoke in today's North Carolina, attracted by the plethora of grapes growing in wild profusion. Sir Walter was acting on behalf of Queen Elizabeth, who was determined to gain an independent source of wine without being endlessly beholden to England's eternal enemies, the French and the Spanish.

Elizabeth's successor, King James I, was so fond of wine that he gave standing orders to the royal cellar master to deliver twelve gallons of Sherry per day to the King's table. Like Elizabeth, James was equally determined to create an independent source of wine, free of foreign interference. James established the first English colony in Jamestown with the express purpose of making wine. The very first official meeting of the English colonists in 1619, and the first law passed in the New World, was to enforce all men who headed a household to grow European grapes:

261

"... every household doe yearly plante and maintaine ten vines, until they have attained to the arte and experience of dressing a Vineyard, either by their owne industry, or by the Instruction of some Vigneron. And that upon what penalty soever the Gouvernour and Counsell of Estate shall thinke fitt to impose upon the neglecters of this acte."

It was later decided that the penalty for failing to follow this law should be "on paine of death."

From Captain John Smith to Lord Baltimore and William Penn, the English were determined to create an independent source of wine in America, and throughout the sixteenth, seventeenth, and eighteenth centuries, the English colonists endlessly tried making wine from the Native American vines, *Vitis labrusca* and *Vitis riparia*. They also tried importing and growing the European vine *Vitis vinifera*, but all to no avail. The European vines died, while the wine made from American vines was undrinkable. Wines made from *Vitis labrusca* and other Native American vines are always described as having a "foxy" taste—*le goût de Reynard* or, less politely, *pissat de Reynard*—"fox piss."

Thomas Jefferson continued the quest as Ambassador, as President, and as landowner, but though he was successful at all his other ventures, he was a complete failure in the cultivation of wine. In all his thirty-six years of dedicated trying, he never produced a single bottle. Apart from loving wine personally as a connoisseur, Jefferson believed passionately in the civilizing effects of wine on the population. As ambassador to France, he was more than familiar with the moderating effects of wine on sophisticated French culture when compared to the rough savagery of the gin and whiskey culture back home in the colonies. If the common people drank wine instead of spirits, he argued, life would be less violent and more civilized: "No nation is drunken where wine is cheap; and none sober where the dearness of wine substitutes ardent spirits as the common beverage. It is, in truth, the only antidote to the bane of whiskey." But despite his best efforts, all Jefferson's vineyard plantings eventually died, and he never produced any American wine that was drinkable.

The French, in New France, which at one point contained most of North America—a vast tract east of the Rockies and west of the Appalachians, from New Orleans to the north of Quebec—had no more luck than the English in successfully planting vines. They all died. It was not until the Spanish sent missionaries up the Californian coast in the eighteenth century that European vines finally took successful root in North America.

Although California produces a disproportionate 90 percent of the total, at the start of the twenty-first century, vines are now grown and wine is made in all of the fifty United States. After the colonists' well-documented failures on the East Coast, the first successful winery opened in Cincinnati, Ohio, in the 1830s, and by 1850, the wines of Ohio were being rivaled by the wines of Missouri, where German winemakers had developed several successful wineries centered on the German colony of Herman. Unfortunately, the twin disasters of Phylloxera and Prohibition at the end of the century, as discussed in more detail elsewhere, completely destroyed the US wine industry, which only began to recover in the latter half of the twentieth century.

U.S. STATE	WINERIES
California	3532
Washington	670
Oregon	544
New York	310
Virginia	222
Texas	204

Pensylvania	160
Ohio	142
Michigan	131
North Carolina	129
Missouri	125
Illinois	103

Figure 7: US Wineries by State

If only to honor the memory of Thomas Jefferson, wine is finally being grown and made in Virginia, and there are even vineyards at his Monticello estate producing Chardonnay, Viognier, Cabernet Franc, and even Nebbiolo. New York, too, over the past two decades, has seen an increase in the number of wineries and in the quality of wine produced, especially around the Finger Lakes region, which is noted for its production of Riesling, Chardonnay, Gewürztraminer, and Pinot Noir. Because the wineries of New York, Virginia, and most of the other states like Michigan, Texas, New Jersey, and Pennsylvania, are small family-owned enterprises, they lack distribution networks and are thus little known outside their immediate neighborhood. Many of the wineries east of the Rockies also use the Native American grape, *Vitis labrusca*, either by itself or cloned or blended with the European *Vitis vinifera*. The Canadians also experiment with *Vitis labrusca,* which is probably the original vine that the Vikings saw growing on the shores of Newfoundland more than a thousand years ago.

Canada produces a certain amount of wine, but more than 50 percent of the wine consumed in Canada is imported—which might reflect a local perception of the quality of the domestic product. The most notable and deservedly sought after Canadian wine is the ice wine, a sweet and powerful dessert wine made from grapes that have been allowed to freeze on the vine before fermentation. Canada also allows wineries to import grapes and juice from other countries, and to label it as "Cellared in Canada."

Although this book is dedicated to wine, not cider, I must make an exception by mentioning La Face Cachée de la Pomme, a small-boutique Canadian winery in Quebec which uses apples to produce a range of unctuously delicious, fruity, mouth-filling ice wines called Neige.

The only North American wines which have achieved success on the international market are all on the West Coast, and of these, the most important is, of course, California.

California

California produces 90 percent of the wine in North America, and if California was a separate country, it would be the world's fourth largest wine producer after France, Spain, and Italy. The three most important dates in the history of Californian wine are 1769, 1920, and 1976.

> *1769 Missions:* In 1769, Spanish Franciscan missionaries led by Father Junipero Serra started moving up the Pacific Coast from Baja California. Their plan was to found a string of missions along the coast, each located a single day's horseback ride from the next, along a single road which they called El Camino Real. The first mission was founded at San Diego in 1769, and fifty-four years later, the twenty-first and final mission was founded at San Francisco in 1823. In order to celebrate Mass, each mission planted a vineyard to produce wine for the Eucharist. The vine that the monks planted was the same Palomino vine that Cortez had brought with him from Spain in 1524. Not having any other name, it was called Mission, and remained the dominant wine in California until the twentieth century.

The Californian Gold Rush of 1849 brought thousands of thirsty miners from Europe, and so the demand for wine increased dramatically, especially in Northern California around the new mission of San Francisco. Many of the "49ers" came from the wine-producing parts of France, Spain, and Italy, and brought their winemaking skills with them. The first commercial winery, Buena Vista, was opened in Sonoma in 1857 by a Hungarian adventurer named Count Haraszthy, often referred to as the "Father of the Californian Wine Industry," who certainly improved the quality of the local wine and imported many European vines, but whose biographic details remain as elusive as those of Keyser Söze, his compatriot from *The Usual Suspects.* In addition to their winemaking skills, immigrants like Haraszthy brought their native vines with them also, and so the ubiquitous Mission grape began to give way to other, better-quality vines.

When the great Phylloxera blight destroyed the vineyards of Europe in the late nineteenth century, it was Californian root stock which saved the day and allowed the vineyards to be replanted. By the end of the nineteenth century, wine production was a major part of the Californian economy, and Californian wines were gaining recognition and winning prizes internationally. Napa Valley in particular was quickly recognized for producing quality wine. At the Exposition Universelle in Paris in 1889, Napa Valley wines won twenty of the thirty-four medals or awards (including four gold medals) won by California entries. This was the high point that was followed by forty years of natural and human-caused disasters: severe frosts, an economic depression, the San Francisco earthquake that destroyed an estimated thirty million US gallons of wine in storage, and the disaster of national Prohibition from 1920 through 1933.

1920 Prohibition: In January 1920, as discussed in Chapter Three, the 18th Amendment to the Constitution, the Volstead

Act, banned the manufacture, importation, transportation, and sale of intoxicating beverages within the United States—but not their consumption.

Just when the Californian wine industry was achieving international recognition and respect, the government ordered all the vineyards to be torn up. Certain wineries, such as The Christian Brothers, were permitted to continue making wine for "sacramental purposes," and Beaulieu Vineyard, for example, had the approval of the Archbishop of San Francisco to provide altar wine for the archdiocese. Vineyards were, however, permitted to grow grapes for private consumption, and so farmers ripped up all their more delicate vines and replaced them with Alicante Bouschet, a coarse varietal that produced thick-skinned grapes which were easier to transport from California to the East Coast without bruising or rotting. Other winegrowers would use the prolific Alicante Bouschet grapes to produce semi-solid grape concentrates, often called "wine bricks" or "wine blocks," which were labeled with a very clear warning to consumers not to add yeast or sugar, and "after dissolving the brick in a gallon of water, do not place the liquid in a jug away in the cupboard for twenty days, and do not store in temperatures above seventy degrees because then it would turn into wine." A free packet of yeast was usually attached to the wine block.

Farmers made so much money selling unfermented grape juice and grape blocks during Prohibition that land devoted to vineyards in California increased by 700 percent. By 1928, approximately 27,900 railroad carloads of grapes left California bound for New York alone. The volume was so great that the Pennsylvania Railroad expanded its Jersey City freight terminal solely to accommodate the thousands of grape-laden boxcars. Prices increased as well as volume. During the first four years of Prohibition, a ton of grapes went from a pre-Prohibition price of less than $30 to a staggering

267

$375, and land prices for vineyards during Prohibition increased seven-fold.

The repeal of Prohibition in 1933 left California with an excess of vineyards producing a surplus of bad juice. The Californian wine industry was dead. Americans in general had once again developed a taste for spirits and cocktails rather than wine. Consumers now demanded cheap "jug wine" (so-called dago red) and sweet, fortified (high alcohol) wine. Before Prohibition, dry table wines outsold sweet wines by three to one, but after Prohibition the ratio had more than reversed. In 1935, 81 percent of California's production was sweet wines. The reputation of the state's wines suffered accordingly.

For the next thirty years, the Californian wine industry was in complete disarray, producing such American classics as E&J Gallo's Thunderbird and other wines normally served in a brown paper bag. But during the 1960s, a new wave of winemakers began to emerge and help sponsor a renaissance in California wine with a focus on new winemaking technologies and an emphasis on quality. Several well-known wineries were founded in this decade, including Robert Mondavi, Heitz Wine Cellars (both in Napa Valley), and David Bruce Winery in the Santa Cruz Mountains. As the quality of Californian wine improved, the region started to receive more international attention.

1976 Judgment of Paris: A watershed moment for the industry occurred in 1976 (discussed in more detail in Chapter Three), when British wine merchant Steven Spurrier invited several Californian wineries to participate in a blind tasting event in Paris to compare the best of California with the best of Bordeaux and Burgundy. In an event known as The Judgment of Paris, Californian wines shocked the world by sweeping the wine competition in both the red and white wine categories. Throughout the wine world, perspectives about the potential of California wines dramatically changed.

Once he had recovered from the shock of seeing his Premier Cru, Mouton Rothschild, voted second place to the unknown Californian wine from Stag's Leap, Baron Phillippe de Rothschild flew to California and signed a fifty-fifty partnership deal with Robert Mondavi. The result was the wine Opus One.

As George M. Taber explains so well in his book *The Judgment of Paris*, California wine has never been the same; the French are still struggling to recover, and the ripple effect of that blind tasting in Paris is still being felt around the world. The wine critic Robert Parker had started writing his wine guide one year earlier in 1975, and started publishing his newsletter, *The Wine Advocate*, in 1979. Parker is an unabashed advocate of the big-bodied, fruit-forward, alcoholic wines that first emerged in California and are now defined as New World wines. It was Parker who criticized winemakers for imitating French wines and "going against what Mother Nature has given California." If you want to make French wines, he said, do it in France. It was Parker who enthused that the strength of Californian wines "lies in power, exuberance, and gloriously ripe fruit;" and of course by "gloriously ripe" he meant high in alcohol.

Parker's rise to being the world's undisputed and most-influential wine critic parallels the incredible rise of the Californian wine industry. Although wine is grown in some fifty states, California is responsible for nearly all of it.

Californian Varietals: For much of its history, California was dominated by the Mission grape until the late nineteenth century when European immigrants started to introduce French and Italian vines. As described previously, most of these quality varietals were replaced during Prohibition by Alicante Bouschet grapes, but by the middle of the twentieth century a new wave of immigrants started replanting other vines, such as Cabernet Sauvignon and Chardonnay.

Initially the winemakers tried to imitate European wines, and even labeled their own wine with recognizable European names such as Burgundy, Chablis, or Chianti. But under pressure from innovators like Frank Schoonmaker and Robert Mondavi, Californian wines began to be labeled with the name of their varietal—in the same way that the wines of Alsace are labeled.

Today, there is probably not a wine varietal in existence which somebody is not trying to grow in California. Every type of varietal can be found in California, including many different hybrid grapes and new *Vitis vinifera* varieties developed at the UC Davis Department of Viticulture and Enology. The only varietal which was perceived as being unique to California was Zinfandel, which recent DNA analysis shows to be descended from the Croatian grape Crljenak Kaštelanski and the Primitivo grape from Puglia in Italy. The Zinfandel was declining in popularity in the mid-twentieth century and might as well have vanished if it was not for the sudden and surprising success of White Zinfandel in 1975, when Sutter Home accidentally created a pink, sweet, soft jug wine with low alcohol. It became an overnight success and remains the third most popular wine, accounting for 10 percent of all the wine consumed in America. White Zinfandel outsells red Zinfandel by six to one.

Ironically, after promoting "varietal" over "terroir" for so many years, different regions of California are increasingly starting to focus on specific varietals, and thus California is now developing its own terroirs.

Californian Terroirs: Over the past hundred years, as experience has shown which varietals thrive under what specific local conditions, a series of Californian terroirs has started to emerge. At the same time, the US government introduced the American Viticultural Area (AVA), which is a designated wine-growing area defined by its geographic boundaries. As of March 2015, there were 230 AVAs in the United States. However, AVAs are much more like the German Grosslage than the French AOC definition of terroir.

Ignoring the vast wine-producing region of the Central Valley where most of California's grapes are grown, the other two major regions are the North Coast and the Central Coast. California's most notable terroirs include the following very abbreviated list, from north to south down the coast, where the very cold waters of the Pacific Ocean temper the warm, sunny climate and bring on the cooling evening fog:

• North Coast (North of San Francisco Bay)

Mendocino: The summer fogs coming in from the coast create German-like conditions, and so favor white wines like Riesling and Gewürztraminer, while above the fog line of the Anderson Valley the area has long been noted for its great old-vine Zinfandels, which were long thought to be native to California. Not famous just for its cannabis, Mendocino wines are increasingly competing in reputation with its southern neighbors in Napa and Sonoma, and producing some of the nation's very best Zinfandels and Petit Syrahs.

Sonoma: The Alexander Valley in the north of Sonoma is most famous for its red wines, Cabernet Sauvignon, and Merlot, but, receiving less sun, they are often not as powerful as the reds from the adjoining Napa Valley. Some vineyards, such as Silver Oak, cross the border, and are able to blend grapes from both Sonoma's Alexander Valley with grapes from Napa Valley. The Russian River, subject to cooling fog rolling in from the ocean, is noted for its Pinot Noirs and Chardonnays. Further south, Dry Creek Valley, again above the fog line, is noted, not just for its powerful Zinfandels, but also Sauvignon Blanc and, increasingly, Barbera and Syrah.

271

The southern part of Sonoma, Los Carneros, where it borders Napa Valley, was always famous for its Californian Champagne. The cool fog and consistent breezes from the bay create the perfect climate for Pinot Noir and Chardonnay grapes to thrive, as they do on the limestone plains of northern France. What is interesting is that after the European Union prevented use of the word Champagne outside of its historic geographic region, many of the big French Champagne and Spanish Cava makers, such as Taitinger, Freixante, Cordonieu, Moet Chandon, and Mum's, have all purchased vineyards in Los Carneros to make sparkling wine. After you beat 'em, join, 'em!

Napa Valley: Despite its large international fame, Napa Valley is relatively small, being only one-eighth the size of Bordeaux. Much hotter in the north of the valley, the southern half is cooled by the fog coming through the Golden Gate Bridge and up from San Francisco Bay. Widely recognized, except by the French, as producing the best Cabernet Sauvignons in the world, the names of the following Napa Valley AVAs (from north to south) are almost as well-known as many of France's AOCs: Spring Mountain, St. Helena, Rutherford, Oakville, Yountville, and, of course, Stags Leap.

Oakville is the home of the famed Ulysses Vineyard and its acclaimed Cabernet Sauvignon wines. The literary reference is neither to Homer nor James Joyce, but to Alfred Lord Tennyson and his poem "*Ulysses*," with its praise of the hero's determination "to strive, to seek, to find, and not to yield."

Stag's Leap was named after a rocky peak in the southern part of Napa Valley associated with various legends involving stags escaping capture or alternatively being slaughtered by leaping off the cliff. In any event, it was the Cabernet Sauvignon from the

Stag's Leap winery owned by Warren Winiarski that won the 1976 Judgment of Paris, putting Californian wines on the map and making Stag's Leap the most famous wine in California. The neighboring vineyard of Stags' Leap (note the apostrophe), owned by Carl Doumani, obviously benefitted from the confusion over the name, and this resulted in decades of bitter and expensive lawsuits between the two wine owners. Eventually, when the lawsuits ended, Doumani and Winiarski became friends and joined forces to produce a wine with grapes made from both estates, called Accord. When the US government created the American Viticultural Area in 1989, it wisely decided to ignore the apostrophe, which is why the AVA is Stags Leap. Stag's Leap is now owned by Foster's (the Australian beer giant), and Stags' Leap is now owned by Château St. Michelle.

Interestingly, after selling the Stags' Leap winery, Carl Doumani opened a smaller winery inspired by Miguel de Cervantes. His wines include an organic Petit Syrah called Sancho Panza, as well as a robust Cabernet Sauvignon called Quixote, like the name of his winery.

• Central Coast (From Santa Cruz to Los Angeles)

Santa Cruz Mountains: South of San Francisco, close to Monterey Bay, the vineyards are surrounded by protective forests, and benefit from the higher-elevation Californian sun during the growing season and from the cooling fog off the bay during the evenings. David Bruce Winery is noted for his full-bodied and powerful Cabernet Sauvignons (despite getting the lowest score for his Chardonnay in the 1976 Paris tasting). Nearby Bonny Doon Winery is noted for its uniquely quirky labels by Ralph Steadman, its focus on terroir, its successful blends of Rhône style wines, biodynamic practices, and its pioneering use of the screw-top seal for its bottles.

The Bonny Doon Winery also produces an interesting Grenache wine, Clos de Gilroy, also known as "The Proust Wine." Gilroy is a town just south of Santa Cruz, which is known as the "Garlic Capital" of the world. The label of Clos de Gilroy features a picture of Marcel Proust and a reference to the famous opening sentence of his seven volume masterwork, *In Search of Lost Time*: "For a long time I would go to bed early." The label on the bottle includes the line: "For a long time I would go to bed aioli," meaning smelling of Gilroy's oil and garlic sauce. This is not the only link between Proust and wine; Virginia Woolf once said of reading Proust, "the pleasure becomes physical—like sun and wine and grapes."

Paso Robles: In the past twenty years, Paso Robles wineries have grown from less than twenty to more than two hundred. Robert Parker believes that it is a wine-growing area of considerable potential, and its growing importance is reflected by the recent decision to sub-divide it into eleven AVA subregions. Known originally for its hearty Zinfandels, Paso Robles has also been long-recognized for its Bordeaux-style Cabernet Sauvignons. The most recent trend in the region is for GSM-style wines, with plantings of Grenache, Syrah, Mourvèdre, and Carignan, as well as Viognier and Rousanne. The emerging popularity of the region's focus on Rhône wines led it to become the first site of the annual "Hospice du Rhône" conference on Rhône-style wine. Today, Paso Robles Wine Country is receiving attention for its unique Paso blends. These wines are unique to the area and include varietal blendings that do not follow the traditional rules of more conventional winemaking.

Santa Barbara: Famous, of course, for its Pinot Noirs as immortalized by the 2004 movie *Sideways*, set in the Santa Maria Valley, Santa Barbara is also famous for its full-bodied and oaky Chardonnays, which can fetch the highest prices in the state. Like nearby Paso Robles, Santa Barbara is building a reputation for its Northern Rhône-style wines with its planting of Viognier and Syrah.

Oregon

Although the early pioneers planted grapes to make wine on the Oregon Trail as far back as 1847, because the state did not have the history of the Spanish Missions, winemaking was never as important as it was in California. With the arrival of Prohibition in 1920, whatever winemaking existed was wiped out for the next forty years.

Just as the wine industry in California started to revive in the 1960s, so too people started opening wineries in Oregon and experimenting with quality wines at that same time. It soon became apparent that while the more southerly valleys of California had the perfect conditions to compete with Bordeaux, the more northerly valleys of Oregon had the cooler and wetter conditions to compete with Burgundy. Following California's 1976 success in the Judgment of Paris, a bottle of 1975 South Block Reserve Pinot Noir from David Lett's Eyrie Vineyards was entered into the Gault-Millau 1979 Wine Olympics and won top prize, being voted among the best Pinot Noirs in the world.

Since the 1980s, Oregon, particularly the Willamette Valley, has been recognized as a world leader for Pinot Noir. Even the French acknowledge the quality of Oregon Pinot Noirs, being far more like the reds of Burgundy than the more alcoholic, fruit-forward Pinots from California.

At forty-five degrees north, Oregon is on the same latitude as Lyon in southern Burgundy, and not only has Oregon's Governor been officially welcomed in Burgundy, but one of Burgundy's most respected négociants and winemakers, from the Joseph Drouhin family, has purchased land in the Willamette Valley where they produce elegant and refined Pinot Noirs that age gracefully. The close relationship between Oregon and Burgundy continues to expand, and Oregon is increasingly being recognized for its Chardonnay—Burgundy's other wine—which again, is far less fruity and oaky than Californian Chardonnay.

Washington

Most people, especially those living in South Florida, think of Washington State as being in the far, distant north, far too cold to make wine. In fact, at forty-seven degrees north, Seattle is on the same latitude as Beaune in central Burgundy, and Washington, with 670 wineries, is second only to California in the production of American wine.

Most of Washington's wine is produced in the dry, almost desert-like conditions of the eastern part of the state, irrigated by the mighty Colombia River. Although visitors to Seattle may think that Washington is permanently raining, the eastern side of the Cascade Mountains is protected by the "rain-shadow," and provides perfect conditions for growing vines. Although the state's largest and best-known producer, Château Ste. Michelle, is located just an hour's drive outside of Seattle, most of its grapes are actually grown further east and trucked back over the Cascades after harvesting. Walla Walla in southeast Washington, bordering on Oregon, produces some of the state's best Cabernets, Merlots, and Syrahs—truly great wines at very reasonable prices. Château Ste. Michelle offers a full range of varietals, but its crowning glory is to be found in its whites; the Sémillons compare with the best from Bordeaux and the Rieslings with the best from Germany.

As in California and Oregon, modern wine production began in the late 1960s, and by 1988, Château Ste. Michelle was named "Best American Winery." The following year, five Washington wines made the Wine Spectator's "Top 100 List". But despite its successes and despite its large production, the wines of Washington are not so well-known outside the state. One of the reasons is that people think of Château Ste. Michelle as being a French or Californian wine, and the other reason is that people confuse the state with Washington, DC. "Which side of the Potomac are your vineyards?" they ask. Another possible reason that Washington remains unrecognized is because it does not have a signature wine which identifies it. Australia has Shiraz, Oregon and Burgundy have Pinot Noir, Germany has Riesling, New Zealand has Sauvignon Blanc—but Washington has no identifying varietal. If anything, Washington has focused on Merlots, but the 1990s craze for Merlots has long abated.

Although it was UC Davis which first started serious research into winemaking, Oregon State University and Washington State University have both contributed to the continuing research, which has resulted in those states' recent oenological successes.

Chapter

6

VARIETALS

Chapter Six: VARIETALS

"Having spent so much of my life with Shakespeare's world, passions and ideas in my head and in my mouth, he feels like a friend — someone who just went out of the room to get another bottle of wine." — Patrick Stewart

---

Terroir refers to the soil, the climate, and the cultural traditions of the place where a wine is made—in the same way that varietal refers to the specific variety of grape used. These are both French expressions which represent two rival schools of thought concerning the most important influence on the quality of the wine. Terroir was discussed in the previous chapter.

There are hundreds of different varieties of vine in the world, but it is only the *Vitis vinifera*, originally from the Middle East and Europe, which provides the hundreds of different grape varieties from which wine can be made. In this guide we examine just the most common— the top seventy out of the hundreds of different possible varietals. A few "international" varieties have become so popular that they are now grown everywhere in the world, from Europe to North America and New Zealand. Most other "regional" varieties remain identified with the geographic regions in which they originated.

Over the past twenty or thirty years, there has been a remarkable change in the quality of grapes being cultivated around the world, as the high-yielding but low-quality grapes used for jug wine are being replaced with the lower yielding grapes used for high-quality wines. As recently as 1990, the most-cultivated grape in the world was Airen, used mainly for blending or distilling, but twenty years later, it had been replaced by Cabernet Sauvignon. Other jug wine grapes, like the Soviet Union's Rkatsiteli, the Turkish Sultaniye, Carignan, Cinsaut, and even Trebbiano, have been replaced by Merlot, Chardonnay, Syrah, Tempranillo, and Pinot Noir.

THE WORLD'S MOST PLANTED VARIETALS

1990	2010
1. Airen	1. Cabernet Sauvignon
2. Garnacha tinta	2. Merlot
3. Rkatsiteli	3. Airen
4. Sultaniye	4. Tempranillo
5. Trebbiano Toscana	5. Chardonnay
6. Carignan	6. Syrah
7. Merlot	7. Garnacha tinta
8. Cabernet sauvignon	8. Sauvignon blanc
9. Monastrell	9. Trebbiano Toscano
10. Bobal	10. Pinot noir

Figure 8: World's top varietals

Alphabetical list of major varietals—some paired with great writers

The following list of seventy of the world's leading grape varieties for making wine is arranged alphabetically. Some of the better-known varietals have been paired with writers, mainly poets and novelists. The pairings are entirely personal and mostly whimsical, but serve, I hope, to catch those elusive qualities of a wine which are so difficult to capture with mere words. Where appropriate, I have put the name of the writer in parenthesis, following the name of the grape.

Airen (Barbara Cartland): Airen was, until very recently, the world's most planted grape. Like Ugni Blanc in France and Trebbiano in Italy, it produces vast quantities of undistinguished white wines which are used for blending with other, better varietals, or for distilling into industrial alcohol. Grown mainly in Spain, it is gradually being replaced with red varietals, especially Tempranillo.

Dame Barbara Cartland, until her death at the age of ninety-nine in 2000, was one of the world's most prolific writers. Despite the success and popularity of her 723 books, most of her writings, like Airen wines, are considered to be undistinguished.

Agiorgtiko: This is the most-widely grown red varietal in Greece, and its thick-skinned berries are capable of a wide range of styles, from light to full-bodied reds. Grown most notably in the Northeastern Peloponnesian region of Nemea, the wines have succulent tannins, which enable the wines to age well in oak. Delicious with goat roasted over an open flame.

Aglianico: Originally planted near Rome by the Ancient Greeks and whose name is a corruption of *Hellenic* in Latin, this was the grape used for the production of the legendary Falernian wines so treasured and celebrated by the Romans. Even today, in southern Italy, it is valued as a noble grape, like Sangiovese in Tuscany or Nebbiolo in Piedmont. Jancis Robinson, wine critic, regards this vine as, potentially, producing one of Italy's finest wines.

Albariño/Alvarinho (J.R.R. Tolkien): Albariño is a variety of white wine grape grown in Galicia (Northwest Spain) and across the border in Northern Portugal, where it is used to make varietal white wines and Vinho Verde. It is believed to have been brought to Iberia by German Cistercian monks during the twelfth century as they participated in the pilgrimage to St. Jacques de Compostela. Its name Alba-Riño means "the white [wine] from the Rhine," and was probably a Riesling clone originating from the Alsace region of France. The highly floral aroma of the best Albariños recall the Gewurztraminer and Riesling grapes, also from Alsace.

The literary pairing of Albariño with Tolkien is irresistible. Consider the image of hooded monks setting off from their walled monastery on the banks of the Rhine, and crossing the Black Forest to the land of the Franks. There would be perilous days crossing the bleak mountain passes of the Massif-Central before reaching the Spanish border near San Sebastien, and then the long, winding journey along the rocky shoreline of Asturias and Galicia. All the while, they would be carrying their precious offering, the root stock of their delicate vine to be planted, like the body of Saint James, at the end of the Camino de Santiago, near Cape Finistere, the end of the world.

In *The Hobbit* as well as in *The Lord of the Rings,* there are several versions of Bilbo Baggins' walking song:

> *Roads go ever, ever on,*
> *Over rock and under tree,*
> *By caves where never sun has shone,*
> *By streams that never find the sea;*
> *Over snow by winter sown,*
> *And through the merry flowers of June,*
> *Over grass and over stone,*
> *And under mountains in the moon.*

Albariño wines are fresh and energetic, representing a call to adventure with a floral perfume suggesting the distant magic of wizards, elvish princesses, ancient runes, dragon's gold, and faery lands forlorn.

Alicante-Bouschet: A cross between Petit Bouschet and Grenache first cultivated by a French farmer called Henri Bouschet in 1866, when farmers in the Rhône valley were struggling to combat the mysterious arrival of Phylloxera. Because of its ease of growth, productivity, and very dark color, it soon became one of the most planted grapes throughout Southern France, and the twelfth most-planted in the world. It was during America's Prohibition that the grape's popularity really reached its peak, when California's vineyards were ripped up and replanted with acres of Alicante-Bouschet. Its thick skin and extremely dark color meant the grapes could survive the bruising rail journey to New York, where the grapes were auctioned for "home winemakers." The color of Alicante-Bouschet grape juice is so dark that it was claimed you could paint the side of a barn with just one coat. In Europe, this quality made it popular for blending with paler and weaker wines.

Alicante D.O. is a wine region around the town of Alicante on Spain's Mediterranean coast. The wines are traditionally made with Mourverdre and Grenache grapes.

Aligoté: Aligoté is always referred to as Burgundy's other white wine, Chardonnay's ugly sister. Any Burgundy AOC wine is, by definition 100 percent Chardonnay, and therefore there is no need to mention the varietal on the label. However, if the wine contains Aligoté, this must be clearly stated. The advantage of Aligoté over Chardonnay is that it requires less sun, and thus can be planted lower in the valleys which receive less hours of sunlight. Usually in Burgundy, Aligoté is the cheap white wine which is mixed with blackcurrant liquor to make Kir, a late afternoon aperitif. The big surprise about Aligoté is that Maitre Aubert de Villaines, the famous vigneron and legendary owner of France's greatest vineyard, the Domaine de la Romanée-Conti, also has his own small vineyard next to his private residence in the village of Bouzeron, which he works himself. The vines that de Villaine grows and bottles are 100 percent Aligoté, with a yield of only 2.5 tons per acre (45 hl/ha). The wine is so good that it has its own appellation, Aligoté-Bouzeron AOC.

Arneis: A crisp and aromatically floral white wine variety from Piedmont, which has been grown there since the fifteenth century. It is also sometimes known as the "white Barolo," referring to the powerful red Nebbiolo wine from the region. Growing in international recognition, it is becoming more popular in US restaurants.

Assyrtiko (Homer): Assyrtiko is a Greek white wine native to the fabulous and legendary wine-producing island of Santorini, whose volcanic and pumice soils produce a long-lasting, bone dry wine with a refreshing taste of lime and honeysuckle. Because of the harsh Mediterranean winds, the vines grow low to the ground in a circular protective basket shape. Finally, like other Greek wines, Assyrtiko is becoming increasingly recognized and available on the international marketplace.

Although modern Assyrtiko vines are produced to make a dry style of wine, traditionally they were used to make a passito, or raisinated wine. This syrupy-sweet dessert wine is probably how Homer would have drunk it, diluted with water. In most of the ancient world, sweet white wines were always the most valued, partly because they aged better and were higher in alcohol, but also because the ancient diet offered very few sources of sweetness. Homer, of course, is famous for writing of the "wine-dark sea," which is puzzling, since most of the wine he would have drunk was white and the Aegean is famously blue. Scholars still argue over the meaning of the phrase, but one theory is that since the Ancient Greeks never drank their wine neat, the resin and water they diluted it with would have darkened the color.

Barbera is a red Italian wine grape variety that is the third most-planted red grape variety in Italy (after Sangiovese and Montepulciano). Like the Nebiolo grape, it is mainly cultivated in Piedmont and Southern Lombardy, most famously around the towns of Asti, Alba, and Pavia. It produces good yields and is known for a deep color, low tannins, and high levels of acid (which is unusual for a warm climate red grape). Century-old vines which somehow survived the Phylloxera blight of the nineteenth century still exist in many regional vineyards, and allow for the production of long-aging, robust red wines with intense fruit and mild tannic content. The best-known appellation is the DOCG Barbera d'Asti. When young, the wines offer a very intense aroma of fresh red and blackberries. In the lightest versions, notes of cherries, raspberries, blueberries, and black cherries are in wines made of riper grapes.
It used to be said that the wines of Barbera were "what you drank while waiting for the Barolo to be ready." With a new generation of winemakers, this is no longer the case. The wines are now meticulously vinified; aged Barbera is called "Barbera Superiore." Sometimes the wines are aged in French barrels, becoming "Barbera Barricato," and intended for the international market.

Beaujolais: See Gamay.

Boğazkere is a grape variety and a Turkish wine originating from Diyarbakır Province near the Tigris River in Southeastern Turkey. Not widely known outside of Turkey, it is only listed here because it is possibly the world's original grape from the "Garden of Eden." The wine is long finishing, with a dark-red color and dark-blue hue, with very rich, strong aromas of dried red fruits and spices. Good for aging up to ten years. It is recommended for drinking with red meat kebabs, turkey, salmon, and cheese, especially eastern Anatolian cheddar or Gruyere cheese. The most famous Boğazkere wine is called Buzbağ, grown in the Anatolia region near the Euphrates River. It is sometimes produced in an ice wine fashion, with the grapes allowed to hang on the vine until the first frost, and then crushed while the grapes are still frozen. Historically, the area where Buzbağ is produced is considered the probable birthplace of wine. The biblical account of Noah after the flood has him planting a vineyard near the area where the ark landed. This area is presumed to be Mt. Ararat, where Buzbağ is still being produced today by the Turkish state-run vineyards of Tekel near the town of Elazığ, the source of the Euphrates River and the birthplace of civilization.

Bordeaux (Roald Dahl): Strictly speaking, Bordeaux does not belong in this list, as it is the name of a region and a type of wine, not a grape varietal. Bordeaux wines are a traditional blend of six different grapes as described elsewhere under "Claret." In his magnificent short story, "Taste," the English writer Roald Dahl describes a not-so-friendly wager between two men to identify the vineyard and the vintage of a specific bottle of Bordeaux. In describing the thought processes of the man doing the blind tasting, the author proves himself to be a sublime master of the Médoc:

"First, then, which district in Bordeaux does this wine come from? That's not too difficult to guess. It is far too light in the body to be from either St Emilion or Graves. It is obviously a Médoc. There's no doubt about that. Now—from which commune in Médoc does it come? That also, by elimination, should not be too difficult to decide. Margaux? No. It cannot be Margaux. It has not the violent bouquet of a Margaux. Pauillac? It cannot be Pauillac, either. It is too tender, too gentle and wistful for Pauillac. The wine of Pauillac has a character that is almost imperious in its taste, And also, to me, a Pauillac contains just a little pith, a curious dusty, pithy flavour that the grape acquires from the soil of the district. No, no. This—this is a very gentle wine, demure and bashful in the first taste, emerging shyly but quite graciously in the second. A little arch, perhaps, in the second taste, and a little naughty also, teasing the tongue with a trace, just a trace of tannin. Then, in the after-taste, delightful consoling and feminine, with a certain blithely generous quality that one associates only with the wines of the commune of St Julien. Unmistakably this is a St Julien."

The wine expert in this most delightful story, using the same unrelenting logic, finally even identifies the name of the small and little-known vineyard where the wine was grown and bottled.

Brunello (Richard Condon): Brunello is a Sangiovese clone grown around the Tuscan village of Montalcino, where the wine is known as Brunello di Montalcino. It is one of Italy's best-known and most expensive wines. According to the American novelist Richard Condon, Brunello di Montalcino is considered to be the only acceptable wine to offer well-connected New York family men of Sicilian extraction.

Cabernet Franc is a red wine grape that is often used in Bordeaux blends to add acidity and aroma. DNA testing indicates that, crossed with Sauvignon Blanc, it is the parent of Cabernet Sauvignon and makes wines that are lighter and fruitier than Cabernet Sauvignon. Mostly planted in the Bordeaux region for blending, it is actually better known in the Loire valley, particularly Chinon, Anjou, and Saumur, where it produces elegant, earthy wines that accompany just about any food. In Bordeaux, Cabernet Franc is usually employed as a minor (10-15 percent) component in a blend with other varieties. The only notable exception is at Château Cheval Blanc in St.-Émilion which contains 57 percent Cabernet Franc, 40 percent Merlot, and 3 percent Malbec. The American wine critic, Robert Parker, gave an unfavorable review of Château Cheval Blanc's 1981 vintage in a widely circulated article. On Parker's next visit to the Château, the owner's dog bit his leg and drew blood. Parker asked the owner for a bandage, and was handed instead a copy of the offending magazine article and instructed to use that to staunch the bleeding.

Cabernet Sauvignon (Charles Dickens): Whether it was the best of times or whether it was the worst of times; whether the vineyard was north of the Equator or south—the first grape varietal to be planted would usually be Cabernet Sauvignon. If Dickens is the world's most widely-read author, this small, dark, almost black, thick-skinned grape is perhaps the world's best-known and most-widely grown red wine varietal. Originally from the Bordeaux region of France, it is now to be found both north and south of the equator in a wide variety of climatic conditions. Since first being discovered as an accidental cross between Cabernet Franc and Sauvignon Blanc, two of the predominant grapes grown in Southwest France, Cabernet Sauvignon has been the major component of Claret—the red wine blended in Bordeaux for the English market. Traditional Claret (or Bordeaux) is a blend of six grapes—Cabernet Franc, Merlot, Malbec, Petit Verdot, and Carménère—but by far the most important component is Cabernet Sauvignon.

One of the reasons for the popularity of Cabernet Sauvignon is its ease of cultivation. The grapes are small and dark, the skins are thick and tough, the roots are strong and resistant to frost and disease, and the vine is tolerant of a wide range of climatic conditions—with the result that it is grown just about everywhere that wine is made. This is the Charles Dickens of grapes. Dickens' novels are read everywhere, and have been translated into every language on earth. Like the grape, his stories are resilient and universal; originally inspired by the English market, they have now been blended and integrated into a wide variety of cultures. It is hard to imagine any wine-producing country where they do not grow Cabernet Sauvignon and also read Charles Dickens.

A consequence of the small grapes having thick skins is that the resulting juice of Cabernet Sauvignon is high in tannins and phenols. The concentration of phenols and tannins create a powerful complexity of taste and flavors, but also requires many years of aging before the tannins have mellowed enough to be drinkable. Typically, Cabernets taste of dark cherry, cedar, tobacco, and black currant, while cool climate growth can add green pepper or olive flavors. Up to eighteen months of aging in small oak barrels before bottling Cabernet is common in order to achieve more complexity. For exceptional vintages, especially in Bordeaux, the wine spends even longer in the oak.

This need for aging was ideal for the English market. Not only did these more complex wines appeal to the English taste, but both English and Dutch navies would load up with Cabernet Sauvignon-based wines for the long sea voyages to their empires in the Far East.

President Jefferson, by the end of the eighteenth century, was already laying down Bordeaux's Cabernet Sauvignon wines for aging—most notably Château Haut-Brion—and the grape's reputation through the nineteenth and twentieth centuries has been based on its ability to age, to improve, and develop complexities over the decades.

Another factor which increased the tannic nature of the Bordeaux wines was the local habit of allowing maceration (when the juice is exposed to the skins) to continue for as long as three weeks. Southwest France is rich in game, and the local winemakers insisted on enjoying a three week hunting holiday following the hard work of the harvest. Because they had spent so long macerating, these highly tannic wines required as long as twenty years of aging before they were drinkable. Modern winemakers tend to forgo the hunting trip and macerate for just a few days in order to make the wine more immediately accessible.

Cabernet Sauvignon has a natural affinity for oak when it is fermented and/or aged in oak barrels. Not only does the oak absorb and mellow the grape's high tannins—thus speeding the aging process—but the barrel's natural flavors of spice and vanilla perfectly complement the blackcurrant and tobacco flavors of Cabernet Sauvignon.

Although Cabernet Sauvignon will always be associated with the wines of Bordeaux, the grape is now inseparable from California's Napa Valley, where it is bottled as 100 percent Cabernet Sauvignon rather than blended as in Bordeaux. Cabernet Sauvignon also created some controversy in Italy when it was blended with Sangiovese to create Super Tuscans.

Because of its international popularity, historic reputation, and ease of cultivation, Cabernet Sauvignon is now grown all over the world. At the same time, its very popularity has created a certain resistance, and it is often resented as a "foreign" vine and a "colonizer." Dickens, too, during his first visit to America, was widely criticized in the press for complaining that his work was pirated. As a foreigner, the US press argued, he should be grateful that he was popular enough to be copied.

Carignan is a high-yielding red wine grape that was so widely planted in Spain, Italy, and France that it was considered responsible for Europe's "wine lake" until, in the 1990s, farmers were actually paid to uproot and destroy their vines. Too tannic and acidic to be drunk alone, it was traditionally used for blending and adding color to other varietals such as Grenache. Originally planted by the Phoenicians almost three thousand years ago, the varietal is now found all over the world, and until recently was one of the most-widely planted of all varietals.

Carménère (Harper Lee): A member of the Cabernet family of grapes, the name Carménère comes from the French word for crimson (*carmin*), both for the crimson color the leaves display in autumn and also for the dark red color of the wine. The color is so deep and rich that it seems almost black in the bottle and in the glass, until you tilt it, and light filters through and changes the edge to violet. In addition to the deep red color, Carménère wine offers the aromas found in red fruits, spices, and berries. Carménère is also known as Grande Vidure, and is one of the original six varietals from Bordeaux, along with Cabernet Sauvignon, Cabernet Franc, Merlot, Malbec, and Petit Verdot, which were blended by the English to make the wine known as Claret. Carménère produces a medium-body wine with tannins gentler and softer than those in Cabernet Sauvignon, and is best drunk young.

After the ravages of Phylloxera in the late nineteenth century, it was believed that the Carménère vines had all been lost and it was never replanted. However, DNA testing on what was thought to be a type of Merlot found in Chile during the late twentieth century proved it to be the long-lost Carménère. For some reason, Chile is one of the only countries in the world that was not affected by Phylloxera, which is how the varietal survived. As such, Chile produces the vast majority of Carménère wines available today, and as the Chilean wine industry grows, more experimentation is being carried out on Carménère's potential as a blending grape, especially with Cabernet Sauvignon and also with the country's original grape, Pais.

The obvious literary pairing must be with Harper Lee, the much-revered author of that great American classic, *To Kill a Mockingbird*. Since the publication of *Mockingbird* in 1960, Lee had retired from public life to her hometown in Alabama. *Mockingbird* was believed to be her only novel. In fact, she had written an earlier novel in 1957, which was titled *Go Set a Watchman*, but the manuscript had somehow become lost. For the next fifty-seven years, the lost manuscript lay hidden and forgotten in a safety deposit box in Lee's hometown, Monroeville, Alabama. Just as the "lost" Carménère grape was "rediscovered" in

Chile in 1994, so too the "lost" manuscript of *Go Set a Watchman* was rediscovered and published in 2015.

Chardonnay (Jane Austen): Chardonnay is a classic green-skinned, white wine grape grown all around the world. The original fame of Chardonnay comes from its success in the Burgundy and Champagne regions of France. White Burgundy must be made from the Chardonnay grape unless the label indicates it was made from a much less well-known grape, Aligote. Until the 1960s, Chardonnay was almost unknown outside of Burgundy and Champagne, yet suddenly, within twenty years it was being grown everywhere.

Traditionally in Burgundy—especially in Chablis—the limestone soil and the cool climate gives Chardonnay a citrusy and slightly chalky taste with an acidic edge. Chardonnays from the New World, however, are far less austere, and are noted for their riper and more full-bodied texture. This is why many Americans are disappointed when they taste what they perceive as thin and sharp French Chardonnays, and why the French are dismissive of what they perceive as the vulgar and sugary Chardonnays from California. Of all the wine-producing regions of the New World, Oregon, with its cool climate and similar limestone soil, produces a Chardonnay closest to the French original.

More than any other varietal, Chardonnay represents New World winemaking: fruity, full-bodied, flavorful, and delicious. The Australians were the first to produce the new mouth-filling, easy-to-drink Chardonnays, but they were swiftly copied by Californian, South African, and South American winemakers.

Since the first plantings of Chardonnay by the Cistercian monks in twelfth century Chablis, the Chardonnay grape has now spread all over the world and is grown in more wine regions than any other grape—including Cabernet Sauvignon. One reason for its popularity

was of course the success of Californian Chardonnays in the 1976
Judgment of Paris, but more important is its ease of cultivation. Its early-
budding feature makes it well adapted to regions with short growing
seasons, and although it prefers the chalk, clay, and limestone soils
of Burgundy, it adapts to almost any soil conditions. Chardonnay is a
very robustly forgiving grape and extremely malleable, which is why
most new vineyards and wine regions begin by planting Chardonnay.

Chardonnay is described as neutral and "malleable," meaning that its
flavors and texture reflect the terroir where it is grown and the style of
the individual winemaker. There is a very clear difference, for example,
between the delicately mineral tastes of the classic Chardonnays from
the Côtes de Beaune in Burgundy and the powerfully, oaky and fruit-
forward flavors of the Chardonnays from Australia. Chardonnays
grown elsewhere in the world usually try to imitate either the big
Australian-style or the more traditional and delicate Burgundy-style.

Chardonnay takes oak well, and many higher-priced Chardonnays
are typically fermented and aged in oak barrels. When Chardonnay
is aged in oak barrels, it may pick up vanilla overtones in its aromas
and flavor. Chardonnay is also the dominant grape in the best of the
world's sparkling wines. Champagne in France, and some Cava in
Spain, are made from a blend of Chardonnay with Pinot Noir.

Chardonnay also ages well in the bottle, though it will not age as
long as Riesling or many red wines. It likes slightly cooler climates
(warm days/cool nights), and develops less acidity than Sauvignon
Blanc. Some producers put their Chardonnay (or some of it) through
malolactic fermentation, which reduces crispness and brings out a rich,
buttery taste. This usually shortens the life of the wine as far as aging
is concerned. Chardonnay matches very well with chicken and with
dishes that are served with a lot of butter or a cream sauce. Unlike

Sauvignon Blanc or Riesling, most Chardonnays lack the acid to pair well with seafood.

The sudden worldwide popularity of Chardonnay, starting in the 1980s, especially among the "Bridget Jones'" generation of the 1990s, has led to a backlash called the "ABC movement:"Anything But Chardonnay. Nevertheless, Chardonnay remains one of the world's most widely-planted grape varieties.

It is a truth, universally acknowledged, that anywhere in the world that people gather for wine and cheese, Chardonnay is always to be found. In the same way, like Dickens and Cabernet Sauvignon, Jane Austen and Chardonnay have a universal appeal. On the surface, her novels portray the prim gentility of English country life, but the careful reader soon sees the archly humorous and even passionate currents that roil beneath. The original Chardonnays from the limestone vineyards of Burgundy were noted for their acidic edge, but the more recent versions from Australia and California show a softer and more accessible body. Like the oaky and buttery Chardonnays of California, recent costume dramas from the BBC and Hollywood have made straitlaced Jane every girl's bff.

Chasselas: A white wine grape, mostly grown in Switzerland in the Canton of Vaud but also in the Loire valley of France where it is blended with Sauvignon Blanc to produce a wine known as Pouilly-sur-Loire, after the village where it is grown. Chasselas is a full-bodied, dry wine, fruity with a silky texture. An especially delicious example of Chasselas is served on the SBB Swiss Train service, and one of life's finer pleasures is sipping a glass from a chilled bottle of *Aigles les Murailles* while watching the Alps slowly drift past the carriage window.

Chenin Blanc (Rabelais): Chenin Blanc is a white grape that is commonly grown in the middle Loire Valley of France. It is also cultivated in South Africa and California. It makes white wines that are fragrant and high in acid. Chenin Blanc can make wines that range in style, from dry to very sweet, depending on decisions made by the individual winemaker subject to the specific conditions of the season. The town of Vouvray, in Touraine on the Loire, for example, is famous for sweet, dry and sparkling versions of Chenin Blanc. Because of the high acidity in wines made from Chenin Blanc, they tend to age very well. In Saumur, also on the Loire, Chenin Blanc is used to make sparkling wines of notable quality. Between Saumur and Vouvray lies the historic town of Chinon, whose wines were immortalized by Rabelais, the fifteenth century writer, humanist, physician, and philosopher. His writings, most notably *Gargantua and Pantagruel*, are wild, bawdy, and drunken fantasies filled with fornicating friars and naughty nuns, but all of whom swear by the healing powers of the Chenin Blanc wines from the vineyards of Chinon. Just as the Chenin Blanc wine can be extremely dry or extremely sweet, so too the writings of Rabelais range from the most lewd and vulgar to the most profound, and he is regarded as one of the fathers of modern European literature.

Chenin Blanc is known elsewhere as Pineau de la Loire. It is the most-planted grape in South Africa, where its local name is Steen. Chenin Blanc is a high volume producer, so the wines it produces tend to be fairly inexpensive. Western Australia's Margaret River produces some of the world's finest Chenin Blanc, but, because of its remoteness, they are hard to find in America.

Cinsaut is a red wine grape, very heat-tolerant and high-yielding. Both these qualities made it especially popular to French winegrowers in Languedoc-Roussillon and across the sea in Algeria and Morocco. The bulk wines of Cinsaut were used for blending with more prestigious wines, to which they added softness and bouquet. Following the Phylloxera epidemic, most vineyards in South Africa were replanted with Cinsaut, which was locally called Hermitage. Crossed with Pinot Noir, it became Pinotage, the signature wine of South Africa.

Claret (Keats): Claret is the name of the red wine blended in Bordeaux for the English market. Six grapes are permitted to be used in the blend: Cabernet Sauvignon for its tannins, Merlot for its softer fruitiness, Carménère for its rich aromas, Cabernet Franc for its earthiness, Malbec for its dark color, and Petit Verdot for its structure and body. In the Middle Ages, the wine was called "vinum clairum" or "vin clar," from which the English derived the term claret. Today, there is a Bordeaux dark rosé wine called "Clairet," which is full-bodied and deep-colored, and apparently similar to the original claret. Californian winemakers have recently begun blending wines in imitation of this Bordeaux/Claret style, which they label as Meritage.

In terms of literary pairings, there is no question that the honor must go to the English poet John Keats. In the spring of 1819, he wrote to his brother George as follows:

"Now I like Claret and whenever I can have Claret I must drink it. It is the only palate affair that I am at all sensual in. For really it is so fine. It fills the mouth, one's mouth with a gushing freshness, then goes down cool and feverless, then you do not feel it quarrelling with your liver, no it is rather a Peace maker and lies as quiet as it did in the grape. Then it is as fragrant as the Queen Bee; and the more ethereal part of it mounts into the brain, not assaulting the cerebral apartments like a bully in a bad house looking for his trul and hurrying from door to door bouncing against the wainscot; but rather walks like Aladdin about his own enchanted palace so gently that you do not feel his step. Other wines of a heavy and spirituous nature transform a Man into a Silenus;

this makes him a Hermes, and gives a Woman the soul and immortality of Ariadne for whom Bacchus always kept a good cellar of claret."

Colombard: A white grape widely-planted on the west coast of France for making Armagnac and Cognac brandy. It is also grown in California for making jug wines.

Concord: Concord is a grape made from the Native American vine, *Vitis labrusca*. It is mainly used for table grapes and jellies, but is also sometimes used for winemaking in the Eastern USA and Canada. It is said to be distinguished by its "foxy" taste (whatever that might mean).

Corvina (Dante): Along with the varietals Rondinella and Molinara, this is the principal grape which makes the famous wines of Verona, on Lake Garda: Valpolicella and Amarone. Valpolicella wine has dark cherry and spice flavors. After the grapes undergo appassimento (a drying process), the wine is called Amarone and is extremely high in alcohol (16 percent and higher), and full of raisin, prune, and syrupy fruits. Some Amarones can age for over forty years and command spectacular prices. In December 2009, Amarone di Valpolicella was finally awarded its long-deserved DOCG status.

Although Dante Alighieri will forever be associated with Florence and the Chianti wines of Tuscany, he also spent several years of his exile in Verona. His son, Pietro, came to love the beauty of the city and its countryside, and so decided to remain in the area, purchasing the Casal dei Ronchi in Gargagnago estate in the heart of the historic Valpolicella region in 1353. Twenty-one generations later, both house and estate still belong to Dante's direct descendants, the Counts Serego Alighieri. Today, the Villa stands surrounded by Valpolicella vineyards, the center of traditional farming activities associated with a large and flourishing estate, with the nearby Foresteria providing accommodation for guests—no doubt in descending levels of hospitality and comfort.

Crljenak Kaštelanski: (See Zinfandel)

Dolcetto: A grape that grows alongside Barbera and Nebbiolo in Piedmont, its name means "little sweet one," referring not to the taste of the wine, but the ease with which it grows, and makes great wines suitable for everyday drinking. Flavors of licorice, cherry, wild blackberries, and herbs permeate the wine. Because the skins are high in tannins, the wines are very dark, with a bitter finish to the taste.

Gamay (Keats): Perhaps more than any other grape varietal, Gamay identifies with a single geographic location. More than half of the world's Gamay grapes are grown in the Beaujolais region around Lyon in Southern Burgundy. The Gamay vine is far easier to grow than Pinot Noir, for example; it flowers early and produces prolifically, resulting in generous harvest of juice. The city of Lyon is located at the confluence of the Rhône and Saône rivers, and because the Gamay grape produces so much wine, it is known as the "third river of Lyon." But what it offers in quantity, it lacks in quality; the Gamay wines are pale for red wines, high in acid and low in alcohol. They do, however, make a refreshingly light, midday drink, and are the first wines in France permitted to be sold after harvest. Beaujolais Nouveau, made from the Gamay grape, is permitted to be sold as early as the third Thursday in November.

The Gamay grape is the only varietal grown in Beaujolais, just as the Pinot Noir is the only red varietal grown across the border in Burgundy. A July 1395 edict of Philip the Bold, Duke of Burgundy described the Gamay grape as being an "evil and disloyal plant with very great and terrible bitterness … injurious to the human creature." He banned it from the Dukedom and ordered all vines to be "extirpated, destroyed and reduced to nothing."

Despite the poor reputation the wine has developed over the past few decades because of the rage for Beaujolais Nouveau, Beaujolais is still a delightful lunchtime drink, and John Keats, in his *Ode to a Skylark*, can only have been referring to Beaujolais when he wrote:

O for a beaker full of the warm South,
Full of the true, the blushful Hippocrene,
With beaded bubbles winking at the brim,
And purple-stained mouth;

Gewürztraminer (Marcel Proust): Gewürztraminer is noted for its floral fragrance and spicy flavors. It was originally a clone of the Traminer grape from the village of Tramin in the Tyrol of Northern Italy, which was for a long time part of the Austrian empire. The musqué, or more floral version of the Traminer grape, is now so widely grown that Gewürztraminer is now considered a grape variety in its own right. Widely planted in the Rhineland of Germany, it has found its greatest success across the French border in Alsace. Because it thrives best in cool rather than warm climates, it is also grown successfully in Northern California, Oregon, Washington, Germany, and New Zealand. However, the Gewürztraminers of Alsace are in a superior class all by themselves.

Gewürztraminer is often paired with spicy foods, and some argue that it is one of the few wines which can be successfully paired with Asian cuisine. Others disagree strongly. Gewürztraminer can be made in styles that range from completely dry to semi-dry, and can also be made in a late harvest dessert wine style that is delicious. This is especially true in Alsace. When you taste your first glass of Alsatian Gewürztraminer, you will imagine that somebody has entered the room with a bouquet of fresh flowers whose aroma of floral purity acknowledges all your better virtues, and will give you the power and determination to become a more worthy person, better able to live up to all the subtle promises of the wine's bouquet.

As a literary pairing, the Gewürztraminer of Alsace deserves no lesser a writer than Marcel Proust, and not just because his mother, Jeanne Weil's, family came from Alsace. Despite the wine's underlying acidity, its sharpness and acuity is hidden behind a rich, floral bouquet that charms with a mellifluous harmony that simply overwhelms the senses. In the same way, Proust, the writer, hides his sharp and extremely comic insights into human nature behind a screen of poetically seductive images. The first taste from a glass of Gewürztraminer, or a random passage read from *In Search of Lost Time,* leaves us standing alone in ecstasy, inhaling through the rain, the lingering scent of invisible lilacs.

On a personal note, the Gewürztraminer of Alsace is my favorite white wine, and Marcel Proust is my favorite novelist of all time. Case closed!

Grenache/Garnacha is a soft, spicy grape, and is one of the most-widely planted in the world. It is extensively planted along the Mediterranean coast particularly, between Northern Spain and the Rhône valley in France. The Grenache produces wines that, in their youth, are fruity, full of flavor, and have overtones of spice. Wines made from the Grenache are usually light in color and are often blended with other grape varieties. The Grenache grape resists heat and tolerates limited rainfall.

In France, Grenache is used in making red and rosé (Tavel and Lirac) wines in the Rhône river valley where it is widely planted. Grenache is also widely-planted in Spain, where it is known as Garnacha Tinta, and in Catalonia and Mallorca, where it is called Garnatxa. In the United States, it is grown in California, where it is almost exclusively a blending grape for rosé wines. Lacking tannins or color, Grenache is not known for producing wines that age well over a long period of time. This tends to be the "go-to" red wine for white wine drinkers, and are usually best consumed when young.

Grüner Veltliner (Hašek): Gruner Veltliner is the most popular grape variety in Austria—white, light, and peppery. Delicious when young and lively, but it also can be aged as long as five years. If Riesling is the grape of the Rhine, Grüner Veltliner is the grape of the Danube, and grows widely in the Czech Republic, Hungary, and Slovakia, as well as in Austria. Like most of the other white wines, it is best enjoyed young, fresh, and innocent.

What could be more fresh, young, and innocent, than the *Good Soldier Švejk*, stumbling hilariously around the Danube river and Bohemia during the farcical collapse of the Hapsburg Empire during the First World War? Like Joseph Heller's novel *Catch 22*, Jaroslav Hašek's sadly unfinished novel about a Czech dealer in stolen dogs who signs up for the Austrian army is a classic of military satire. Surrounded by the pomposity and inefficiency of the Austro-Hungarian bureaucracy, batman Švejk's hilarious stories and misadventures are as refreshing and peppery as a fresh glass of Gruner Veltliner.

Malbec (Borges): Malbec is one of the six grape varieties approved for making red wines in the Bordeaux region of France where it originated. In Bordeaux, Malbec is used like a spice, blended with other wines for its strong dark color (but making up a very small percentage of the final blend), and is being grown less and less every year. The only place in France where Malbec is bottled unblended is around the town of Cahors, slightly southeast of Bordeaux.

On the other hand, Malbec has found a new home and a new following in Argentina. Some of the best Malbecs can be described as dry, mouth-filling, and sumptuous. Elsewhere in the world, Malbec is only planted in small amounts. Malbec is usually included in plantings and blends simply because of its background in Bordeaux. It is a thin-skinned grape that needs more sun and heat than either Cabernet Sauvignon or Merlot to mature.

For some reason, the hot, dry conditions of the high-altitude Andean vineyards of Argentina and even Bolivia have proved to be perfect for the Malbec grape, and have finally revealed its full, glorious potential. Powerful and full-bodied Malbec wines from Mendoza Province are now the backbone of a rejuvenated Argentinian wine industry.

Just as it was the hitherto ignored Malbec grape which heralded and championed the dramatic arrival of Argentinian wines upon the world stage, so too it was the writings of an obscure Argentinian librarian, Jorge Luis Borges, that introduced the world to Latin American literature. The success of Borges' short stories in the late '50s introduced the world to magical realism, and the writings of Gabriel Garcia Marquez, Mario Vargas Llosa, and Carlos Fuentes.

Borges' stories are filled with extremes: a man who forgets no experience in his life, a library that contains every possible arrangement of letters in a 410 page text, a small sphere from which it is possible to view every single part of the universe, and a garden of forking paths which lead in every possible direction. Malbec too is a vine of extremes; while vineyards in Europe are seldom planted higher than 1,500 feet, Malbec vineyards in Mendoza are planted as high as five thousand feet and more.

In his poetry, Borges often referred to wine and how it flowed through time as well as cultures, linking his own history to that of the Babylonians, with whom he was fascinated and who feature in many of his poems, like "To Wine:":

> *Wine, flows red along with the generations*
> *and on the arduous road like the river of time*
> *pours on us its music, its fire and its lions.*
> *On the night of joy or on the hostile day*
> *it exalts the glee or soothes the horror...*

Malvasia (Shakespeare): Known in France as Malvoisie and related to the ancient Greek grape Malagousia, this light-skinned grape is grown all over the Mediterranean, especially in Italy and Spain and even out in the Atlantic, where it makes Madeira, known by the English as Malmsey. It was, of course, in a barrel of Malmsey that, according to Shakespeare, the Duke of Clarence was drowned by order of his brother, Richard III.

Marsanne & Roussanne: Marsanne and Roussanne are both white grapes mainly grown in the Rhône valley. Though both can be bottled and drunk by themselves, they are more usually blended together or with other varietals. Along with Viognier, these are the only three white grape varietals permitted in the Northern Rhône. Marsanne tends to be full-bodied and deep-colored while Rosanne is noted more for what wine critic Jancis Robinson calls its "haunting aroma."

Melon de Bourgogne: See Muscadet

Meritage: See Claret.

Merlot (F. Scott Fitzgerald): Unlike the small dark berries of Cabernet Sauvignon, Merlot grapes are characterized by loose bunches of lighter-hued grapes with thinner skins and thus less tannin and malic acids, but more sugar. Like the Chardonnay grape, Merlot is an early-ripening, easily-grown, and forgiving varietal. Originally grown in Bordeaux, it was traditionally used for blending and adding more softness and fleshiness to the harsher and more tannic Cabernet Sauvignon. Not only is Merlot usually grown in the same regions and often blended with Cabernet Sauvignon, but the two varietals are close cousins and share many characteristics. Though grown in the same regions as Cabernet Sauvignon, Merlot is usually grown in the cooler part of the region so as not to ripen too early. Lower in tannins, Merlot makes wines that mature faster and are softer in texture, both of which have caused its surge in popularity since the early 1990s. At its best, Merlot makes a wine that is dry, rich in flavor, and smooth, as it settles in your throat. At its worst, Merlot makes wine that is dry but thin in taste and texture, and disappointingly mediocre to drink.

Merlot usually has ripe berry components in the bouquet. Its wines tend to be soft, fruity, and smooth in texture, but vary widely in quality around the world depending on location and producer. Although it is more susceptible to fungus and mold diseases, and therefore more challenging to grow, Merlot is able to mature in regions that are cooler than those required for Cabernet Sauvignon. Select Merlots can have long aging potential, but most are ready to consume in four to eight years. Wherever it is grown, Merlot is usually bottled in a Bordeaux (high shouldered) bottle.

First recognized internationally for its success on the right bank of Bordeaux, in the Saint-Émilion and Pomerol AOCs, Merlot has recently become one of the most popular and widely-planted varietals in the world. Not even included in the 1855 Bordeaux classification of great wines, which were dominated by the Cabernet Sauvignons of the left bank, certain Pomerols and St.-Émilions now command higher prices than even the Medoc first growths. Château Petrus from Pomerol is the stellar example of fine Merlot. When the garagiste revolution occurred in Bordeaux in the 1990s, it was in Pomerol, using Merlot grapes, that the movement began.

Morley Safer's *60 Minutes* broadcast in 1991 exploring "The French Paradox" of why French people are so slim and healthy, even though they eat rich foods and drink lots of red wine, suggested that the key was Merlot. Following the broadcast, many Americans concluded, they could live longer, happier, slimmer, more elegant, and sexually-fulfilled lives by drinking lots of Merlot. Merlot enjoyed an immediate surge in popularity, and additional acreage was planted in many major wine-producing regions. Merlot has since become the major red wine grape in Washington State, where the long days of sunshine and the cool nights provide ideal growing conditions. Not coincidently, Washington State is just a couple degrees north of Bordeaux—the original home of Merlot.

Merlot is the F. Scott Fitzgerald of the wine world. Merlot was suddenly "discovered" and became all the rage in America during the final decade of the twentieth century, just as Fitzgerald, with the publication of *This Side of Paradise,* had became all the rage during the second decade. Because it was softer on the palette and matured far sooner, there was a widespread belief that Merlot would supplant Cabernet Sauvignon as the grape of choice for great red wines. Indeed, during the Merlot wine craze of the 1990s, many Californian vineyards were torn up and replanted exclusively with Merlot vines. Unfortunately, the vine did not live up to expectations, and by 2004, with the release of the movie *Sideways,* California had a surplus glut of Merlot vines.

Similarly, Fitzgerald, hailed as the "chronicler of the Jazz Age," was expected to follow his first novel with a string of best-sellers, but proved a disappointment. His talents were dissipated in less successful novels and a string of short stories for magazines, and hack-work for Hollywood. However, with his glamorous and opulent lifestyle and productive literary output, he seemed full of promise at the time, and it is only with hindsight that we sense our disappointment both for the wine and the writer. Nonetheless, despite the mediocre bottles of Merlot, and the pages of mediocre writings, some masterpieces stand out. Château Petrus, a Merlot wine from Pomerol, is one of the greatest—if not the most expensive—wines on the market, while Fitzgerald's novel *The Great Gatsby* is still regarded as one of the greatest and most popular American novels ever written.

Mission: The Mission grape is the name given to the European grape first introduced into the New World by the Spanish Conquistador Herman Cortez in 1524. Cortez insisted that in return for land, all Spanish settlers had to plant a vineyard with the original vines he had brought from Spain. Vineyards were planted in Mexico, Peru, Bolivia, and Chile, where the vine was named Pais and remained the most common wine varietal in Chile until the twenty-first Century. In Argentina and Bolivia, the same grape is known as Criolla Chica. When the Spanish moved north, into what is now California, they took these original vines with them, and planted vineyards at each of the twenty-one missions they founded along the Pacific coastline, from San Diego to San Francisco. Since nobody knew what else to call these grapes, they were called Mission grapes, and were used to make the first wine in North America.

Since all the Spanish Atlantic Fleets sailed from Cadiz, the ships would have been provisioned locally with food, wine, and other supplies. The local vine in the Cadiz region is the Palomino grape from which Sherry is made. Recent DNA testing has shown that these original American grapes—whether known as "Pais," "Criolla," "Mission," or "Spanish Black,"—just like the Listán Negro grapes of the Canary Islands, are all descendants of the Palomino grape of Cadiz, grown in vineyards first planted by the Phoenicians in AD 1100—more than three thousand years ago!

The other vine that Cortez imported was Muscat of Alexandria, a white wine grape that is considered to be the oldest unmodified varietal in the world. These two grape varietals are the parental source of all South American grape varietals.

In a detailed DNA analysis of all South American vines entitled "Determining the Spanish Origin of Representative Ancient American

Grapevine Varieties" by professors Alejandra Milla Tapia, et al., they make the following conclusion:

"Genotypic analysis of ancient grapevine accessions from Argentina, Bolivia, Chile, Peru, and the United States reveals that most correspond to two ancient cultivars still cultivated in Spain: Muscat of Alexandria and Listán Prieto (or Palomino). The latter is grown throughout North and South America under different names such as País, Criolla Chica, Negra Peruana, Misión, and Mission. Most remaining ancient American cultivar genotypes analyzed correspond to hybrid progeny of Muscat of Alexandria, Palomino / Listán Prieto, or both. We conclude that these two cultivars are major founders of ancient American viticulture."

Montepulciano is a red Italian wine grape that is most noted for being the primary grape behind the Denominazione di Origine Controllata e Garantita (DOCG) wine Montepulciano d'Abruzzo, and the DOC wines Colline Teramane, Rosso Conero, and Rosso Piceno. It should not be confused with the similarly named Tuscan wine Vino Nobile di Montepulciano, which is made predominantly from Sangiovese grapes and is named for the village it is produced in, rather than for the grape it is made from.

The grape is widely planted throughout central and southern Italy, most notably in Abruzzi, Latium, Marche, Molise, Umbria, and Apulia, and is a permitted variety in DOC wines produced in twenty of Italy's ninety-five provinces. Montepulciano is rarely found in Northern Italy, because the grape has a tendency to ripen late and can be excessively "green" if harvested too early. When fully ripened, Montepulciano can produce deeply colored wines with moderate acidity and noticeable alcohol levels.

Moschofilero: This pink-skinned grape from the high plateau of the Greek central Peloponnesian peninsula produces notably aromatic white and rose wines which are light, crisp, and low in alcohol. With fresh scents of limes and roses, this makes the perfect al fresco wine for summer picnics.

Mourvèdre / Monastrell is a late-ripening red grape variety that is widely planted along the French and Spanish coasts of the Mediterranean Sea. It is used in the Rhône river valley of France, where it is typically blended with Syrah and Grenache in wines such as Côtes du Rhône and Châteauneuf du Pape. Mourvèdre performs well in warmer growing areas and well-drained (even stony) soils. Its wines are medium-bodied tannic wines high in alcohol, deeply colored and full of fruit (cherry and berries). Thanks to the tannins, it can improve for up to ten years when stored properly. In Australia and California, Mourvèdre is increasingly being blended with Grenache and Syrah in a Rhône-style blend known as GSM.

Müller-Thurgau: Müller-Thurgau is an alternative but inferior grape to Riesling that growers have been using in Germany. Unlike the long ripening time of Riesling, this grape variety only requires one hundred days to ripen, can be planted on more sites, and is higher yielding. However, this grape has a more neutral flavor than Riesling and, as the main ingredient of *Liebfraumilch,* its reputation has taken a beating together with that particular wine. Germany's most planted variety from the 1970s to the mid-1990s, it has been losing ground for a number of years to Sylvaner and Riesling. Dry Müller-Thurgau is usually labeled Rivaner. For a while, Müller-Thurgau was planted all over New Zealand with disastrous results. Any bottle of German wine which is not labeled "Riesling" is probably made from Müller-Thurgau.

Muscadet/Melon is a white French wine. It is made at the western end of the Loire Valley, near the city of Nantes. More Muscadet is produced than any other Loire wine. It is made from the Melon de Bourgogne grape, often referred to simply as Melon. As a rule, in France, Appellation D'Origine Contrôlée wines are named either after their growing region or after their varietal (the latter in Alsace only). The name "Muscadet" is, therefore, an exception. The name seems to refer to a characteristic of the wine produced by the melon grape varietal: *vin qui a un goût musqué*, wine with a musk-like taste. The sole varietal used to produce Muscadet, Melon de Bourgogne, was initially planted in the region sometime in or before the seventeenth century. It became dominant after a hard freeze in 1709 killed most of the region's other vines. Dutch traders who were major players in the local wine trade encouraged the planting of this varietal, and distilled much of the wine produced into *eau de vie*, brandy, for sale in Northern Europe.

Muscat/Moscato: The Muscat family includes many varieties of grapes that produce big crops and make wines that are generally sweet and very floral. The fact that Muscat wines are so hardy and hearty and able to survive in the driest and most difficult conditions, explains why they are considered to be the oldest grapes in the world. It is known as Moscato in Italy and Moscatel in Spain. It is the grape used to produce Asti Spumante, the sweet sparkling wine from Italy, as well as Tokaji, the sweet botrytized wine of Hungary. Grown mainly in Piedmont, it is used in the slightly sparkling (frizzante), semi-sweet Moscato d'Asti. Not to be confused with Moscato giallo and Moscato rosa, two Germanic varietals that are grown in Trentino Alto-Adige of northeastern Italy.

Muscat of Alexandria is considered to be one of the oldest genetically unmodified vines still in existence, and along with Palomino, was one of the two grape varietals first brought from Spain by the Conquistadores. Muscat of Alexandria is still an important wine in South America, especially Bolivia and Argentina, where, along with

Palomino, it is the parental vine of most American varietals such as Torrontés (see Mission).

Musqué (C.K. Scott Moncrieff): Musqué is not an actual grape varietal; it is a French term used to describe certain sub-varietals, or clones of grapes, which are highly aromatic. Just like the Muscat family of grapes, the Musqué wines are perfumed and decidedly floral. Chardonnay Musqué or Sauvignon Blanc Musqué are notably perfumed versions of the original grape. Gewürztraminer is perhaps the most well-known example of a Musqué varietal, being an aromatic clone of the Traminer grape originally found in the northern Italian region of Tyrol.

Because it is not an actual varietal itself, merely a version of the original, then the literary pairing should be with a translator rather than the original writer. C.K. Scott Moncrief was a much-decorated soldier in the Great War, and was also an inter-war British intelligence agent as well as being a close friend of most of the literary figures of his time. It was Moncrieff who created the very first, and many argue, the very best, translation of Proust's *A la recherché du temps perdu.* Joseph Conrad, among others, said that Moncrieff's translation was even better than the original. Certainly, no translator would ever match the lush and honeyed silkiness of Moncrieff's sweet and sumptuous prose.

Nebbiolo (Baudelaire): Nebbiolo is an Italian red grape known for its success in the Piedmont region of Northwest Italy, where it is used to make Barbaresco and Barolo. These DOCG wines are noted for their powerful and full-bodied flavors, as well as their ability to age well. Although it is rightly regarded as the jewel in the crown of Piedmont, Nebbiolo is a difficult grape variety to cultivate, and is not considered a significant varietal in other growing areas.

Nebbiolo is acclaimed as the most noble of Italy's varieties. The name (meaning "little fog") refers to the autumn fog that blankets most of Piedmont where Nebbiolo is chiefly grown, and where it achieves the most successful results. The wines are known for their elegance and power, with a bouquet of wild mushroom, truffle, roses, and tar. Traditionally produced Barolo can age for fifty years-plus, and is regarded by many wine enthusiasts as the greatest wine of Italy. Unfortunately, both Barbaresco and Barolo have been discovered by Robert Parker and, as usual, the curse of his blessing is that the prices of both wines have soared astronomically.

Like the Nebbiolo grape, the French poet Charles Baudelaire was regarded as being difficult and demanding. Although his poems have been translated into other languages, they have never been adopted by any other culture—any more than the Nebbiolo grape has been much-planted outside of Piedmont. But despite their rough and unrefined appearance, both the wine and the poet have the ability to inspire, and even to make the heart sing with thoughts of divine love:

My nectar falls in your fertility,
A precious seed whose Sower is divine,
So from our love is born rare poetry,
Thrusting towards God the blossom on its vine!

Nero d'Avola (Lampedusa): Nero d'Avola is the preeminent wine of Sicily, and the name translates as "the black grape of Avola," a town on the south coast. As the dark, purple color suggests, the wine is full-bodied and voluptuous, velvety in the mouth with a taste of plum and cherry. It ages extremely well and can be matured for a long time in the barrel. Long ignored as a "peasant" wine, it is finally receiving the international attention it deserves. Prince Don Fabrizio Salina, the hero of Giuseppe Tomasi di Lampedusa's great novel, *The Leopard*, sadly observes the decline of the feudal aristocracy in the face of modern changes. As the revolutionary forces of Garibaldi advance, he reflects that, "I belong to an unlucky generation, astride between two worlds and ill-at-ease in both. And what is more, I am completely without illusions." His sole consolation is to drink Nero d'Avola, a wine as dark, voluptuous, and intoxicating as his nephew's beautiful fiancée, played by Claudia Cardinale in the movie version of the novel. The Prince and his fellow aristocrats are long "gone with the wind," swept away from the modern world, but Nero d'Avola continues to fortify and delight.

Pais: The traditional red grape of Chile. (See Mission.)

Palomino: (Also known as Listán Prieto.) Palomino grapes are grown in the Jerez-triangle, close to the Southern Spanish city of Cadiz. This is a white wine grape used to produce Sherry. As a result of both varietal and terroir, Palamino grapes fermented in this specific location produce a unique yeast called "Flor," which coats the surface of the wine and is responsible for the dry and delicate "fino" and "manzanillo" styles of Sherry. (See also Mission, and Fortified Wines.)

Pedro Ximenez is the sweet grape of Andalucía in the subregion of Montilla-Moriles, further inland from Cadiz. It is used by itself or blended with the Palomino grape to produce the sweetest Sherry, and is labeled PX. Before fermentation, the grapes are often left to dry in the sun for a few days, thus raisinating them and concentrating the sugars.

Petit Verdot: One of the six varietals traditionally blended to make classic Bordeaux, to which, in small amounts, it adds structure. Unfortunately, because it ripens very late in the season, often too late to be used, it is increasingly being left out of the blend.

Picpoul /Piquepoul: This is an ancient vine found all over Languedoc, and can produce both red and white wines, though the white varietal is much more common. The name literally means "lip-stinger" because of its high acidity. It is mainly used for blending to add crispness, though it is often bottled unblended as the tart but lemony Picpoul de Pinet.

Pinot Blanc/Pinot Bianco grapes are used to produce light, dry, pleasant white wines. It is grown in Alsace (France), Northern California, Italy, Germany, and Austria. It has been grown in Burgundy and was sometimes mistaken for Chardonnay. The two varieties look very similar, and there are some similarities in the wines they make. Pinot Blanc is often referred to as "poor man's Chardonnay." These wines should be consumed young before the fruit flavors diminish. In Austria, the Pinot Blanc grape is known locally as Weissburgunder—white Burgundy, again like Chardonnay.

Pinot Gris/Pinot Grigio: The grape variety is known as Pinot Grigio in Italy, Pinot Gris in France, and Rulander in Germany. In general, it produces wines of average quality—an everyday drinking wine and a popular alternative to the more full-bodied Chardonnays on the American market. By far the best Pinot Grigios come from Northeast Italy in the Venezia region, where the grapes are protected from harsh winter conditions by the Alps. It makes wines that are delightfully refreshing, well-balanced, and with subtle floral aromas. These inexpensive wines are perfect with antipasti.

As a hugely mass-produced wine, it is often bland and mild, but in a good producers' hands, the wine can prove more full-bodied and complex. The main problem with the grape is that to satisfy the commercial demand, the grapes are harvested too early every year, leading to bottles without character and reinforcing the wine's reputation as Chardonnay's bland and boring sister at the typical wine-and-cheese gathering.

Pinot Noir (King Solomon & Pablo Neruda): Pinot Noir grapes are tightly clustered, dark purple, pine cone-shaped bunches of fruit, whose name probably refers to the French words for "pine" and "black." Pinot Noir is one of the most difficult grapes to grow and make into fine wine. It is also one of the very best when it is done properly. It has very specific requirements for its growing conditions: it needs warm days and cool nights. If Pinot Noir receives too little heat in the growing season, its wines are thin and pale. If the growing season is too warm, the wines have an overripe, cooked flavor.

The contrast between the classic wines of Bordeaux with the fruit-bomb Cabernets of Napa Valley is even more extreme when the delicate Pinot Noirs of Burgundy are compared with the vulgar jammy quality of the New World versions. It is only in Oregon and some parts of New Zealand, where climatic (and even cultural) conditions are similar, that Pinot Noirs can attain the magical delicacy of Burgundy's Côte de Nuits.

As anyone who has seen the movie *Sideways* will already know, Pinot Noir is a grape that inspires great passion. The acclaimed wine critic Jancis Robinson calls Pinot a "minx of a vine," and legendary winemaker André Tchelistcheff declared that "God made Cabernet Sauvignon whereas the devil made Pinot Noir." Other critics, however, offer a completely different perspective. Joel Fleischman of *Vanity Fair* describes Pinot Noir as "the most romantic of wines, with so voluptuous a perfume, so sweet an edge, and so powerful a punch that, like falling in love, they make the blood run hot and the soul wax embarrassingly poetic." Master Sommelier, Madeline Triffon, calls Pinot Noir "sex in a glass," while Peter Richardson of OenoStyle christened it "a seductive yet fickle mistress!" Robert Parker has said of Pinot Noir "When it's great, Pinot Noir produces the most complex, hedonistic, and remarkably thrilling red wine in the world." The children's author, Roald Dahl, once wrote that "to drink a Romanée-

Conti [Pinot Noir] is like having an orgasm in the mouth and nose at the same time."

A grape which can inspire such passions can be paired only with a writer of sublime and sensuous sensitivity, such as King Solomon and his *Song of Songs*:

"Let him kiss me with the kisses of his mouth! For your love is better than wine ... How graceful are your feet in sandals, O queenly maiden! Your rounded thighs are like jewels, the work of a master hand. Your navel is a rounded bowl that never lacks mixed wine. Your belly is a heap of wheat, encircled with lilies. Your two breasts are like two fawns, twins of a gazelle. ... You are stately as a palm tree, and your breasts are like its clusters. I say I will climb the palm tree and lay hold of its branches. Oh, may your breasts be like clusters of the vine, and the scent of your breath like apples, and your kisses like the best wine that goes down smoothly, gliding over lips and teeth. I am my beloved's, and his desire is for me. Come, my beloved, let us go forth into the fields, and lodge in the villages; let us go out early to the vineyards, and see whether the vines have budded, whether the grape blossoms have opened and the pomegranates are in bloom. There I will give you my love."

Obviously inspired by the *Song of Songs*, and possibly a glass of Pinot Noir as well, the Chilean poet Pablo Neruda wrote in his "Ode to Wine:"

> *My darling, suddenly*
> *the line of your hip*
> *becomes the brimming curve*
> *of the wine goblet,*
> *your breast is the grape cluster,*
> *your nipples are the grapes,*

the gleam of spirits lights your hair,
and your navel is a chaste seal
stamped on the vessel of your belly,
your love an inexhaustible
cascade of wine

Pinot Noir produces a small crop. It has low amounts of tannin and relatively high acid levels for a red grape. Pinot Noir found its fame in the Burgundy region of France, where it is the primary grape used for red wines. During the Middle Ages, the monks and aristocracy of Burgundy grew an older form of Pinot in the most-favored land, while the peasants grew a more hardy Gouais Blanc in the lowlands. Over the centuries, cross pollination resulted in the two varieties that we know today as Pinot Noir and Chardonnay. In the fourteenth century, the Duke of Burgundy forbade the cultivation of any red grape other than Pinot Noir.

Pinot Noir is also a major component, with Chardonnay, in the production of most fine-quality Champagne. Most of the Pinot Noir cultivated in France is planted in the Champagne region. The state of Oregon in the United States appears to be an upcoming growing area with the right conditions for Pinot Noir. Some promising wines are also starting to come out of New Zealand. It is known as Spatburgunder, or Burgundy-style, in Germany, where the cooler climate produces wines that are crisper and lighter than elsewhere.

Strong cherry and strawberry aromas and flavors are often the most notable components in these wines. The aging potential can range from three to twenty years, depending on the quality and style of the wine. The very best Pinot Noirs from the Côte d'Or region of Burgundy often don't begin to reach maturity for fifteen to twenty years after bottling. Pinot Noir is very versatile in its ability to match up with foods.

Grilled seafood is an especially good match with most wines made from Pinot Noir.

Pinotage is a red wine grape that is South Africa's signature variety. The grape is a viticultural cross of two varieties of *Vitis vinifera*, not a hybrid. It was bred there in 1925 as a cross between Pinot Noir and Cinsaut (Cinsaut was known as Hermitage in South Africa during that time, hence the portmanteau name of Pinotage). It typically produces deep-red varietal wines with smoky, bramble, and earthy flavors, sometimes with notes of bananas and tropical fruit, but has been criticized for sometimes smelling of acetone. Pinotage is often blended, and also made into fortified wine and even red sparkling wine.

Primitivo (See Zinfandel)

Riesling (Schiller): Originally from the Rhine river valley in Germany, the Riesling grape is now cultivated worldwide wherever growing conditions are sufficiently cool. Riesling does best in cool climates and is very resistant to frost. It is planted very widely in Northern European growing regions, and is increasingly popular in other areas of the world, such as Oregon, Chile, and New Zealand. Among international wines, Riesling is rated one of the top three white wines, with Chardonnay and Sauvignon Blanc. Along with Muscat, Gewürztraminer and Pinot Gris, Riesling is one of the "noble" vines authorized in the Grand Cru sites of France's Alsace region. The "terroir expressive" nature of Riesling, meaning its sensitivity to where it is grown, can be seen by comparing Rieslings from Alsace to Rieslings grown just a few miles away, over the German border in Pfalz.

An aromatic grape, its wine displays a floral, almost perfumed aroma with high, crisp acidity. Seldom blended with other varietals and seldom "oaked" in barrels, Riesling usually shows fresh fruit flavors and a zesty character. The grape has the ability to produce wines that run

319

the gamut from bone-dry to very sweet, but are usually made in dry or semi-dry styles. It has a perfumed aroma with peach and honeysuckle notes, and although it can be enjoyed young, it also ages well. The grape's natural acidity allows the wine to improve for decades, and many German Rieslings are still being drunk after more than one hundred years in the bottle. In the German town of Bremen, there are barrels of Riesling dating back to 1653. Dry Rieslings can be aged from five to fifteen years, semi-sweet aged for ten to twenty years, and very sweet can be aged from thirty to one hundred plus years. But, this variability depends upon the winemaker, the vineyard location, vineyard practices, and the vintage year.

In drier Rieslings, citrus flavors diminish, and characteristics of mineral, smoke, and petrol become more prominent. Those that are not overtly fruity, with relatively high initial acid levels, some residual sugar (2-2.5 percent) and sealed with screw-caps or a good quality natural cork, are most likely to age well. Modern Rieslings can be classified as "aged" after three years, and many will last for at least twenty years if stored in ideal cellar conditions. It was during the Middle Ages that the botrytized Rieslings, produced and aged in giant oak tuns by the Cistercian Monks along the valleys of the Rhine and the Moselle, became so famous and sought after for their longevity.

In the right circumstances, some of the finest sweet wines in the world can be made from Riesling that has been affected by Botrytis cinerea, or noble rot. This mold attacks the skin of the grape and concentrates the sugars in the grape by allowing the water to evaporate. This is especially true in the Moselle and Rhine river valleys of Germany, as well as the Alsace region of France. These wines, known as Trockenbeerenauslese, are very rare, very long-lived, extremely expensive, and absolutely delicious.

Just as Riesling is Germany's most famous wine and Beethoven is Germany's most famous composer, so Friedrich von Schiller is Germany's most famous poet. Schiller's poem "Ode to Joy" not only provided the words for Beethoven's greatest and final symphony, but also celebrated the glories of Riesling:

> *Joy within the goblet flushes,*
> *For the golden nectar, wine,*
> *Every fierce emotion hushes, —*
> *Fills the breast with fire divine.*
> *Brethren, thus in rapture meeting,*
> *Send ye round the brimming cup, —*
> *Yonder kindly spirit greeting,*
> *While the foam to heaven mounts up!*

Rkatsiteli, from Georgia, is one of the world's oldest vines, and traces, dating back over five thousand years, have been found by archeologists in the Caucus Mountains. Because of its popularity in the Soviet Union for making cheap fortified wines, it became one of the most-planted varietals in the world. It is still a popular grape for making wines in Russia and Eastern Europe.

Roussanne: (See Marsanne & Roussanne)

Sangiovese (Dante, Petrarch, Boccaccio): Sangiovese is the primary grape used in Central Italy in the region of Tuscany to make such well-known wines as Chianti, Brunello di Montalcino, and Vino Nobile di Montepulciano. Its Roman name was originally *sanguis Jovis,* or blood of Jove.

Sangiovese produces wines that are spicy, with good acid levels, smooth texture and medium body. In the right climates and with controlled yields, Sangiovese can be made into very structured and full-bodied wines. It is often blended with other grapes for best results. During the later decades of the twentieth century, Sangiovese was often blended with Cabernet Sauvignon to create a Super Tuscan blend, and was typically aged in French oak barrels. This resulted in a wine primed for the international market in the style of a typical California Cabernet: oaky, high-alcohol, and a ripe, jammy, fruit-forward profile. Although these Super Tuscans eventually won official recognition, the trend in Tuscany now is increasingly to focus on the native Sangiovese grape.

Sangiovese is experiencing increased interest and plantings in California and elsewhere. Because of its ability, like Merlot and Carménère, to create smoother wines with acid levels that pair well with many foods, a great deal of experimentation is taking place with it as a blending agent with several red varieties.

For a Sangiovese literary pairing, there are three obvious contenders, all of them Tuscan writers of the fourteenth century, and all born in the city of Florence or close nearby.

Durante degli Alighieri, Dante, the Florentine poet, being the oldest and the best known, should obviously pair with Chianti, the most well-known of all the Tuscan wines. Dante's *Divine Comedy* is as representative of Italian literature as the straw-covered Chianti bottles were characteristic of Italian wine.

Francesco Petrarch, whose father was a friend of Dante, should be paired with the Vino Nobile di Montepulciano. The Sangiovese wines from the village of Montepulciano were popular with the educated and refined classes of Tuscany (hence the name). Since Petrarch's father was a professor, and he himself, along with Shakespeare, is regarded as the father of the sonnet form, then the Vino Nobile wine would seem an appropriate pairing.

Giovani Boccaccio, a friend of Petrarch, is most famous for the *Decameron*, a series of about one hundred witty and often erotic stories offering a glimpse into the reality of everyday Tuscan life in the fourteenth century. The perfect Sangiovese pairing for such a rich and earthy writer is clearly the rich and powerful wines of Brunello di Montalcino.

Sauvignon Blanc (Saki): Sauvignon Blanc is a green-skinned varietal, high in acidity, which produces a white wine of great distinction. The grape is widely grown around the world, partly because of its high yield and low costs, and also because it can tolerate greater heat than many other varieties. Depending on the climate, the flavor can range from aggressively grassy to sweetly tropical; the wines often exhibit "melon" in the nose and taste, and are usually described as crisp, elegant, and fresh. If grown in too cool a climate, it can develop a herbaceous character in its aromas. Karen MacNeil memorably wrote that "if Chardonnay were Marilyn Monroe then Sauvignon Blanc would be Jamie Lee Curtis."

Sauvignon Blanc originated on the west coast of France in the Loire and Bordeaux regions. Although it can gain additional complexity and richness after some limited time in the barrel, it is seldom aged in wood because it can get overpowered by the oak flavors. Some of the best Sauvignon Blanc in France comes from two villages in the upper Loire Valley, called Sancerre and Pouilly-sur-Loire. The wine from the second village is called Pouilly Fumé, and so, for marketing purposes, US winegrowers often called the wine made from the grape Fumé-Blanc.

New Zealand is currently having notable success with Sauvignon Blanc, and produces wines that have very high levels of acidity and complexity. Wineries from Cloudy Bay in Marlborough on the South Island have won many international prizes, and are regarded by many as some of the best Sauvignon Blanc in the world. The asparagus, gooseberry, and green flavor commonly associated with New Zealand Sauvignon Blanc is derived from flavor compounds known as *methoxypyrazines* that become more pronounced and concentrated in wines from cooler climate regions.

While it is usually unblended when bottled in the Loire valley, in Bordeaux Sauvignon Blanc is blended with Sémillon, Muscadelle, and Ugni Blanc to produce Bordeaux Blanc and Entre-Deux-Meres. In the Bordeaux subregion of Sauternes, it is blended with Sémillon alone. The Sémillon rounds out the acid of the Sauvignon Blanc, and the two late harvested grapes, after undergoing noble rot (Botrytis cinerea), produce a powerfully sweet and alcoholic wine of which Château d'Yquem is the most famous and sought after.

A common saying in the upper Loire is "any land not perfect for vines is perfect for goats." Sauvignon Blanc is especially good when served with chèvre, goat cheeses, or seafood, and is one of the few wines that pairs well with sushi—not that sushi is especially common in the villages of the upper Loire.

Saki was the nom de plume of H.H. Munro, an Edwardian short story writer who was killed on the Western Front in 1916. Like Sauvignon Blanc wines which are widely accessible and refreshingly easy to drink, Saki's short stories were widely popular and dealt amusingly with the everyday concerns of upper-middle class English life. A chilled glass of Sauvignon Blanc is the perfect accompaniment to a lazy summer afternoon, relaxed in a deckchair overlooking the croquet lawn. And for the accompanying reading material, nothing could possibly be more appropriate than a new story from Saki. Like the wine, Saki's stories dazzle and delight, entertaining and refreshing. But beneath the soft hints of melon and gooseberry, Sauvignon Blanc wines can have a sharp acidity that accosts the palate with a surprising jolt. In the same way, the graceful French-windows of Saki's witty and elegant Edwardian drawing rooms open to an outside world of surprising and savage cruelty. The realm of the Great God Pan is never far from the well-tended gardens of the vicarage.

Sémillon (James Joyce): Sémillon is a golden-skinned grape used to make both dry and sweet white wines, most notably in France and Australia. Sémillon ripens earlier in the season than most grapes, and is less-likely to be damaged by rains or frost. It produces wines that are full-flavored, rich, and aromatic, and is most often blended with other varieties (especially Sauvignon Blanc) to add body to more acidic varietals.

In France, Sémillon is grown mainly in the Bordeaux region where it is used for blending, adding softness and body to the more acidic Sauvignon Blanc. When it is blended with Sauvignon Blanc, Muscadelle, and Ugni Blanc to make Bordeaux Blanc, Graves or Entre-deux-mers, Sémillon is a minor component in the blend. However, when blended with Sauvignon Blanc alone to make Sauternes or Barsac, then it is usually the major component. For example, Château d'Yquem is usually 20 percent Sauvignon Blanc and 80 percent Sémillon. As discussed elsewhere, in such wines the vine is exposed to the noble rot of Botrytis cinerea, which consumes the water content of the fruit and concentrates the sugar present in its pulp. When exposed to Botrytis cinerea, the grapes shrivel and the acid and sugar levels are intensified producing powerfully sweet and highly alcoholic wines. Whether in the sweet wines or in dryer styles, Sémillon has the ability to age for a very long time.

James Joyce spent much of his life struggling to be published. Much of his early work, such as *Portrait of the Artist as a Young Man* and *Dubliners*, are decent examples of the writer's art, just as the Sémillon grape makes a fairly decent white wine. These short stories of Joyce usually appear, along with the work of other writers, in anthologies, just as Sémillon is usually drunk when it has been blended with other grapes to produce wines such as Entre-Deux-Mers.

However, when exposed to the fungus Botrytis cinerea, there is a magical transformation which elevates the humble Sémillon grape to the realm of the divine and gives us such masterpieces as Château d'Yquem. In the same way, a combination of the First World War and exile life in Paris transformed the struggling Joyce into an avant-garde giant and his masterpiece *Ulysses* became one of the two greatest novels of the twentieth century. Leopold Bloom, the hero of Ulysses, regarded the taste of wine as an affirmation of life:

"Glowing wine on his palate lingered swallowed. Crushing in the winepress grapes of Burgundy. Sun's heat it is. Seems to a secret touch telling me memory. Touched his sense moistened remembered. Hidden under wild ferns on Howth below us bay sleeping: sky. No sound. The sky... O wonder! Coolsoft with ointments her hand touched me, caressed: her eyes upon me did not turn away. Ravished over her I lay, full lips full open, kissed her mouth. Yum.... She kissed me. I was kissed. All yielding she tossed my hair. Kissed, she kissed me."

Unlike France, where it is almost always blended with other varietals, in Australia Sémillon is gaining renown under its own name. North of Sydney, in Hunter Valley, four styles of Sémillon wines are being produced: a commercial style, often blended with Chardonnay or Sauvignon Blanc; a sweet style, similar to Sauternes; a complex, early picked style, which has great longevity; and an equally high-quality, dry style, which can be released soon after vintage. Once the Australians have decided on which cuddly animal to use on the label, we should begin to see more Sémillon on our supermarket shelves.

Shiraz/Syrah (Sebastian Faulks and Richard Flanagan): This grape is known as Syrah in France and Shiraz in Australia. In the United States, it can appear under either name depending on the style of the winery. The grape was long thought to be named either for a city in Sicily, Syracuse (Syrah), or for a city in Persia (Shiraz), in either of which it possibly originated. It produces full, rich wines of intense color and flavor. In warmer climates like Australia, the grape produces wines that are sweeter and riper tasting; in cooler climates like the Rhône valley of France, it often has more pepper and spice aromas and flavors. Syrah wines usually becomes drinkable at an early age, and most are produced for consumption within a year after release (second year after harvest). On the other hand, there are Syrah/Shiraz examples of very long-lived wines, such as Hermitage in France and Penfold's Grange in Australia.

Like Sebastian Faulk's brilliant novel *Birdsong*, Richard Flanagan's *The Narrow Road to the Deep North* intertwines a tragic love story of infidelity with unbearable images of the brutality of war. Each novel features a protagonist who simultaneously inhabits two different worlds; one of banal normalcy and the other of indescribable horrors. His experience, whether in the trenches of Flanders or the jungles of Burma, is something each man is unable to share after returning home. Flanagan's hero returns home to Australia, tormented by his memories, unable to share them, unable to move on.

Legend has it that a crusading French knight, Chevalier Guy De Sterimberg, returned to the Rhône Valley from a visit to Persia, with some vines from Shiraz. Wearied from the horrors of war, he became a hermit, built a stone chapel and developed a vineyard on the steep hill where he lived. It became known as the Hermitage, by which name the wine is known to this day. The use of the crusader's vine, Syrah, spread throughout the Rhône region, and it is now the dominant varietal of the Rhône valley. It is often blended with Grenache and Mourvedre, and is an essential grape in the production of Châteauneuf du Pape (which can include as many as nineteen different varietals).

There are many reasons to question this story of the world-weary Chevalier, if not to dismiss it entirely; but some romantic tales just deserve to be repeated—if only to be savored in the telling over a precious glass of Hermitage. Unfortunately for us romantics, recent DNA testing has shown that, despite tales of crusaders from Persia, Shiraz is indigenous to France, a genetic cross of two relatively obscure varieties, Mondeuse Blanche and Dureza. Nonetheless, the theme of war-weary warriors and the wine's Australian revival, makes Flanagan and Shiraz the perfect literary pairing.

Until the Iranian revolution in 1979, Shiraz was still well known for its extensive vineyards and for the quality of its wines. I visited Shiraz in the mid-1970s, inspected the lush vineyards and tasted the deliciously sweet white wines, but never imagined that something so rich and so ancient could be so swiftly destroyed or that such deeply ingrained cultural traditions could be so suddenly terminated. The Shah is gone and now the Mullah reigns; there are no more vines growing, and no birds sing.

Syrah was introduced to Australia in 1832 by Dr. James Busby, who imported vines of several varieties from Europe. For a while, the Australians called it Hermitage, but when the French finally objected, they started calling it Shiraz, and for at least its first hundred years, it was used as a "field blend" variety rather than being vine-ified separately. Its late-blooming nature suited the warmer growing conditions found in Australia. Shiraz wines from Australia, compared to those from France, tend to be full-bodied with higher alcohol and tannin levels.

Some Californian and Israeli winemakers offer a variety called Petite Syrah. This name probably originally applied to Syrah vines that were brought from the Rhône valley around 1870. In the years since that time, the name has been applied to a great many old red grape vines in California, including what we now know to be Durif, Peloursin, and other less common varietals. In America, Petite Syrah has now become a generic name rather than a unique grape variety.

Sylvaner (Goethe): Sylvaner or Silvaner is a variety of white wine grape grown mainly in Alsace and Germany, where its official name is Grüner Sylvaner. In Germany, it is best-known as a component of Liebfraumilch and production boomed in the 1970s to the detriment of quality. While the Alsatian versions have primarily been considered simpler wines, not included among the four noble grapes of Alsace, it was recently included among the varieties that can be used to produce Alsace Grand Cru wine, together with the four noble grapes of Alsace, although only in one vineyard—Zotzenberg.

This hesitation is explained by the vigor of the Sylvaner vine and the grape's neutral flavor, which can lead to blandness unless yields are controlled. On the other hand, it gives a blank canvas for the expression of terroir, and on good sites with skilled winemaking, Sylvaner can produce elegant wines.

A good example is Sylvaner from the town of Würtzburg, in its distinctive *bocksbeutal*, round bottle. This was the favorite wine of Germany's most famous writer, Johann Wolfgang von Goethe. In a desperate letter, Goethe once wrote to his wife, "send me some Würzburg wine, no other tastes as nice, and I am in a surly mood if I lack my usual favorite drink." In another letter he famously observed that, "life is too short to drink bad wine."

Tempranillo (Cervantes): Tempranillo is only grown on the Iberian Peninsula in Spain and Portugal. It is known as Tinta Roriz in the Douro river area of Portugal. In Spain, Tempranillo is the most important red varietal, and is the major grape in Rioja red wines and in the wines of Toro and Ribera. In Toro, it is known as Tinta-Toro, and in the Ribera it is known as Tinto-Fino. Tempranillo makes wines that are medium-bodied with moderate tannins and acids. They are distinguished by dark colors and deliciously earthy flavors of plum and black currants, truffles and autumn decay.

More than any other wine, Tempranillo, will always be associated with the Ingenious Gentleman, Don Quixote of La Mancha, and his faithful servant, Sancho Panza, as they travel around the Kingdom of Castile pursuing justice, saving damsels in distress, and attacking windmills. The Castile-La Mancha setting of Cervantes' novel is actually the largest continuous vine-growing area in the world, and Tempranillo is the main varietal grown—and was certainly the wine that was drunk locally. Quite probably, it was the Tempranillo wine, as much as the excess reading of books, that transformed the humble Alonso Quixano into the proud knight-errant, Don Quixote. The mixture of wine and books always has ennobling results.

Torrontes (Tasker): Torrontes is a white grape from the Salta province of Argentina, grown in the highest vineyards of the Andes, sometimes at elevations in excess of ten thousand feet. The grape is descended from a cross between the two vines originally brought from Spain by the Conquistadores, Palomino (Pais/Criola/Mission), and Muscat of Alexandria. It is a deliciously aromatic and refreshing wine, with marked acidity, a satisfying mouth-feel, and a distinctive lingering aftertaste of peaches. Torrontés is so aromatic, so perfumed with scents of orange blossoms, honeysuckle, and lavender, that, according to the *Miami Herald*'s wine writer, Fred Tasker, you could put a dab behind each ear and go out for an evening of fun and romance.

Torrontes is also the name of a distinctively flavored grape varietal native to Galicia. Although there was large-scale emigration to Argentina from Galicia, this did not significantly occur till the early twentieth century, long after the Torrontes vine was established in the

Andes. Recent DNA testing shows there is no relationship between the two varietals other than the name.

Touriga Nacional is the best of the grapes that are blended to make Port. It has been used in Port making as far back as the eighteenth century. Touriga Nacional is an early maturing grape that makes wines of especially deep color, intense fruity aroma, and tannin. This variety grows rapidly, and is adaptable to a wide range of growing conditions including limited rainfall. It is grown almost exclusively in Portugal, on the granite plateau of the Dao, and also the remote, steep sides of the upper Douro river valley, near the Spanish border.

The Touriga Nacional variety makes the best of the Ports, but its yields are small (less than half of other key varieties), and it is the most expensive of the grapes to use. It is used in high percentages only in the best Ports. This grape produces wines with smooth, soft textures that have excellent aging potential.

Trebbiano: Although not well-known, Trebbiano was for a long time the second most widely planted grape in the world. It produces good yields, but makes undistinguished wine at best. It can be fresh and fruity, but doesn't age for long. Its high acidity makes it important in Cognac production. Also known as Ugni Blanc, in particular in France, it has many other names reflecting a family of local subtypes. Trebbiano is also the most widely planted white varietal in Italy. It is grown throughout the country, with a special focus on the wines from Abruzzo and from Lazio, including Frascati. Mostly, they are pale, easy-drinking wines, but a few select Trebbiano wines from producers such as Valentini have been known to age for over fifteen years.

Ugni Blanc (See Trebbiano)

Verdelho is the most popular white wine grape in Portugal, especially on the island of Madeira—recently the grape has been successful in the vineyards of Australia, particularly the South Burnett wine region in Queensland, Hunter Valley region, Langhorne Creek, and the Swan Valley. Australian versions of Verdelho are noted for their intense flavors, with hints of lime and honeysuckle, and the oily texture that the wines can get after some aging.

Verdejo is a Spanish white wine grape found mainly in the Rueda region between Toro and Ribera in Castile and Leon. Rueda DO wines must contain a minimum of 50 percent Verdejo grapes, and wines labeled Rueda Verdejo must contain a minimum of 85 percent. The Marques de Riscal has begun developing a fresher style of wine to replace the traditional heavy and oxidized style, and this new style is becoming popular in the USA.

Verdicchio is grown in the areas of Castelli di Jesi and Matelica in the Marche region of Italy, and gives its name to the varietal white wine made from it. The name comes from "verde" (green). The white wines are noted for their high acidity and a characteristic nutty flavor with a hint of honey.

Vernaccia (Patricia Highsmith): Vernaccia is an undistinguished grape from central Italy, used for blending with other grapes such as Trebianno, to make the local white table wines. However, the Vernaccia grapes, which are grown around the central Tuscan town of San Gimignano, have raised and distinguished themselves above their humble origins to make sophisticated wines of distinction. Since the Renaissance, Vernaccia di San Gimignano has been considered one of Italy's finest white wines. It was the first Italian wine to be awarded DOC status, which was later upgraded to DOCG. The grape was immortalized in *Dante's Divine Comedy,* in which the poet described the gluttonous Pope Martin IV drowning a plate of Bolsena eels in a flask of Vernaccia before swallowing them and then slowly savoring the wine.

The grape pairs most beautifully with the American writer Patricia Highsmith, who also rose from humble origins to literary eminence. Coming from distinctly non-literary and unsophisticated rural Texas, like her hero Mr. Ripley, Ms. Highsmith quickly became the epitome of the sophisticated and cosmopolitan European literary elite. Like Highsmith's writing, the Vernaccia di San Gimignano are noted for their crisp, dryness, complexity, and a certain salty fruitiness. The story of Pope Martin and the eels perfectly reflects the gleeful cruelty of Ms. Highsmith's delightfully complex plots.

Vin Du Pays (Ernest Hemingway): *Vin du Pays* is a French expression, meaning "the local wine." When traveling around France (or Spain or Italy), it is always the best thing to order in a bar or restaurant. It's just the ordinary wine of the region, which probably does not travel, and is not available elsewhere. As Hemingway wrote in *A Movable Feast*:

"In Europe then we thought of wine as something healthy and normal as food and also a great giver of happiness and well-being and delight. Drinking wine was not a snobbism nor a sign of sophistication nor a cult; it was as natural as eating and to me as necessary, and I would not have thought of eating a meal without drinking either wine or cider or beer. I loved all wines except sweet or sweetish wines and wines that were too heavy."

Viognier was once a little-used varietal best known in the commune of Condrieu, and limited to the northern Rhône valley where it is the dominant white grape. It is experiencing a resurgence in popularity as more of it is being planted in California and elsewhere in the world. Often mistaken for Chardonnay, Viognier makes fruity wines of medium body. Stone fruit aromas (peach and apricot) are often found in wines made from Viognier, along with a bit of spice. Depending on the producer, the wine can range from exquisite to ordinary. Also, depending on the producer's style, the wine matches well with "Asian Infusion" dishes, as well as many foods that are often served with Chardonnay.

Viura: Known elsewhere as Macabeo, Viura is the white grape of the Rioja, and produces a light refreshing drink for early consumption. It is also one of the main varietals used in the blending of Cava sparkling wines in Spain's Catalonia region.

Xinomavro: The most famous wines made with the Xinomavro grape come from Naoussa in the Macedonian region of northern Greece. Xinomavro means acid-black in Greek, which aptly describes both the color of the grapes and the resulting wine. The wines, with their lingering taste of olives, are high in both tannins and acid, which means they can be aged for a very long time. Perfect with Greek salad and feta cheese.

Zinfandel is a grape variety that has been important almost exclusively in California. The Zinfandel grape can make solid red wines with good fruit and structure. It was a popular variety with home winemakers during the American Prohibition era because its thick skins allowed the grapes to ship without damage. It later (in the late 1970s and early 1980s) became popular for the wines produced from it, with fruit-forward flavors and spicy overtones. There are vines in Sonoma Valley that are probably the oldest grafted vines in California, going back to 1888, and there may be even older vines on their own roots in Amador County. Zinfandel declined in popularity in the mid-1980s, and became unprofitable to grow until "White Zinfandel" was accidentally introduced. Red Zinfandel has regained popularity since the turn of the century, partly as a reaction against mediocre Merlots, and partly as a growing appreciation of the full-body, high alcohol qualities of "old-vine zins."

Based on DNA evidence, California Zinfandel originated in Croatia. Zinfandel has been in Croatia a very long time, perhaps as early as 1300. This fact makes it one of the oldest grape cultivars that we make wine from today. The name of Zinfandel in Croatia is Crljenak Kaštelanski ("black grape of Kastel"), but nobody knows why it was named Zinfandel when it arrived in America. Zinfandel is genetically identical to Primativo, which probably migrated from Croatia, across the Adriatic Sea to Puglia in Italy in the late 1700s. Once regarded as an unimportant South Italian wine, since the discovery of the sexy Californian Zinfandel connection, Primitivo is now being proudly and successfully marketed all over the world.

Zinfandel (White): In 1975, Sutter Home accidentally created a pink, sweet, and easy-drinking jug wine with low alcohol and an acid balance. The wine can be compared to Mateus Rosé, Snapple, Lancers Sparkling Rosé, and other rather saccharine beverages. To everyone's surprise, it became an overnight success, and remains the third most popular wine, accounting for ten percent of all the wine consumed in America. White Zinfandel outsells red Zinfandel by six to one. As a result, many otherwise well-educated Americans still associate Zinfandel wines with those sickly, sweet, pink glasses that Aunt Elsie still insists on serving at family gatherings.

Non-Grape Wines (Ray Bradbury and Edward Thomas): Probably because it is not a grape-growing country, the English have a long tradition of making wine from flowers. It was a tradition that they took with them to their colonies across the Atlantic. Dandelion wine was so popular as a country-wine that Ray Bradbury used it as the title of one of his most moving and enchanting novels, describing the boyhood magic of a long-distant, small-town summer of Illinois. Back in England, perhaps the most popular of country wines is made from elder flowers and elderberries. Recently, a French company has been using elder flowers to distill a sublimely aromatic liqueur called St. Germain. But nothing will ever evoke English wine and the English countryside more than Edward Thomas' poem, "Adlestrop:"

> Yes. I remember Adlestrop—
> The name, because one afternoon
> Of heat the express-train drew up there
> Unwontedly. It was late June.
>
> The steam hissed. Someone cleared his throat.
> No one left and no one came
> On the bare platform. What I saw
> Was Adlestrop—only the name
>
> And willows, willow-herb, and grass,
> And meadowsweet, and haycocks dry,
> No whit less still and lonely fair
> Than the high cloudlets in the sky.
>
> And for that minute a blackbird sang
> Close by, and round him, mistier,
> Farther and farther, all the birds
> Of Oxfordshire and Gloucestershire.

Chapter Six: VARIETALS

Chapter

7

FORTIFIED WINE

*"The only advice I can give to aspiring writers
is don't do it unless you're willing to give your
whole life to it. Red wine and garlic also helps."*
— Jim Harrison

Fortified wines are regular wines to which brandy has been added. The process was developed in the seventeenth and eighteenth centuries by the Dutch and the English, who both had large overseas colonies which involved long ocean voyages. Both nations discovered that by fortifying the wines with brandy, they would better survive the journey. By happy chance, they also discovered that the wines thus treated significantly improved in taste.

Brandy: Brandy simply means distilled wine. Although first discovered by the Moors in Andalusia and used for making perfumes and medicines, the process was first used commercially by the Dutch. Both the Dutch and the English had long been closely involved in the Bordeaux wine trade and Dutch engineers were very involved in the draining of marshes and reclaiming land on the west coast of France. Vast areas of land to the north of Bordeaux in Cognac and south of Bordeaux in Armagnac were planted with Ugni Blanc or Trebbiano grapes, which made poor but high-yielding white wines. The Dutch distilled the wines, primarily as a way of transporting them more economically, and also to minimize export and import taxes, which were based on liquid quantity. However, after discovering that the resulting *brandewijn* (Dutch for "burned wine") tasted better after being aged in the oak barrels, it soon became sought after for its own sake. The two most famous brandies are obviously Cognac and Armagnac, but brandy is found everywhere that wine is made; Mexico and Spain are also well known for their brandy. At the end of the fermentation process, most winemakers will distill the pomace residue of skins and juice into homemade brandy for personal use. In France, this is called

Marc. Many regions use a variant of the name "water of life" for brandy; for example *eau de vie, aqua vitae, and aguardiente.* Adding brandy back into the original wine from which it was distilled results in the following fortified wines.

Sherry: Sherry is a fortified white wine grown and produced exclusively in a very small region called Jerez, just outside Cadiz in Southern Andalusia. Unfortunately, because the name was not legally protected until 1996, "Sherry" has become synonymous with sickly, sweet wines from South Africa, California, and Cyprus. Sherry is now defined by law as the English name for the wines of Jerez, and, far from being sweet, most Sherry is among the driest of all wines.

Sherry is made primarily from the Palomino grape and sometimes, for sweet versions, with Pedro Ximenez. The wine is fermented to about 11 percent alcohol, and then blended with brandy to bring it to 15 percent or higher. The four most common styles of Sherry are:

Fino: This is the palest and driest. Alcohol 15-17. Sugar grams per liter: 0 – 5

Amontillado: Slightly darker than Fino. Alcohol 16-17%. Sugar g/l: 0 – 5

Oloroso: Darker, fuller bodied slightly oxidized. Alcohol 17-22%. Sugar g/l: 0 – 5

Pedro Ximénez: Dark, full-bodied and *very* sweet. Alcohol 15-22%. Sugar g/l: 212+

After fermentation and the fortification with brandy, the Sherry is aged using the solera system in which the barrels of aging wine are stored in a pyramid style with the oldest on the bottom and newest barrels on top. Wine to be bottled is drawn from one third of the oldest, bottom barrels, which are then topped-up with wine from the layer above and so on, until there is space in the top layer of barrels for the new wine to be added. Consequently, over the years and decades, the wines of various vintages are blended together, which is why a bottle of Sherry never has a vintage year on the label. In some cases, some of the content of the bottle could be more than a hundred years old. Dry Sherry is a popular drink all over Spain, not just in Andalusia, and has been extremely popular in England since long before Shakespeare celebrated it in his plays.

Sherry is the Shakespeare of wines. Both offer the widest variety of styles, from the driest Fino to the sweetest Pedro Ximenez, or the broadest comedy of Bottom to the most sublime tragedy of Lear. They are both unique and have no peers; the solera system is unique to Sherry, and the sheer volume and range of the written word is unique to Shakespeare. Not only does Shakespeare make more than thirty-five direct references to Sherry in his plays, but during his lifetime, Sir Francis Drake "liberated" 2,900 butts of Sherry (2.25 million bottles) from the King of Spain, and brought them home to England. The richness, the range, the historic parallels, will forever unite the Bard of Avon with the sack of Jerez.

Shakespeare's most famous Sherry drinker, of course, was Sir John Falstaff, who called it "sac" and attributes the bravery and military success of Prince Hal to his consumption of Sherry. He also adds that Sherry produces "excellent wit," while it "warms the blood." In conclusion, Sir John avows that if he had a thousand sons, the first thing he would teach them is to reject all small thin wines and to devote themselves to Sherry.

Part of the payment to England's Poet Laureate, since the time of Shakespeare's drinking companion, Ben Johnson, has traditionally been a barrel of Sherry. England's current Poet Laureate, Carol Anne

Duffy, was presented with 720 bottles of Sherry in 2012. Sherry is typically drunk as an aperitif before meals.

Port: Like Sherry, Port is a fortified wine developed for and largely controlled by the English market, even today. It is made from the Touriga National grapes, which are grown in the remote reaches of the River Douro after it crosses the border from Spain. Because of the steep slopes of the vineyards, the grapes are harvested by hand and pressed with human feet in order to thoroughly macerate the grape skins in the juice, thus imparting the dark color to the wine. Fermentation is interrupted by the addition of aguardiente (brandy) before all the sugar is converted, which means that the wine is high in both alcohol and residual sugar.

Although there are a dozen different styles of Port which are tightly controlled and regulated by the various Port houses down-river in Porto, they can be divided into two general types.

Wood-Aged Port: As the name implies, these are wines that are aged in wooden barrels before being bottled. They include the cheapest and most common, Ruby Port, which is dark and fruity and ready for immediate drinking. Late Bottled Vintage Ports are aged in the vat for between four and six years minimum. More delicate than Ruby, rich and mellow Tawney Port is a blend from several vintages, which are aged in wood from ten to forty years, and whose delicious nuttiness and aromas of butterscotch and fine oak intensify the longer they spend in wood. White Ports are made from white grapes, and are aged for at least three years before bottling.

Bottle-Aged Vintage and Crusted Port: As the name implies, these wines are aged in the bottle after a minimum of just two years in oak casks. This Port should not be drunk until at least fifteen or twenty years after the date, usually stenciled in white paint, on the bottle. Because the wine has not been filtered, it will form a crust of natural sediment in the bottle and will need to be carefully decanted before serving. Port wines are among the longest lasting, most structured, and most powerful of all wines.

The English, who have been deeply involved in the development of the Port trade since the 1670s, traditionally present a new-born baby with a bottle of Port to be opened at the child's twenty-first birthday.

Madeira: Madeira is a fortified wine made from the Malvasia grape in the Madeira Islands off the west coast of Africa, where European sailors would stop and load up with provisions on their way across the Atlantic or south to The Cape. In both instances, the local wine, fortified with rum or brandy, was not only able to weather the long ocean-crossing but actually improved with the heat of the sun and the rolling of the ship.

Less popular now, Madeira used to be the most-popular wine imported to America, and its devoted drinkers included Thomas Jefferson, George Washington, Alexander Hamilton, Benjamin Franklin, John Hancock, John Rutledge, and John Adams, who all used it to toast the Declaration of Independence. During colonial times, one of the early Church of England commissaries, the Reverend Gideon Johnston, discovered the joys of Madeira when appointed to Charleston, South Carolina, by the Bishop of London. Whilst crossing the Atlantic to take his official post, he found himself abandoned on the island, having become totally addicted to Madeira and being too drunk to leave. When the Reverend gentleman did eventually arrive in Charleston, he was delighted to discover that his parishioners, like the citizens of Savannah, were all equally addicted to the pleasures of Madeira.

Madeira had already long been popular in England, where it was known as Malmsey. According to Shakespeare, when King Richard III needed to get rid of his brother, George Duke of Clarence, in 1477, he had him drowned in a barrel of Malmsey. When the two murderers arrived at the Tower of London to carry out the task, the unsuspecting Duke of Clarence asked for a cup of wine. The second murderer made the famous response: "You shall have wine enough, my lord, anon."

Marsala: The town of Marsala in Sicily had long produced a popular white table wine which an English visitor in 1773 decided would be greatly improved by fortifying with extra alcohol, so that it would survive the long sea voyage to England. The wine is aged using *the in perpetuum* method, similar to the solera process already in use to make Sherry. Marsala can be either sweet or dry, and ranges in color from amber, golden, or ruby. The alcohol content is usually between 15-20 percent.

Banyuls: Banyuls is a French AOC for the fortified dessert wine from Banyuls in Roussilon, near the Spanish border of Catalonia. The process, called *Mutage* in French, is similar to the production of Port, in which the fermentation is interrupted by the addition of brandy, thus retaining the residual sugars while increasing the alcohol level to about 16 percent. François Hollande, the recent President of France, served a bottle of Banyuls to President Obama during a state visit to Paris in 2016.

Chapter Seven: FORTIFIED WINE

Chapter

8

WINE PAIRING, SERVING & BUYING

"Most people whom you may view as wine experts are usually just good at just one thing: winemakers are good at making wine, sommeliers at talking about it, and wine writers at drinking it for free." —
Olivier Magny

What sort of food?

When selecting wine for a meal, the very first and most important step is to decide whether your food is going to be delicate and mild tasting or hearty and flavorful. Is it going to be fatty or lean? Will it be rich, buttery, and creamy, or will it be thin, sharp, and acidic? The wine and the food must balance each other, so that a hearty dish will match a hearty wine, while a mild-flavored food will require a delicate wine. What is important is that neither the wine nor the food should overwhelm the other.

So a delicate Dover Sole, for example, would go well with a Sauvignon Blanc or Pinot Grigio, but not with a Chardonnay; while a hearty steak-and-kidney pie would complement a Malbec but probably overwhelm a Beaujolais. However, the Beaujolais would go well with a light lunch, such as cold ham, charcuterie, and salad, while the Chardonnay would be the perfect match for a rich chicken in cream sauce. As noted elsewhere, when in doubt, Champagne goes well with everything.

Traditional Red/meat: White/ fish rule

Some fish, such as cod, haddock, and mackerel, as well as all shellfish, are high in iodine, which is why red wines don't do well with them. The iodine content reacts with the tannins in red wine and makes both the fish and the wine taste metallic and nasty. However, red wines like Pinot Noir, Beaujolais, or even certain Chiantis that are not high in tannins, go very well with fish, such as salmon or sea bass.

Meats like chicken or pork go very well with full-bodied white wines like Chardonnay, Riesling, or even Gewürztraminer. Rich patés, like foie gras in Perigord, are traditionally enjoyed with a late harvest white wine, like Monbazillac or Sauternes.

Tannins and Acids

Tannins not only enhance the complexity of the wine itself but are also very useful for cleansing the palette of fatty foods. Lamb chops, for example, or a grilled beef steak, will both be improved with a Cabernet Sauvignon from Bordeaux, whose astringent tannins will strip away the fatty-coating inside your mouth.

Acids perform the same function as tannins in cutting through fat, and so a fried chicken or smoked salmon, which would be overwhelmed by the tannins of a Cabernet, would respond well to the cleansing acids of a crisp Sauvignon Blanc.

Acids in wine should also match the acid in food. Pasta with a tomato sauce—or indeed any food over which you squeeze lime or lemon juice—should be paired with a light acidic wine such as Riesling, Pinot

Grigio, or even Alvarinho. Cream sauces, on the other hand, will react badly to acid, and so should be paired with richer, more full-bodied whites, such as Chardonnay and Viognier.

Wines which are lower in alcohol tend to be higher in acidity, and thus go better with food since the acids and tannins cleanse the palette. For the same reason, many New World wines with their fruit-forward and high alcohol content tend to overwhelm the food, however hearty it might be. Many of these "hedonistic fruit-bombs," therefore, are best drunk by themselves and not paired with food at all.

Sometimes it's okay for the wine to overwhelm. If you are serving a bottle of Château Latour or a Screaming Eagle, for example, you probably want your guests to notice the wine. The accompanying food should be simple and not spicy, so it does not distract while you slowly savor the expensive pleasures of these legends of the winemaker's art, and your friends savor the pleasures of knowing so generous a host.

National pairings and wine

When in doubt, just match the wine with the nationality of the food. The two have evolved together over generations and—within the obvious rules listed above—will always complement each other. For example, a pasta dish will almost always do well with Chianti, and a Boeuf Bourguignon will always improve with Pinot Noir from Burgundy.

As for Asian food, while many Japanese dishes, especially sushi and some Chinese dishes, pair well with Champagne and light dry wines from Alsace, the Loire and Burgundy. For spicy Vietnamese, Korean and Indian food, ignore the wine and serve cold Asian beer.

The next section lists twenty-four different varietals in order of lightness, with the more full-bodied and heavier wines listed last. However, bear in mind that varietals often vary depending on their origin. For example, a Chardonnay from Chablis, which is fairly flinty and austere, would go well with snails or a fish simply grilled with butter and garlic, but not with a chicken in cream sauce. Chicken and cream sauce requires a more full-bodied Chardonnay from California or Australia, as well as a non-tannic red, such as Chianti or even Merlot.

Top Forty Wines to Try Before You Die (24 Varietals)

White: *Listed from light to more full-bodied*

Sauvignon Blanc. Compare Pouilly Fumé or Sancerre, France with Marlborough, NZ.

Pinot Grigio from Venetia, Italy.

Vinho Verde from northern Portugal.

Albarino from Rías Baixas, Galicia, north western Spain.

Chenin Blanc. Compare Vouvray, Loire wines with South Africa and Margaret River, Australia.

Torrontes from northern Argentina.

Riesling, Compare wines from Moselle, Germany, with Alsace, France.

Gewürztraminer from Alsace, France.

Viognier from northern Rhône Valley, France.

Chardonnay. Compare Chablis or Pouilly Fuissé with Californian or Australian wines.

Late Harvest wines from Monbazillac or Sauterne* in France; or Tokaji* from Hungary.

Red: *Listed from light to more full-bodied*

Gamay. From Beaujolais, France.

Pinot Noir. Compare Burgundy with Willamette Valley, OR and Santa Rita Hills, CA.

Sangiovese. Compare Chianti with Brunello di Montalcino* or Vino Nobile di Montepulciano.

Syrah. Compare Syrah from Rhône, France with Shiraz from Australia.

Merlot. Compare St. Émilion* or Pomerol* with Californian Merlot and compare both with Carménère (Chile)

Rioja Reserva. Compare with a Tempranillo from Toro (Spain)

Zinfandel. Compare a Californian Zin with a Primitivo from Puglia, Italy.

Bordeaux. Compare a Medoc with a Cabernet Sauvignon from Napa, California.

Malbec. Compare a Cahors, France, with a Malbec from Mendoza, Argentina.

Barolo* from Piedmont, Italy.

GSM Compare a Cotes de Rhône, France, with a GSM from Paso Robles, CA.

Châteauneuf-du-Pape*, France

Amarone-di-Valpolicella* Italy.

Vintage Port * Portugal

All these wines can be found for around $10 except for those marked with an asterisk, which are more expensive.

Wine Serving Temperatures

In most parts of the world, serving wine at "room temperature" is an easy rule of thumb to follow. However, those of us who live in South Florida are torn between freezing A/C units and cloying humidity and thus need more guidance.

As with most things concerning wine, people can be too rigid and pedantic in their rules about what is "correct." There is no correct temperature for serving wine, but over the years certain preferences have proved more popular and enjoyable than others. What works best on a brisk October evening in Tuscany might not be what works best in the humid heat of Miami—even in the cool environs of Books & Books. Personal tastes are also not to be ignored. My personal preference is always on the warmer side, while other people prefer their wine more chilled.

In general, full-bodied reds such as Cabernet Sauvignons and Zinfandels should be served between 61°F and 65 °F. Medium bodied reds such as Sangiovese and Pinot Noir should be served between 59°F and 60°F while young wines from Beaujolais should be served slightly chilled at 54°F.

Full bodied whites such as Californian Chardonnay should be served barely chilled at 53°F, while lighter whites like Sauvignon Blanc or Pinot Grigio taste freshest at 47°F or 48°F. Sweet and sparkling wines like Sauternes and Champagne are best served cold, around 44°F.

Choosing and buying wine

So, having read this book—what is the next step? What is the best way to broaden your experience in wine and take advantage of what you have been reading?

I have two basic rules:

Experiment with as many different styles of wine as possible. Ignore any pre-conceptions you may have; you will be pleasantly surprised by how many unexpected and different styles you might enjoyably discover.

You can purchase a decent example of most wines for around $10 or less per bottle. While you are learning the different varietals, you should try to stay around this $10 to $15 range.

Gaining experience:

Buy a glass or bottle and sample every wine listed my list of "40 Wines." (Separately; not all in the same evening.)

If possible, do this with a friend, so that you can share the bottle, share the expense, but most of all, share the experience; discuss and share notes.

Work methodically; use a scoring chart to keep a record of the wines you drink.

Compare and compare. Buy a Sauvignon Blanc from New Zealand and one from the Loire and compare them side by side. You don't need to finish both bottles—they will survive a night in the fridge! Do this with Cabernets, Chardonnays, and Pinots: compare Old World with New World as suggested in my 40 Wines list.

Try the wines by themselves and then incorporate them into a meal, and see how they adapt and how your perception changes.

Purchasing wine:

While you are in the experimental stage, the $10 to $15 range allows you to be adventurous and, in fact, you will often find great wines at less than $10.

By all means, read reviews and listen to recommendations, but try to ignore the shelf-talkers in wine stores and numerical ratings of wine critics. Make your own judgment.

After you have found a wine that you really like at $10, try buying a $20 or $25 version and see if there is a difference. If there is, is it worth the extra money?

Some wines—especially those blessed (cursed) by Robert Parker, simply can no longer be purchased for under $20 (hence the curse); especially the big-bodied reds like Amarone, Barolo, Barbaresco, Brunello, and Châteauneuf du Pape. So, for those, you have no choice, bite the bullet and venture into the $40+ range. (Marked with a * on my Top 40 list.)

Other wines, like Romani Conti, Stag's Leap, and Château Latour, you might as well accept and resign yourself to the fact that you can only dream about them unless you win the lottery—or cultivate rich friends and, by using this book, impress them with your superior knowledge and appreciation of wine.

Otherwise, by being open to experiment, you can drink a wide variety of very fine wines from all over the world between the $5 and $15 price range with the occasional $25+ splurge for that special wine on a special occasion.

In most parts of the US, you should be able to find a local wine store where you can develop a relationship with the staff or the owner—but to begin with, please do not dismiss the big box retailers or your local supermarket. Wine has become a consumer commodity; it is widely available, and the big retailers are all competing to sell it to you—take advantage and embrace it!

America in the 21st century is a wine drinker's paradise. Enjoy.

Conclusion:

If you have read this far, you will now be aware of many serious facts about the history and culture of wine, where it is grown, and how it is made. I have written this book and you have presumably read it in the belief that such knowledge increases the pleasure we get from wine. But never forget that we drink wine for pleasure—for our own pleasure, and for the pleasure of the people we drink it with. Don't take it too seriously—drinking wine is fun. Perhaps nobody puts this in better perspective than that great Floridian writer and philosopher, Dave Barry.

"How to Order a Bottle of Wine in a Restaurant," by Dave Barry

1. Look at the wine list and tell the waiter which wine you want.
2. When the waiter brings it to you, take a sip.
3. If it's OK, say it's OK.
4. Then shut up about the wine.
5. Don't talk about the wine anymore.
6. Nobody gives a damn how much you know about wine, OK?
7. And above all, don't keep sloshing the wine around and looking at

it as if it's magical unicorn blood.

8. It's wine, for God's sake.

9. In an hour it will be urine, same as Bud Light.

Acknowledgements

"I have drunken deep of joy, And I will taste no other wine tonight." — Percy Bysshe Shelley

---

I could not have written this book without Mitchell Kaplan, the owner of Books & Books in Coral Gables, Florida, who offered me his legendary bookstore to host the wine appreciation course I'd originally developed for the University of Miami. So it is to Mitchell and his supportive staff, especially his greatly-loved restaurant manager Irving Fields, that I offer my thanks for over six years of wonderful classes. And of course it was Mitchell, the incorrigible booklover, who suggested that the six week class would also make a great book.

I will always be indebted to a number of far more experienced wine writers; giants, upon whose shoulders I have been standing, in order to write this book.

Hugh Johnston has been writing and rewriting *The World Atlas of Wine* since 1971 when I bought my first copy. He is by far my favorite writer on wine. He is passionate, amusing, and has a strong sense of history. His *Vintage: The Story of Wine* is a marvelously fascinating exploration of the history of the grape that no other writer can surpass. Like Johnson, Paul Lukacs is another wonderful historian, and his *Inventing Wine* has proved invaluable to my understanding of wine's commercial development as an industry. Another favorite writer is Jancis Robinson, whose expertise on varietals in particular is second to none. Karen MacNeil's *Wine Bible* is another favorite book, and her creative metaphors when describing wines are as delightful as they are descriptive. George Tabor's *Judgment of Paris* gives not only one of the best background descriptions of the development of the California Wine industry, but also offers the only glass-by-glass, eyewitness description of that watershed moment in 1976 when the world of wine changed forever.

The books of Mike Veseth and Tyler Colman in particular have helped unravel for me the economics and the politics of the modern wine industry, and they are listed, with a few other wine authors, in the bibliography—to all of whom I am greatly indebted, and from each of whom I have learned a great deal. And of course, I owe an immeasurable debt to my faithful and tireless fact checkers, Google and Wikipedia—who are never wrong!

I will be forever grateful to my most patient and eagle-eyed editors at Mango Publishing, Brenda Knight and Sara Giusti, whose good natured encouragement and professional advice helped turn a rough manuscript into a finished book,

Finally, I must thank my wonderful and supportive wife Jude, who has so selflessly helped me research all the many bottles of wine which were so necessary in order to complete this book.

Any mistakes or omissions are obviously my wife's fault.

Appendix

APPENDIX A: All 45 Bordeaux AOC Appellations

"Wine is constant proof that God loves us and loves to see us happy." — Benjamin Franklin

BORDEAUX APPELLATION CONTROLE		
Appelation	Hectares under vine	Bottles per annum (millions)
Médoc		
Médoc	5300	37.1m
Haut-Médoc	4600	28.0m
Listrac	664	3.8m
Moulis	607	3.6m
St. Estèphe	1254	7.0m
Pauillac	1209	6.5m
St. Julien	909	4.8m
Margaux	1403	7.1m
Red Graves & Pessac-Léognan		
Graves	2568	16.2m
Red Pessac-Léognan	1263	6.0m
St. Emilion, Pomerol & Fronsac		
St. Emilion Grand Cru	3719	18.1m
St. Emilion	1773	10.9m
Montagne St. Emilion	1590	9.3m
Lussac-St. Emilion	1447	8.7m
Puisseguin St. Emilion	745	4.5m
St Georges St. Emilion	185	1.0m
Lalande de Pomerol	1131	6.3m
Pomerol	764	3.6m

Fronsac	843	4.3m
Canon-Fronsac	318	1.7m
Sweet White Wines		
Sauternes	1669	4.3m
Sainte-Croix-du-Mont	393	1.7m
Loupiac	404	1.8m
Barsac	594	1.6m
Cadillac	215	0.7m
Cérons	63	0.2m
Bordeaux & Bordeaux Supérieur		
Red Bordeaux	41,775	282.3m
Bordeaux Supérieur	11,317	67.1m
Bordeaux & Dry White Wines		
Bordeaux Blanc	6721	48.8m
Entre-Deux-Mers	1571	11.8m
Graves	802	4.7m
Crémant de Bordeaux	122	1.0m
Pessac-Léognan	267	1.3m
Premières Côtes de Blaye	216	1.4m
Blaye	90	0.6m
Graves-de-Vayres	95	0.7m
Côtes de Bourg	22	0.1m
Côtes de Blaye	216	0.3m
Côtes des Francs	9	1200
Red Wines From The Côtes		
Premières Côtes de Blaye	5773	35.7m
Côtes de Bourg	3951	24.2m
Premières Côtes de Bordeaux	3496	20.0m
Côtes de Castillon	3044	17.5m
Graves-de-Vayres	537	3.4m
Côtes de Francs	506	2.9m

APPENDIX B: All 33 Grand Crus of Burgundy

The thirty-three Grand Cru vineyards of Burgundy do not show the name of the village or commune on their label, just the name of the vineyard. Some vineyards (Batard-Montrachet, Montrachet, Bonnes-Mares, Charlemagne, Corton and Corton-Carlemagne) are divided between two or more villages, which is why the following list appears to show forty-one grand crus. The village of Gevrey-Chambertin has nine grand-crus, and the village of Vosne-Romanée has six. To further complicate things, although Chablis is listed as a single grand-cru, it does in fact include seven official grand-cru climats, or individual vineyards. The 585 premier-cru labels show both the name of the vineyard and the village where it is located. Burgundy has a total of 106 different AOCs. These include the thirty-three Grand Crus listed below, each of which has its own individual AOC. The 585 Premier Cru vineyards are spread among the remaining seventy-three village AOCs. For example, the village of Chassagne-Montrachet has three Grand-Crus listed here, but in any list of all the AOCs, the village itself has just the single AOC, Chassagney-Montrachet. However, this single AOC has fifty-one Premier-Cru vineyards, and about another fifty regular vineyards. The Premier-Cru vineyards can include the name of the vineyard as well as the village, Chassgne-Montrachet, on the label. The regular vineyards can only put the name of the village, Chassgne-Montrachet AOC, on the label. Thus:

Montrachet, Grand-Cru AOC (one of 3 vineyards)

La Grande Borne, Premier-Cru, Cassagney-Montrachet, AOC (one of 51 vineyards)

Chassagney-Montrachet, AOC (from 50 possible vineyards)

Another example is the village of Gevrey-Chambertin, which has an extraordinary nine Grand-Crus listed here, but again, in any list of

French AOCs, has only a single AOC for the village. This single village classification includes twenty-six Premier-Cru vineyards, and about another sixty-nine regular vineyards. Thus:

Chambertin, Grand-Cru (one of 9 vineyards)

Clos Saint Jacques, Premier-Cru, Gevery-Chambertin, AOC (one of 26 vineyards)

Gevery-Chambertin, AOC (from 69 possible vineyards)

GRAND CRU	REGION	VILLAGE
Bâtard-Montrachet	Côte de Beaune	Puligny-Montrachet
Bâtard-Montrachet	Côte de Beaune	Chassagne-Montrachet
Bienvenues-Bâtard-Montrachet	Côte de Beaune	Puligny-Montrachet
Bonnes-Mares	Côte de Nuits	Morey-Saint-Denis
Bonnes-Mares	Côte de Nuits	Chambolle-Musigny
Chablis Grand Cru	Chablis	Chablis
Chambertin	Côte de Nuits	Gevrey-Chambertin
Chambertin-Clos de Bèze	Côte de Nuits	Gevrey-Chambertin
Chapelle-Chambertin	Côte de Nuits	Gevrey-Chambertin
Charlemagne	Côte de Beaune	Pernand-Vergelesses
Charlemagne	Côte de Beaune	Aloxe-Corton
Charmes-Chambertin	Côte de Nuits	Gevrey-Chambertin
Chevalier-Montrachet	Côte de Beaune	Puligny-Montrachet
Clos de la Roche	Côte de Nuits	Morey-Saint-Denis
Clos de Tart	Côte de Nuits	Morey-Saint-Denis
Clos de Vougeot	Côte de Nuits	Vougeot
Clos des Lambrays	Côte de Nuits	Morey-Saint-Denis

Clos Saint-Denis	Côte de Nuits	Morey-Saint-Denis
Corton	Côte de Beaune	Pernand-Vergelesses
Corton	Côte de Beaune	Ladoix-Serrigny
Corton	Côte de Beaune	Aloxe-Corton
Corton-Charlemagne	Côte de Beaune	Pernand-Vergelesses
Corton-Charlemagne	Côte de Beaune	Ladoix-Serrigny
Corton-Charlemagne	Côte de Beaune	Aloxe-Corton
Criots-Bâtard-Montrachet	Côte de Beaune	Chassagne-Montrachet
Échezeaux	Côte de Nuits	Flagey-Echézeaux
Grands Échezeaux	Côte de Nuits	Flagey-Echézeaux
Griotte-Chambertin	Côte de Nuits	Gevrey-Chambertin
La Grande Rue	Côte de Nuits	Vosne-Romanée
La Romanée	Côte de Nuits	Vosne-Romanée
La Tâche	Côte de Nuits	Vosne-Romanée
Latricières-Chambertin	Côte de Nuits	Gevrey-Chambertin
Mazis-Chambertin	Côte de Nuits	Gevrey-Chambertin
Mazoyères-Chambertin	Côte de Nuits	Gevrey-Chambertin
Montrachet	Côte de Beaune	Puligny-Montrachet
Montrachet	Côte de Beaune	Chassagne-Montrachet
Musigny	Côte de Nuits	Chambolle-Musigny
Richebourg	Côte de Nuits	Vosne-Romanée
Romanée-Conti	Côte de Nuits	Vosne-Romanée
Romanée-Saint-Vivant	Côte de Nuits	Vosne-Romanée
Ruchottes-Chambertin	Côte de Nuits	Gevrey-Chambertin

The 33 Grand Crus of Burgundy

APPENDIX C: 1976 Judgment of Paris final results

VINEYARD	VARIETAL	COUNTRY	RESULT	
			white	red
Chateau Montelena, 1973		California	1	
Mersault Charmes Roulot, 1973		France	2	
Chalone Vinyard, 1974		California	3	
Spring Mountain, 1973		California	4	
Beaune, Clos de Mouches, 1973		France	5	
Freemark Abbey Winery, 1972	Chardonnay	California	6	
Batard-Montrachet Ramonet-Prudhon,1973		France	7	
Puligny-Montrachet les Pucelles 1972		France	8	
Veedercrest Vinyards, 1972		California	9	
David Bruce, 1973		California	10	
Stag's Leap Wine Cellars, 1973		California		1
Chateau Mouton Rothschild, 1970		France		2
Chateau Montrose, 1970		France		3
Chateau Haut-Brion, 1970		France		4
Ridge Vinyards Monte Bello, 1971	Cabernet Sauvignon	California		5
Chateau Leoville-Las-Cases, 1971		France		6
Heitz Cellars, Martha's Vinyard, 1970		California		7
Clos du Val Winery, 1972		California		8
Mayacamas Vinyards, 1971		California		9
Freemark Abbey Winery, 1969		California		10

Bibliography

Books about wine

This selection of books has been specifically chosen for having informed and influenced my own knowledge and love of wine, and for inspiring my own book.

Butler, Joel, and Randall Heskett: *Divine Vintage*, Palgrave Macmillan, 2012.

Campbell, Christy: *The Botanist and the Vintner*, Algonquin Books, 2006.

Clarke, Oz: *The History of wine in 100 Bottles*, Sterling Publishing, 2015.

Colman, Tyler: *Wine Politics*, University of California Press, 2010.

Dovaz, Michel, and Michel Guillard: *Bordeaux: Legendary Wines*, Assouline, 2014.

Johnson, Hugh, and Jancis Robinson, *World Atlas of Wine*, Mitchell Beazley, 2014.

Johnson, Hugh: *Pocket Wine Book*, Mitchell Beazley, 2015

Johnson, Hugh: *Vintage – The Story of Wine*, Simon & Schuster, 1989.

Keevil, Susan: *Wines of the World*, Metro Books, 2010.

Kliman, Todd: *The Wild Vine*, Clarkson Potter Publishers, 2010.

Lukacs, Paul: *Inventing Wine*, W.W. Norton & Company, 2013.

MacNeil, Karen: *The Wine Bible*, Workman Publishing, 2000.

McGovern, Patrick K.: *Ancient Wines*, Princeton University Press, 2003

Ordish, George: **The Great Wine Blight**, Sidgewick & Jackson, 1987

Osborne, Lawrence: **The Accidental Connoisseur**, North Point Press, 2004.

Pitte, Jean-Robert: **Bordeaux/Burgundy**, University of California Press, 2012.

Potter, Maximillian: **Shadows in the Vineyard**, Twelve, 2014.

Robinson, Jancis: **Guide to Wine Grapes**, Oxford University Press, 1996.

Robinson, Jancis, editor: **The Oxford Companion to Wine**, Oxford University Press, 2006.

Saporta, Isabelle: **Vino Business**, Grove Press, 2015.

Steinberger, Michael: **The Wine Savant**, W.W. Norton & Company, 2014.

Taber, George: **Judgment of Paris**, Scribner, 2006.

Veseth, Mike: **Wine Wars**, Rowman & Littlefield, 2011.

Wallace, Benjamin: **The Billionaire's Vinegar**, Three Rivers Press, 2009.

Movies about wine (all highly recommended)**:**

Red Obsession (2013 documentary): Beautiful and splendid study of Bordeaux wines and China.

A Year in Burgundy (2013 documentary): Martine Saunier follows seven Burgundian winemaking families through twelve months of work.

A Year In Champagne (2015 documentary): Martine Saunier does the same thing for the winemakers of Champagne.

Mondovino (2004 documentary): The globalization of the world's wine industry.

SOM (2012 documentary): The training and trials of becoming a certified sommelier.

Sideways (2004 comedy): A paean to Pinot Noir and an attack on Merlot.

Bottleshock (2008 comedy): Roughly based on *The Judgment of Paris*

Index

A

ABC: Anything But Chardonnay, 296
AFWE: Anti Flavor Wine Elite, 44
Aging: Effect on wine, 76, 80, 86, 187
Aigles les Murailles: Chasselas, 296
Amarone: 71, 203, 299
Amis, Kingsley: English writer, 212
Amphorae: 101, 103-104, 150
Anbaugebeite: German wine region, 213-214
d'Annunzio, Gabriele: Italian poet, 208
Apollo: Greek God, 210
Appassimento: Raisinated wine, 26, 112, 202, 210,
AOC: Appellation d'Origin Controlée: Defined, 85, 136
Arnaud de Pontac: Branded Haut-Brion, 118
Auslese: 215
Ausonius: Roman poet, 157
Austen, Jane: 258, 294, 296
AVA: American Viticultural Area, 86, 270, 273

B

Bacchus: Roman God of Wine and Rebirth, 105, 107, 299
Balearic Islands: 191
Banyuls: 346
Barrel size: Bordeaux and Burgundy barrels, 66, 74, 76, 78
Barry, Dave: How to order wine, 359
Baudelaire, Charles: 258, 312-313
Beaune classification: ranking of 1861, 122, 152, 165
Beerenauslese: 215
Bergerac: my home, 161, 162
Bernkastel: 220
Bishop of Norwich: 197
Blending and fining: 75
Boccaccio: 109, 321-323
Bolivia: 121, 239, 241
Bollinger: 125, 179,
Bordeaux: 82, 109, 118, 121, 133, 155-162, 173
Bordeaux blend: defined, 298

Bordeaux, 1855 ranking of: 120, 121-122
Borges, Jorge Luis: 303-304
Botrytis cinerea: Noble Rot, 68, 161, 208, 320, 324-326
Bradbury, Ray: 335
Brandy: 26, 115, 341
Brillat-Savarin: 175,
Britain: and Bordeaux, 109, 158
British Influence: on world of wine, 132
Brunello di Montalcino: 206
Burgundy and Monasteries: 106, 108,

C

Cartland, Barbara: 283
Casablanca Valley: 251
Catalonia: 190
Cato: 106, 150,
Catullus: Roman poet, 105
Cava: 190, 334
Cèpe: 38
Cervantes, Miguel de: 273, 329
Champagne: 176
Champagne: famous widows, 178
Champagne bottles: names of different sizes, 84
Charlemagne: 218
Chasselas: 183, 296
Château Chunder: 242
Château D'Yquem: 70, 114, 153, 161, 325,
Château Haut-Brion: 118-119, 255, 290,
Château Latour: 119, 121, 142, 156, 159
Château Monbazillac: 67, 162,
Château Pape Clement: 158, 160, 185
Châteauneuf-du-Pape: 158, 184-185
Chaucer: 109
Chianti: 204
Cicero: 106
Cistercian: monasteries, 78, 109, 113, 150, 212
Cleese, John: 255
Climate Change: effects on vineyards, 60

Climats: 149, 172, 369
Clos: defined, 153
Clos de Vougeot: 109
Cloudy Bay: NZ Sauvignon Blanc, 256, 323
Condon, Richard: Brunello di Montalcino, 206, 288
Constantia: Famous sweet white wine, 230, 258, 260
Constantine: Emperor and Burgundy wines, 106, 163, 165
Constellation Brands: 233-234
Cortez: ; Spanish Conquistador, 265, 308
Costco: 89, 137, 233
Côte de Nuits: 109, 168, 170-171
Crianza: 75, 187
Criolla Chica: 236, 238, 308
Crljenak Kaštelanski: Zinfandel or Primativo, 209, 225, 270, 335
Cru: defined, 153

D

Dahl: English writer, 40, 174, 288, 316
Dally-Plonk: Dalmation/NZ wine, 256
Dante: 299, 321, 332
Describing Wine: 36
Dibdin, Michael: 39
Dickens, Charles: 258, 290
Dionysus: God of Wine and Rebirth, 70, 100, 106-107
DOCG: Denominazione di Origine Controllata e Garantita, 86, 200
Dom Pérignon: 134, 178
Dormancy: Growth of vine, 62, 70
Drake, Sir Francis: 133, 343
Drought: 232
Duke Phillip the Bold: 164

E

E&J Gallo: 182, 234, 268
Egon Müller: white Rieslings, 221
Egyptian wine: styles of, 98
Einzellagen: German vineyard, 213-214
Eiswein: 69

En Primeur: 158
English 'champagnes': best in world, 60
Errázuriz: father of Chilean wine, 247, 249
Eubulus: Poet of Greek moderation, 45, 100
Eucharist: wine sacrifice, 107, 163, 229, 265

F

Falernian: Favorite Roman Wine, 104, 105, 108, 112, 283
Faulks, Sebastian: 326
Fermentation: 25, 71
Fino Sherry: 314, 342
Fitzgerald, F. Scott: 305-307
Flanagan, Richard: 326
Flowering: Growth of vine, 63-64
Flying Winemakers: 43, 61, 181, 248, 259
French Paradox: 45, 306
Frosts: Growth of vine, 62
Fruit bombs: 44, 231, 253
Fruit Set: Growth of vine, 65
Fuentes, Carlos: 304
Furnaces: glass bottles, 76, 81, 118

G

Galicia: Albarino, 187, 192, 195, 283
Garagistes: 160, 181,
Gilgamesh: Earliest reference to wine, 98
Giol winery: was world's largest, 237
Gold Rush: thirsty miners, 265
Grapes needed to make one bottle of wine: Vineyard Yield, 65
Grosslage: German wine district, 213
GSM wines: 244, 274, 310
Guyot, Dr. Jules: 20

H

Hašek, Jaroslav: The Good Soldier Svejk, 303
Haut-Brion: 1st branded wine estate, 118-119, 255, 290
Heller, Joseph: 303

Hemingway, Ernest: 15, 333
Highsmith, Patricia: 332
Homer: Wine dark sea, 99, 286
Hops: improved taste of beer in 16th century, 114
Horace: 19, 106, 150
Hundred Years War: 110, 133, 158

I

IGT: Indicazione Geografica Tipica, 86, 200, 205, 210
INAO: 1935 French classification, 165

J

Jefferson: Thomas, 113, 115, 119, 158, 262, 291
Johnson, Ben: 343
Joyce, James: 325
Judgment of Paris: 130, 135, 181, 243, 248, 256, 268, 363, 372, 376

K

Keats, John: 25, 298, 300,
Keynes, John Maynard: 179
King Solomon: Song of Songs, 316
Kvevri: earliest wine making, 96, 224

L

Late Harvest Wines: Passerillage, Noble Rot, Eiswein, 68, 215
Latitude: effects on vineyards, 58, 150-151
Lee, Harper: 292
Locke, John: 119, 158
LVMH: Louis Vuitton Moet Hennessey, 235, 254

M

MacNeil, Karen: 39, 238, 322, 363
McWine: 142
Madeira: 305, 332, 345
Mago: Phoenecian wine expert, 99, 102, 106
Maipo: 251

Malagousia: 305
Malmsey: 305, 345
Malolactic fermentation: 58, 73
Malvasia: 113, 305
Malvoisie: 305
Mandela: Nelson, 259, 260
Marc: 73, 342
Marquez, Garcia: 304
Marquis de Ségur: Lafitte, Latour & Mouton, 119
Marsala: 209, 346
Masefield, John: 202
Mateus Rosé: 196
Mendocino: 271
Mendoza: 240
Meritage: Californian claret, 76, 305
Merret, Christopher: 134, 178
Missions: Californian missions, 265, 308
Mollydocker: Powerful Australian reds, 246
Monasteries: and Burgundy, 106, 108
Monbazillac: Sweet white wine of SW France, 67, 162
Moncrieff, Scott: Literary translator, 312
Mondavi: Robert, 77, 89, 132, 154, 249, 268
Monte Testaccio: 104
Montepulciano: 206, 309
Monty Python: Australian wine tasting, 241
Morley Safer: French Paradox, 45, 306
Mosel-Saar-Ruwer: 219
Mount Ararat: Origin of wine, 95, 288
Muller Thurgau: 310

N

Nahe: 218
Napa Valley: 272
Napoleon, Bonaparte: 76, 114, 178
Napoleon III: 121, 123
Negociants: 88, 169
Neruda, Pablo: 316
Nile flood cycle: importance of, 98

Ningxia Province: Chinese wine region, 253
Noah: First winemaker, 96, 224, 288
Noble Rot: Botrytis cinerea, 68, 161, 208, 320, 324-326

O

Oak Barrels: background in wine making, 74, 76-78
One percent rule of thumb: 67, 140
Olfactory cortex: amygdala, 32, 37
Orvieto: 208
Osiris: God of wine and rebirth, 70, 99, 106
Ovid: 106

P

Parker, Robert M.: 41, 42, 162, 231, 269, 289
Paso Robles: 274
Passerillage: 68
Pasteur, Louis: 122
Penfolds Grange: 148
Pepys, Samuel: 119, 158
Petrarch: 185, 321
Peynaud, Émile: 73
Pfalz: (Palentine), 218, 319
Philippe the Bold: Duke of Burgundy, 109
Phylloxera: attacks European vineyards, 123-125
Plato: 100
Pliny: 150, 157
Police des Vins: tax codes favoring Bordeaux, 110, 157, 162
Pommerey: Louise, 178
Port Wines: 196-198
Porto Factory House: English traditions, 197
Pouilly Fumé: 136, 147, 183, 207
Prädikatswein: 214
Pre-Fermentation: 71
Price: Retail price of wine, 140-141
Priorat: 191
Prohibition: 127, 266
Prosecco: 201

Proust, Marcel: 13, 16, 32, 126, 274, 301, 312
Puglia: 208

R

Rabelais: 297
Racking: 74
Raleigh, Sir Walter: 261
Rapel/Colchagua: 252
Retsina: 93, 222
Rheingau: 218
Rheinhessen: 219
Ribera del Duero: 190
Riddler: 176
Riesling: 217, 319
Rioja: 124, 187
Ripasso della Valpolicella: 203
Room temperature: 356
Rothschild: 131, 238, 248, 251, 254
Rueda: 189, 332
Ruwer: 221

S

Saar: 220
Saki, H.H. Munro: 323
Sancerre: 147, 183, 323
Sangiovese: 'sanguis Jovis', 204, 321
Santa Barbara: 275
Santa Cruz Mountains: 273
Santorini: 112, 207, 222, 285
Schoonmaker, Frank: 233, 270
Scoring and Rating Wine: 40
Secondary (Malolactic) Fermentation: 73
Shakespeare: and Sherry, 15, 133, 305, 343
Shandong Province: Chinese wine region, 254
Sherry: 314, 342
Shooting: Growth of vine, 64
Sicily: 209

Six-O-Clock-Swill: New Zealand "Happy Hour", 242, 255
Soil and drainage: effects on vineyards, 59
Sonoma: 271
South Australia: 245
Spätburgunder: 217, 318
Spätlese: 215
Spurrier: Stephen, 130, 134, 268
Stag's Leap: and all the apostrophes, 269, 272
Sulphites: 55
Super Tuscans: 205
Sweet White Wine, 112
Swift, Johnathan: 119
Sylvaner: 217, 329
Symposium: Greek wine drinking, 100, 105

T

Tannins: 54
Tasker, Fred: fun and romance, 330
Tasting wine: Smell, 31
Tasting wine: Mouthfeel; Taste 34
Tasting wine: Sight 29
Terroir: 147, 149
Tesco: 135, 137, 233
The Bacchae: Euripides and wine, 107
Thomas, Edward: Adlestrop, 336
Three-Tier: US wine distribution system, 129
Tokaji: sweet Hungarian wine, 69, 113, 223, 311
Tolkien, J.R.R.: Albarino wine, 283
Top ten wine-exporting countries: 137
Top ten wine-importing countries: 138
Toro: 189
Trockenbeerenauslese: TBA, 216
Truffles: 38, 330
Tuns: German wine barrels, 78, 113, 212
Turgot: Louis XIV finance minister, 110
Two Buck Chuck: 78, 234

U

UC Davis: 130, 149, 243, 270
Ullage: 74, 207

V

Valpolicella: Recioto, Amarone, Ripasso, 202, 207, 299
Vargas Llosa, Mario: 304
Varietal: 60, 87, 147, 149, 279
Veraison: 65
Verre anglais: 76
Vineland: 261
Vineyard Yield: 66
Vinho Verde: 192, 194
Viniculture: Making the Wine, 70
Vinification: 53
Vino Santo: 207
Vintner: effects on wine, 53, 61, 70
Virgil: 106, 150
Viticulture: How Vines are Grown: Sun + Grape = Sugar, 53, 61
Vitis riparia: 53, 125, 262
Vitis silvestris: 54, 94
Vitis vinifera: development of, 25, 53, 94, 101

W

Wall of Wine: daunting selection of wines, 136
Walla Walla: Washington wine, 276
Walpole: British Prime Minister, 119
Water: dangers of, 93
Willamette Valley: 275
Wine: 25
Wine Aroma Wheel: 39
Wine Bottle Shapes: description of various shapes, 81
Wine Labels: How to read, 85
Winemaker: Different types of, 88
Wine Spectator's: top wines for 2014, 198, 247
Wine with food: 231, 349

Epilogue

"Strategy is buying a bottle of fine wine when you take a lady out for dinner. Tactics is getting her to drink it."
Frank Muir

"We are all mortal until the first kiss and the second glass of wine." —
Eduardo Galeano

"Wine comes in at the mouth And love comes in at the eye; That's all we shall know for truth Before we grow old and die."
William Butler Yeats

"The wine urges me on, the bewitching wine, which sets even a wise man to singing and to laughing gently and rouses him up to dance and brings forth words which were better unspoken."
Homer, The Odyssey

"Give me wine to wash me clean of the weather-stains of cares."
Ralph Waldo Emerson

The Soul Of Wine
One night, from bottles, sang the soul of wine:
'O misfit man, I send you for your good
Out of the glass and wax where I'm confined,
A melody of light and brotherhood!

I know you must, out on the blazing hill,
Suffer and sweat beneath the piercing rays
To grow my life in me, my soul and will;
I'm grateful to you, and I will not play

You false, since I feel joy when I can fall
Into the throat of some old working man,

And his warm belly suits me overall
As resting place more than cold cellars can.

And do you hear the songs that hope believes,
The Sunday music, throbbing from my breast?
Elbows on table, rolling up your sleeves
You praise me, and I'll put your cares to rest;

I'll fire the eyes of your enraptured wife;
I'll grant a force and colour to your son,
And will for this frail athlete of life
Be oil that makes the straining muscles run.

My nectar falls in your fertility,
A precious seed whose Sower is divine,
So from our love is born rare poetry,
Thrusting towards God the blossom on its vine!'
Charles Baudelaire

CPSIA information can be obtained
at www.ICGtesting.com
Printed in the USA
BVHW01s0430121217
502582BV00003B/3/P